THE
Art
OF THE
Actor

THE
Art
OF THE
Actor

The essential
history of acting,
from classical times
to the present day

JEAN BENEDETTI

Routledge
Taylor & Francis Group
New York

Routledge is an imprint of the
Taylor & Francis Group, an informa business

Routledge
Taylor & Francis Group
270 Madison Avenue
New York, NY 10016

Routledge
Taylor & Francis Group
2 Park Square
Milton Park, Abingdon
Oxon OX14 4RN

© 2007 by Jean Benedetti
Routledge is an imprint of Taylor & Francis Group, an Informa business

Printed in the United States of America on acid-free paper
10 9 8 7 6 5 4 3 2 1

International Standard Book Number-10: 0-87830-204-2 (Softcover) 0-87830-203-4 (Hardcover)
International Standard Book Number-13: 978-0-87830-204-8 (Softcover) 978-0-87830-203-1 (Hardcover)

Visit the Taylor & Francis Web site at
http://www.taylorandfrancis.com

and the Routledge Web site at
http://www.routledge-ny.com

Contents

Foreword

This book is not a formal, narrative history of acting or of individual actors' performances. It is an attempt to trace the evolution of the theories of the actor's art from classical times to the present day, and also to demonstrate the persistence of certain key ideas over a period of 2,500 years.

The book is in broad sections to make clear the changing patterns of thought. It moves from a discussion of the relationship of acting to rhetoric, then to acting seen as declamation, and thence to acting in the modern sense and so to realism and finally to the notion of the ritual, 'holy' actor.

It does not proceed in strict chronological order. Sections are arranged so that readers can follow the discussions and debates on major issues and see how key figures relate to each other in their theory and practice.

The Art of the Actor is intended as a working tool and a sourcebook for all those studying the theatre at whatever level. There is a large margin on each page so that readers can make notes and comments.

Through my teaching both at undergraduate and postgraduate level, I have become aware of the difficulties students experience when key texts are difficult to obtain, out of print or have not been translated. Much of the material presented here is, therefore, not accessible elsewhere. Major extracts can either be read separately or after the main body of the commentary or consulted as the need arises.

All translations, unless otherwise stated, are my own. They do not claim to be scholarly or academic. My intention has been to produce clear, modern translations of sometimes difficult texts so that readers may become aware of the recurrence of certain ideas, of quotes and allusions and thus of the continuity of a tradition of concerns. The extracts from Brecht's plays are taken from the Methuen editions.

Once again, my grateful thanks are due to John Collis and Elinor Skedgell of the Rose Bruford College library for their generous and unfailing help in obtaining source material.

Jean Benedetti, 2005

Acknowledgements

I would like to thank Suhrkamp Verlag for permission to translate texts by Brecht, Hans Bunge, Kaethe Ruelicke and Angelika Hurwicz. I would also like to thank the editorial board of the Société d'Histoire du Théâtre for permission to translate extracts from the classes given by Louis Jouvet at the Conservatoire in Paris.

Introduction

Acting is a normal human activity. Everybody acts in one way or another almost every day. Children play and learn. Adults act and learn. Acting is a way of showing our understanding of the world and passing it on to other people. When they are telling a story, people start to 'act' bits of it, imitating voices, actions, gestures, giving out signs. They do so spontaneously and nobody is surprised. Indeed, they respond sympathetically. The 'acting' is part of a shared experience. It is only when attempting to be impartial, objective, such as when conveying factual information, that people attempt to drain all the personal elements out of what they are saying. In professional acting there is a crucial leap. The basic impulse is there: the desire to communicate an experience of something that has happened, or might have happened, but it is done by pretending to be someone we are not. The ancient Greek word for actor is 'hypocrite'. The difference between acting in life and professional acting proper is that the latter is planned, artistically shaped. The signs are selected.

The art of the professional actor needs to be considered under two main headings:

- the inner creative process

- the conventions and codes, the performance spaces which shape the outward expression of that inner process

What is a professional actor? The professional actor in the Western tradition is defined in two ways:

- anyone who earns a living by being employed to perform in plays

- anyone who has achieved a level of technical skill which enables him to guarantee a certain quality of performance, no matter what the play or frequency of presentation

But within that profession there are a variety of artists. There is also the question not of how actors perceive themselves but how they are seen by their audiences.

From a contemporary point of view, what is an actor?

- Is an actor one kind of person?

- Or several kinds?

- What do they have in common?

- What are the differences between them?

- Is there an unconscious hierarchy of values?

- What is the difference between an actor and a star?

- Who is more admirable, the classical actor who can play Hamlet or Cleopatra, or someone who appears only in soap operas? And why?

- Is the actor who can play the great tragic and dramatic roles superior to the actor in comedy?

- Are theatre actors necessarily superior to actors who appear only in movies or on TV?

- Has sexual magnetism any role to play?

In one form or other, actors have always been classified as to range and type, usually according to the genre or characters in which they specialise.

In studying the nature of the actor's art four main areas need to be examined:

- the permanent elements inherent in the creative process itself

- the changing social factors which condition it

- the conflict between the actor's creative aspirations and the codes of conduct and morality of his period

- the performing space

Theatre is the most public, the most obviously social, of all the arts. Acting takes place in a specific area, a space that has been agreed by audience and actor alike as being set apart, in which actions are performed and observed from the outside. A *theatre* is a place where things are seen. It can be anywhere – a room, a street, a pub, the National Theatre – provided there is an agreement by a group that it is an area set aside for acting, a *designated space*.* A *drama* (from the Greek verb *dron*, to do) is something that is done. There is an essential division of function between an actor (someone who does) and a spectator (someone who sees).

Once a performer moves into the designated space, his performance is governed by certain basic rules: he must be seen, heard, his actions must be clear and readable, allowing an audience to understand the reasons for his conduct, the coherence of his behaviour. We cannot, therefore, consider the actor in isolation from his audience or the space in which he works.

But what the performer does in the designated space, what he is expected to do, or allowed to do, what is recognised as good or bad acting change from period to period, as society and taste change. Modern actors are accustomed to taking off their clothes. That would have been unthinkable (as well as illegal) before the 1960s.

The actor is part of the community. He shares a common culture with his fellow citizens, a set of values. His status, however, is ambivalent. He is both inside and outside the group. He may present the audience members with a picture of their own aspirations, or he may present them with a critical view of themselves. He is and is not 'one of us'. He is both a creative artist and a citizen, one who inspires and also serves as his community requires. But those requirements change.

The techniques, styles, conventions of performance are not only determined by time and place but also by the technical equipment in the theatre. For example, in Greece, where theatres could hold 12,000–20,000 people, the acoustic was so perfect that no special skills of projection were necessary. If a match is struck on a Greek stage, it can be heard in the back row, tens of metres away. But a modern actor, working, say, in the Olivier Theatre, will need a vocal technique that has been developed as a result of a long and rigorous period of training. He will need also to be able to negotiate the complex combinations of sets, lights and sounds that are an integral art of a modern production. He may only be a part of that production and not the dominant part.

But whatever the historical changes in performance conventions and conditions, we can say that the fundamental elements of a theatre event are:

* This term was created by the French sociologist Jean Duvignaud.

3

- an actor

- an action

- a space

- a spectator

We can define the actor's situation using the following diagram:

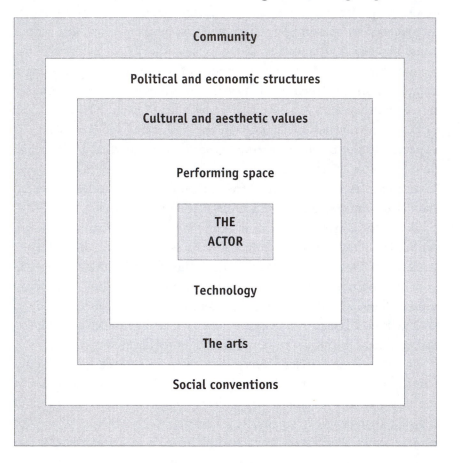

Community

Political and economic structures

Cultural and aesthetic values

Performing space

THE
ACTOR

Technology

The arts

Social conventions

In general, an acting *profession* can only emerge when there is a regular demand for entertainment. This was not always the case.

The professional actor (men only in England),* as we have defined him, only emerges in the sixteenth century in response to economic and social change.

We need to be aware of our own historic position and realise how different our expectations with regard to entertainment are from any previous period. We expect theatres to be open all year, with eight

* The status of women in the theatre is a highly complex question which requires a detailed study of its own. It has more to do with social than artistic considerations.

performances a week. We expect twenty-four-hour television on multi-channels with endless dramatic entertainment.

We need to stand back from those expectations and imagine a world in which there would only be limited entertainment, perhaps for two or three hours over four days once a year – with only one programme.

A fundamental question that has to be asked is: despite all the changes of form and presentation that have taken place over two hundred years, are there elements in the actor's art that are permanent, and linked to his own and others' psycho-physical processes?

1 Classical Rhetoric

Up until the early twentieth century education was based on the study of Greek and Latin. In the Middle Ages, and long after, Latin became the language of theology, law and diplomacy. Scholars, statesmen and diplomats could travel across Europe and be understood. Classical texts were assumed to be the ultimate repository of all knowledge. Wisdom ended there. Like sacred texts, they formed a body of learning and truth that was to be studied and learned as absolute. The same books were read, discussed and commented on generation after generation, so creating an intellectual tradition that was almost impossible to break. Educated men might study the same small range of works – Homer, Aeschylus, Sophocles, Euripides, Plato, Aristotle, Virgil, Ovid, Horace, Livy, Cicero, Caesar, Catullus, Quintilian, Seneca. They thus shared a common frame of reference, so that their own writings and reflections are often reworkings of these same texts and are full of allusions and half-quotations to these basic books. It is impossible to understand the prevailing ideas about acting up to our own era without a proper recognition of the strength of the classical tradition.

The tradition of classical rhetoric is of central importance. All early discussions of the actor's art were made in terms of the precepts of rhetorical delivery laid down in Greece and Rome, together with the prescriptions for body language and gestures that accompanied them.

Rhetoric is the art of persuasion, of convincing other people that what you are saying is true. You can persuade in two ways: by perfect logical argument, or by attracting a sympathetic emotional response. The best speeches do both.

Rhetoric is public. It grew with the development of Greek democracy. Once there is no absolute ruler, no king, no emperor, decisions have to be made by the community. They are public whether it be in a political assembly or the courtroom. They are arrived at through debate and discussion. That means that the community has to be persuaded, one way or another, that a certain course of action is right. The man who speaks the most convincingly will carry the day. His words, his oratory, his rhetoric will be a mixture of cool logic, cleverness and emotional blackmail. All classical authors agree that it is the power to influence, to sway, that matters most. And who better to capture and control someone else's sympathy than an actor?

This was recognised by Aristotle, the first thinker to make a serious, scientific study of theatre.

Aristotle laid the foundations for the study of theatre and performance. He also provided the first comprehensive study of human emotion and social behaviour, which remained the dominant statement until the creation of individual psychology in the late nineteenth century. This he did in two major works: *The Poetics* and *The Art of Rhetoric*.

His approach was scientific, he dissected and analysed. He did not theorise.

What kind of actor did Aristotle see?

The actor in Greek tragedy – a complex spectacle combining singing, dance and acting – had a different function from the modern actor. He was not the centre of attention as an individual. Aristotle had an order of priorities in defining the nature of tragedy, which is entirely different from our own. For Aristotle, first and foremost, there is the plot, the action. This is defined as an imitation or, rather, a *mimesis* – not a copy, a replica, but a structure that resembles a set of life events, one that is self-contained, with a beginning, a middle and an end, and which is, therefore, intelligible.

Second come the characters whose function it is to carry the action, who are its agents. Each person is conceived as having a disposition, an *ethos*, which has been given to him and which inclines him to certain actions. The primary concern is with what people do, what decisions, given their natural disposition, they take in the circumstances in which they are placed, and with the ethical and moral validity of those decisions. The conflict in classical Greek tragedy is not between individual interests but between the sets of values, the conflicting moralities which the individuals represent. Thus, in the *Antigone* of Sophocles, Creon represents a kind of realpolitik, which he believes serves the good of the state, while Antigone represents a set of religious beliefs and values, which Creon is supposed to share.

Third, there is the writing, which must be consistent, and which rounds out the action in human terms.

The actor's function is to live out the dilemma in which the character is placed in the terms the writer has given, and to move the audience in a process of moral education.

We know little about actors in ancient Greece. The most famous were both highly respected and highly paid. Wearing masks, walking on built-up shoes, they had to command the attention of an audience of several thousands. Their movements were restricted but we can obtain some idea of their gestures from painted vases. They had to rely for their effect on the voice. Given the perfect acoustic of the Greek and later Roman theatres they did not need to 'project' in the modern sense. A commonplace experiment is to strike a match in the acting area. It can be clearly heard in the highest seat furthest from the stage. We do not know in detail how they trained. We have accounts of actors using gymnastics to gain control over their bodies. Cicero describes Greek actors as sitting, speaking quietly, slowly rising to their feet and increasing the volume until they reached the loudest point when they were at full height, then putting the process into reverse. But he was writing three hundred years after Aristotle.

It was Aristotle's complaint that no set of principles for training the orator had been laid down. The great actor, who could move thousands, provided a model and a criterion by which to be judged. Aristotle knew how violently audiences could react. One woman is reported to have been so moved that she miscarried. The theatre's power of persuasion could, therefore, in modified form, be transferred to the courtroom.

Aristotle's principles of rhetorical delivery are explicitly derived from the best actor's practice. Control and command of pitch, dynamics, stress, rhythm, range, flexibility, together with appropriate body language, were essential. Aristotle was aware that logical, legal, factual argument needed to be supported by sympathetic presentation, in which the advocate played on his emotions so that he could play upon the judge.

Thus, by a significant reversal, actors' practice was enshrined in the principles of rhetoric, which then, historically, became a prescriptive set of rules for actors.

The role of emotion both in the theatre and in the courtroom was central. For Aristotle it was a cardinal principle that the most successful writers were those who actually experienced the emotions they were describing.

> When constructing their plots and giving them shape and form in words, writers should try to visualise the events as clearly as possible. If they see them as vividly as though they had actually been there, they can discern what makes sense and avoid the incongruous . . . We all share a common nature and so the most effective writer is someone who experiences the emotions he portrays. If he is caught up in a storm of feelings, he can represent them with maximum truth. Poetry belongs to the genius or the madman. The first becomes his characters, the second is beside himself (in a state of ecstasy).
>
> (*The Poetics*, 17)

This, by extension, was true of actors and orators.

The nature of the emotions or, rather, as they were to be known for many hundreds of years, the Passions, became an essential object of study.

The Passions were assumed to exist independently, in fixed form. They waited to be activated and were experienced, as it were, passively. Their exact location was a matter of discussion – the head, the heart, the belly? The important factor was that they could be activated.

In Book II of *The Art of Rhetoric*, Aristotle was the first to define and classify them. His approach as always is analytical and forensic.

The Passions are ten in number, sometimes single, sometimes linked:

- Anger

- Calm

- Friendship and Enmity

- Fear and Confidence

- Shame

- Favour

- Pity

- Indignation

- Envy

- Jealousy

They can be pleasurable or painful or both. Some he defines as positive – Calm, Friendship, Favour, Pity – others as negative – Anger, Fear, Shame, Indignation, Envy, Jealousy.

Aristotle's descriptions of how, why and when emotions occur is extremely detailed. Each of them is examined in depth. Significantly, it is often questions of social relations that dominate, questions of status and class. In other words it is the situation that produces the emotion.

Thus, emotion only appears under certain conditions, depending on:

- the individual's state of mind

- the object of his feeling

- the circumstances in which the feeling arises

Without a knowledge of all three, it is impossible to arouse emotion.

Aristotle establishes this method in his discussion of Anger. All subsequent discussions follow the same pattern.

Anger

Anger is a desire, not without some pain, for overt revenge for an overt and undeserved slight on oneself or a member of one's family.

We are always angry with some man in particular (not with Man in general), because he has done or is about to do something against ourselves or our family.

In all anger there is an element of pleasure arising from the prospect of the revenge we conceive in our imagination, as in a dream.

A slight is an open display of opinion about things considered to be worthless. This can take three forms – contempt, spite, insolence.

To show contempt is to belittle something considered unimportant.

To spite is to thwart another man's wishes, not for your personal gain, but for his personal loss.

To show wanton insolence is to do or say things to shame the victim, not because of any injury suffered, but for the pure pleasure of doing it. To render like with like is not to smear, but to take revenge. Those who delight in insolence imagine they do so because they are superior to the person they are insulting.

We are angry when in pain, for men in pain always have some end in view.

We are angry with people who oppose us, or do not help us, or thwart our desire in some manner. If we are ill, poor, in love, at war, thirsty, or generally obsessed with a desire we cannot fulfil, we are bad-tempered and ready to get angry above all with people who show no concern for our situation. For example, when we are ill, with those who disregard our illness, when we are at war, with those who disregard our war, when we are in love, with those who disregard our love, and so on . . . For with each individual, the path to anger has been beaten by emotion.

Men are angry with:

those who laugh or jeer or scoff at them – this is insult

those who do them all the wrongs that appear insulting. Such actions are not a return in like kind for injuries received so that they seem deliberately insulting

those who disparage or despise things we take seriously. If we have pretensions to philosophy, for example, we are angry with those who speak against it. If we are handsome, with anyone who speaks ill of it. And all the more if we are not sure we have such qualities, or to any great extent, or others do not believe we have them. When we are sure of ourselves, we take no notice. We are much more angry with our friends since we expect better treatment from them

those who do not show the customary respect towards us and seem now to despise us

those who do not return good for good

those who oppose us if they are our inferiors or people of no importance for both obviously despise us. If they demean us we are far more angry because it is not the place of inferiors to demean

friends who do not speak or act sympathetically, or do the opposite, and do not perceive our needs

those who take pleasure in our misfortunes, which is a sign either of hostility or contempt

those who do not realise they are causing pain, which is why we are angry with the bearers of bad news

those who are indifferent to an account or the sight of our faults, for they are then like enemies or those who disregard us; friends share their friends' sorrows and the sight of our own shortcomings makes us all sad

those who discredit us in front of four groups of people: our rivals, those we admire and whom we wish to admire us, who inspire us with respect as we do them. If we are treated with contempt in front of these people, our anger is great

those who have no regard for those whom we are honour-bound to defend: family, children, women, subordinates

those who are ungrateful towards us, for their contempt is the opposite of what they owe us

those who treat matters we take seriously with irony, for there is something contemptuous in irony

those who do good to others but not to us, for it is contemptuous not to do for us what they do for everyone else

A lapse of memory can also produce anger, even if it is only a name, for that lapse is a sign of disdain. Its cause is indifference, which is a form of disdain.

(The Art of Rhetoric, Book II, 1378b–9b)

After his examination of the Passions, Aristotle moves on to broader topics:

- the characteristics of youth, middle age and old age
- characteristics produced by birth, wealth and power

Youth, old age, middle age

Youth

The young are by their nature full of desires and they are inclined to follow their desires. In their bodily desires they are particularly subject to love, which they are powerless to control. They are inconstant, and quickly tire. Their desires are intense but brief (for their desires are urgent, not great, and are like the hunger and thirst of the sick). They are hot-blooded, rash and follow their impulses. They are governed by their ardour. Being ambitious they will not endure disdain and they grow angry if they think they are suffering an injustice. They love recognition but victory even more. For youth desires to be supreme, and victory is supreme. These are their two ambitions rather than a love of money. They have no great love of money since they have not yet experienced need. They are good- rather than ill-natured because they have not seen much evil. They are trusting because they have not often been deceived. They are optimistic (like the confidence of men in wine) because they have not suffered failure.

They live for the most part in hope, for hope embraces the future while memory refers to the past and for the young the future is long and the past short . . . They are more courageous than men of another age since they are rash and hope easily. Their rashness takes away all fear. Hope gives them confidence, for no one is afraid when he is angry and hope for some gain inspires confidence. They are easily embarrassed since they cannot conceive of anything other than what is beautiful having received a conventional upbringing. They are magnanimous. They have not yet been humiliated by life. They have not experienced inescapable necessities and magnanimity means believing oneself capable of great things, and this belongs to someone who is full of hope.

In their deeds they prefer beauty to self-interest, for they live by nature rather than calculation. Calculation deals in self-interest, virtue in beauty.

More than at any other age they love their friends and companions, because they take pleasure in the common life and do not yet judge things by their own self-interest and in consequence neither do their friends. They err always by exaggeration and excessive vehemence, for they do everything to excess; they love to excess, hate to excess and so on.

They believe they know everything and are obstinate in what they say. That is the cause of their excess in everything. They commit their crimes through excess rather than wickedness. They are open to pity because they believe all men to be honest and better than they really are. They apply the yardstick of their own innocence to all men. They imagine that other people's suffering is undeserved.

They love to laugh and to joke, for a joke is excess tempered by good upbringing.

Old age

Old men . . . have characteristics that are almost entirely opposite to the young, because they have lived many years, have been deceived and made mistakes on more than one occasion, because they have seen that human affairs go wrong most of the time, and so they are never affirmative, always over-cautious. They say, 'I think', never, 'I know', and always add 'perhaps', 'possibly'. Everything is qualified.

They are cynical which means they always take the worst view of everything. Moreover they are suspicious of everything because they are mistrustful and they are mistrustful because of their experience.

And so they neither love nor hate strongly.

They are mean-minded because life has humiliated them. They do not desire anything great or above the ordinary. They crave no more than the necessities of life. They are parsimonious because wealth is one of those necessities and they know how difficult it is to acquire and how easy to lose.

They are fearful, they live in a state of permanent apprehension. Age has made them different from the young. They have gone cold, while the young are hot. Old age has led to cowardice, for fear is a kind of cold.

They love life, the more so in the twilight of their days, since we always desire what we do not have, and it is what we lack that causes the most intense desire.

They are more selfish than is right. That, too, is a kind of mean-mindedness. They live, beyond what is reasonable, for their own self-interest not for what is noble. For self-interest has to do with individual good, what is noble with universal good. They do not know shame. Not having as much care for what is noble as for their self-interest they do not mind what people think . . .

Old men are also inclined to pity but not for the same reasons as the young, who feel pity out of human sympathy. They do it out of weakness because they believe they are in constant danger, and that inclines them to pity. Hence their tendency to complain. They do not like fun or laughter.

Middle age

Men in their mature age obviously have a character halfway between the preceding two. They avoid the excesses of either. They are neither too self-assured (for that is foolhardy) nor too fearful but find the middle way, at equal distance from either, neither trustful nor mistrustful, but judging in accord with reality, living neither by what is noble nor what is self-interest, but by both, not by extravagance but by what is seemly. It is the same with passion and desire. They show courage with moderation and moderation with courage . . . All those qualities that youth and old age possess separately are united in middle age.

Advantages of fortune

Birth

It is in the nature of noble birth to make the man who possesses it more ambitious. All men who have possessions add something to it. Good birth is the glorification of one's ancestors. Men of high birth even despise those among their contemporaries who are as good as their own forebears since it is easier to boast of things in the distant past than of things in the present. The word high-born means being true to one's stock, and nobility to that which still maintains their standards. In most cases this is not what happens. The high-born are for the most part worthless, for there are good and bad harvests in the families of men as in the fruits of the earth and sometimes if the stock is good, eminent men arise for a certain time and then there is a decline.

Wealth

The characteristics that arise from wealth are plain to see. Men become arrogant, proud. Their attitude reflects the fact that they possess the good things of life. Wealth is the yardstick by which other things are judged. They are self-indulgent and extravagant; self-indulgent in the upkeep and display of their great wealth, extravagant and insolent.

They believe they have the right to command, since they believe they possess that which makes them fit to rule. The character of a wealthy man is of a happy man devoid of sense.

There are differences between old and new money, the newly rich have all the faults of the old to a much higher degree. It is to be rich without the experience of being rich.

The wrongs they commit are not inspired by the desire to do ill. Some arise from overweening pride, others from intemperance – violence and adultery.

Power

Power has certain characteristics that are similar to wealth and some that are better. Men of power are more ambitious and manly than the rich because they are drawn to exploits which their power enables them to accomplish.

They are also more diligent, because they are always alert, obliged to attend to what concerns their power.

They are more dignified than pompous. Their rank puts them in public view and so their acts are moderate and their dignity is a kind of tempered pomp that is seemly.

If they commit a wrong their misdeeds are not slight but great.

(Book II, 1390b–1b)

Aristotle thus provided future generations with a map, a textbook on psychology and social behaviour that formed the framework for future discussions, and went substantially unchallenged for two thousand years. In it, writers could find character types that were accepted as universal and actors a guide to interpretation.

His pupil Theophrastus provided future generations with another key text, *The Characters*. By characters Theophrastus meant characteristics. His short articles describe certain aspects of behaviour – lying, cheating, gossiping, sponging etc. – which dominate particular individuals who then become types. Future writers were thus provided with a gallery of ready-made characters which they could imitate, with individual variations. Dramatists built plays, particularly comedies, around recognisable types and situations. The New Comedy in Greece, Roman comedy and later the *Commedia* used fixed formulae. The actor could thus easily see what was being asked of him and respond accordingly. A useful shorthand had been created when rehearsals were very brief.

Most actors chose to specialise in one character type. This made them employable. They could be typecast. When professional companies began to be formed they consisted mostly of one-part actors. This enabled them to cover the casting of most of the standard plays in the repertoire. The more talented and skilful actors could almost take possession of a particular type and move from company to company to play it, since they frequently had audience appeal.

Aristotle's manuscripts were lost. Only fragments remained. His ideas were reworked in the Roman world. Educated Romans spoke Greek, which was a sign of superior culture. It is through Rome that his ideas were transmitted until the Renaissance.

There are two key Latin texts: Cicero's *On the Art of Oratory* and Quintilian's *Institutions of Oratory*. Like Aristotle, they took it as axiomatic that both the orator and the actor experienced in some way the emotions of which they spoke. This idea was formulated in some of the most famous and most quoted lines in literary history.

In his *Art of Poetry*, Horace writes:

> When someone laughs, then other men laugh back,
> And when he weeps, then they weep in return. And so,
> If you would have me weep, you first must suffer pain.

Cicero (106–43 BC)

As a renowned advocate, Cicero was concerned with the techniques of delivery, the coordination of voice and body, which made persuasion possible. Like Aristotle, he took good acting as his model: 'When I speak of an orator I do so in the same way as I speak of an actor.' In particular, he took as his model Roscius, whom he immortalised by references to him in his most famous orations. If Cicero's own orations became a model for future speakers, Roscius became synonymous with the supreme actor of his age. Garrick was thus known as the English Roscius.

Roscius had all the necessary gifts for an actor: a handsome figure, a fine voice, an expressive face and penetrating eyes. Above all, he showed moderation. He did not shout or gesticulate. However great his technique, however passionate he appeared, he always seemed a human being, never a player, a performer. This notion of measure, decorum, nobility was important in the classical world and part of its legacy to the future. Good speech, good posture, dignity of gesture, elegance of clothing were essential for the presentation of self in a world in which there were no media. One's medium was oneself.

As an actor, Roscius was the shining exception to the rule. Roman actors did not enjoy anything like the status of their Greek predecessors. They were often slaves. Roman theatre was largely professional and, in addition to tragedies and comedies on the Greek model, served up 'entertainment' often of the crudest kind, low farces and mimes or plays in which, reputedly, live sex and killing occurred. The great Roman tragic author, Seneca, read his plays in public. They were never acted. As a member of the court and tutor to the Emperor Nero, he had to remain aloof and, in so doing, set the model for the 'literary' dramatist. If we consider the extreme violence of the content of Seneca's plays, we realise the vocal skill that was required to convey all the horrors to a society that could see slaughter and butchery every day in the arena.

Cicero set out his ideas in the three books of *On the Art of Oratory*. His analysis and description of delivery fell under two headings:

- the relation of the speaker to his material

- the tones of voice and the gestures appropriate to each emotion

Under the first heading he followed Aristotle and Horace: the orator must to some extent experience his material. A cold advocate makes a cold judge. Under the second heading he catalogued the tone of voice and the body language needed to convey each feeling. Once described, these could be studied and refined to make them aesthetically and socially acceptable. Crucially, he took his examples not from advocacy itself but from plays that he and his readers knew well.

Cicero was the first orator to emphasise the importance of the body. He referred to Greek actors as being 'slaves to the voice' and recommended Roman actors and orators to develop their bodies through martial exercises and dancing to produce strength and fluency of movement

He thus opened up a new field of enquiry. The orator had neither mask nor built-up shoes; he had only himself. Once the actor had abandoned the mask, he was in the same position. His body had also to 'speak'. The physical codes worked out for oratory therefore became crucial.

The art of oratory

I promise you that I have never tried in court to arouse anger or compassion, ill will or enmity without being moved myself by the same feelings I was attempting to evoke in the listener. Just as there is no substance that can take fire without a spark, so there is no mind that can be influenced unless the orator himself is aflame.

The very quality of the words used to arouse the feelings of others, stirs the speaker himself even more deeply than his hearers.

This should not appear to be a marvel to us, for what can be more fictitious than poetry or the stage or plays. I have often been present at a play when the actor's eyes seemed to be ablaze with anger behind his mask . . . or when he lamented I thought I heard sobs of grief in his voice.

(Oratore II, 192–4)

There can be no doubt that the real thing is better than an imitation in all things and if it could present itself unaided, we would have no need for artifice. But because the movements of the mind which mostly have to be shown or imitated through action are often so confused that they are obscured or scarcely visible, we have to dispel the things that obscure them and take up the most important and striking features.

For every emotion has by its nature its own look and tone of voice, its own bearing and the whole of a man's body, the expression on his face, the sound of his voice are like the strings of a lyre and sound according to the way they are touched by each emotion. For the tones of the voice are tuned like the strings of an instrument to respond to every touch, high, low, quick, slow, loud, soft, while there is also a middle note. And there are modifications of all these – smooth or rough, low or full in volume, sustained, detached, weak or shrill, dying away, rising in sound. All can be controlled by technique; they are the colours the actor has at his disposal, like the painter, to create variety.

There is one tone for anger – shrill, rapid, with short, sharp phrases.

There is another for compassion or sorrow – wavering, full, halting and doleful.

There is another for fear – quiet, hesitant, downcast.

There is another for manliness – concentrated, vehement, like an urgent call to seriousness.

There is another for joy – overflowing, smooth, gentle, cheerful and happy.

There is another for dejection – a heaviness of speech with no call for pity, in one long note.

And all these emotions must be accompanied by gesture – not the theatrical kind that illustrates the words but conveying the meaning, the idea by suggestion not show . . .

But everything really depends on the face, and the face is dominated by the eyes. For delivery is entirely the concern of emotions, which are mirrored in the face and expressed by the eyes, for these are the only part of the body capable of producing as many changes as there are emotions and no one can produce the same effect with his eyes shut. [There was an actor] who delivered his lines with eyes in a fixed stare, described as 'turning his back on the audience'. The eyes should therefore be used because facial expression should not be much changed for fear of falling into vulgar contortions. It is the eyes that should be used to show emotions by appearing earnest, then relaxed, then staring, then happy according to the nature of the words. The body speaks through action, so it is all the more needful that it should correspond to the thought.

(*Oratore III*, 214–23)

Roman literature also provides us with the first recorded examples of an actor attempting and succeeding in transferring intense personal emotion into his acting. Aulus Gellus tells us that when the actor Polus played Electra mourning her brother, he brought an urn containing the ashes of his own son who had just died on to the stage with him. As he spoke his lines, he concentrated on the urn and his own grief, so that he wept real tears, forcing the audience to weep with him.

Quintilian (AD 35–95)

Of all the classical writers on rhetoric Quintilian was the most influential. His precepts were taught in schools and universities – the Jesuits in the seventeenth century based much of their education on oratory and drama. They were still under discussion in the eighteenth century when Macklin and Garrick introduced a new style of acting.

The reason for this continued success was the fact that Quintilian wrote the twelve books of the *Institutions of Oratory* for children. It is a manual. Everything concerned with delivery and gesture is spelled out in the smallest detail.

Institutions

Truth of feeling

If you wish to move others, that which is most essential, to my mind, is to be moved yourself.* There are times when it would be ridiculous to appear to feel sorrow, anger and indignation merely by arranging our face and feel nothing in our heart. How do we explain the fact that people who have suffered sudden loss are expressive in their cries? Why does anger make the uneducated eloquent, unless it is because their minds are stirred and their feelings are true? When we wish to give our words an appearance of truth, let us be like those who feel genuine emotions, and let them flow from the state of mind we wish to evoke in the judge. Will he feel sorrow if, as he listens to me, there is no sorrow in my speech? Will he feel anger if the person wanting to rouse him to anger feels none? Will he weep if my eyes are dry? It cannot be. Only fire can burn, only liquid can moisten and nothing can impart to something else another colour than its own. The essential then is that we ourselves be gripped by the feeling we wish to grip the judge, that we should be moved ourselves before we try to move others. But how are we to achieve feeling? Feeling is not ours to command. I will try to explain. There are certain experiences which we call mental images, so that we see in our mind's eye things that do not exist, yet they are so vivid that we believe they are there before our eyes. It is the man who is capable of such experiences who has the greatest power to move. Some writers say that a person who can present things with the greatest truth is naturally endowed with a vivid imagination.† Yet anyone who wants can learn to do this. When our mind is idle, or we are daydreaming, we are haunted by the mental images of which I speak.

We seem to travel, sail, do battle, make speeches, enjoy riches we do not possess. We do not feel we are dreaming, we feel we are doing. Cannot we use this strange state of mind to our advantage? I claim a man has been murdered. Can I not imagine what might actually have happened? See the murderer suddenly leap out? See the victim turn pale, yell, beg for mercy or run away? Can I not see the assailant strike, the victim fall? Will I not see in my mind's eye the blood, the white face, the groans, the victim's last breath, the death-rattle?

This gives rise to what Cicero calls *vividness* and *presence* so that we appear to be not so much telling a story as showing what happened. Our feelings will be no less strongly aroused than if we had been present at the events ourselves.

If we need to arouse pity, let us believe that the sorrows of which we complain have befallen us. We must identify with those we pity for having suffered grievous, undeserved, bitter misfortune. We should not plead their cause as something outside us, but take on their sorrow for a time, and thus we will say what we ourselves would say in similar circumstances. I have often seen actors, both in tragedy and comedy, leave the stage in tears at the end of a demanding role. And if merely speaking words someone else has written can inspire such imagined emotion, what should we do, when we have to think what the accused thinks, so as to be moved in the same way as our client?

(Book VI)

Voice and diction

There is no proof so solid that does not lose its force if it is not spoken with assurance. Emotions flag unless they are fired by the voice, the face, the overall posture of the body. Even then, we shall be lucky if the judge too catches fire. If we lack energy and make no effort, we will not move him, and he will lose interest because we are so apathetic.

We see this in actors. They enhance the poet's work, so that it gives us infinitely more pleasure than when it is just read. At the same time they win an audience for even the weakest writing, so that authors who will never find a place in a library will find a place on the stage. If the spoken word has this power to evoke anger, tears, fears about things we know to be fictitious and unreal how much more potent it must be when we actually believe what we are saying. I have no hesitation in saying that even a mediocre speech well delivered will carry more force than a better one that is not.

There are those, however, who think that untrained speech, prompted by spontaneous feeling, is stronger and the only kind worthy of a man. These are the people who disapprove of taking care, of technique and polish or any kind of study and call it affected and unnatural, and whose own speech is crude, an imitation of antiquity.

I do agree that nature comes first. No one can have good delivery who cannot memorise what he has written, or cannot speak impromptu, or who has an incurable speech defect. Some physical deformities cannot be overcome by any skill. A good, strong voice can be used as we wish, a poor, weak one prevents us from making certain effects, such as rising in a crescendo and giving a loud cry, and forces us to break off, drop the pitch, or fall into some ugly sing-song to give the throat and lungs a rest.

The best thing to do is learn exercises by heart, because when we speak spontaneously, our involvement in the subject matter takes our mind off the voice itself. Learn passages that are as varied as possible, that involve shouting, arguing, talking normally, digressing, those that use the whole range of the voice, so that one single exercise prepares us for all occasions. This is enough.

The most important point is for the voice to match the nature of the subject and our feelings. We should not be monotonous in breathing or tone. I do not just mean that we should not shout everything (that would be madness) or be conversational (which lacks feeling) or mumble (which is weak), but that in passages of a certain emotional colour there should be changes in the voice which are called for by the seriousness of the words, the nature of the thoughts and denote the beginning, the middle and the end. Even artists who painted in monochrome made some things stand out more than others, otherwise the limbs of their figures would not have been visible.

Do not force the voice. It often chokes and the extra effort makes it blur. It sometimes cracks. Be careful not to rush; that destroys the clarity of phrasing and feeling. Sometimes parts of the words are slurred. The opposite mistake is slowness. It shows lack of invention, it drags and kills the listener's concentration. It also means we run out of our allotted time. Speech should be lively not gabbled, temperate not slow.

We should not take a new breath so often that we break up the sense of what we are saying, nor use a single breath until it peters out. That makes an unpleasant noise, like a man who has been held under water for a while, and the new intake is lengthy and out of place, since it happens because we must and not because we want it. So when we embark on a lengthy passage, we should take a breath, not too slowly, or noisily. Elsewhere, the best thing is to take a breath in the natural breaks between phrases. We should train ourselves to take long breaths.

The time has come to explain what good delivery is. It is, of course, one which is right for our subject. It is for the most part ensured by our own feelings. The voice sounds according to the way its strings are struck. Some emotions, however, are real, others are simulated or imitated. Real feelings, like sorrow, anger, indignation, for example, are spontaneous but they are shapeless and need to be disciplined by systematic training. Emotions that are the product of imitation, on the other hand, have form but no roots in nature. So, the first thing we have to do is feel genuine emotion, visualise the situation and let ourselves be moved by it as though it were real. The voice is then the medium which will convey to the judge's mind the feelings we have in our own. It is the mirror of the mind and reflects all its changes.

When the subject is a happy one, it flows full and easy and seems joyful. In a dispute, however, it is roused to its full strength and strains every nerve. In anger it is fierce, harsh, tight, with short breaths because breath doesn't last long when it is expelled with undue force. In envy it is somewhat slower because only the inferior have recourse to it. When flattering, confessing, apologising or requesting, it is gentle and submissive. When persuading, warning, promising or consoling, a deep voice is needed. In fear and shame, it should be restrained, in exhortation loud, in debate precise, in compassion flexible, tearful and deliberately subdued. In a digression the voice expands, is more confident and resonant. In narrative or conversation it is pitched in the middle register. It is raised when emotions are strong and lowered when they are calmer. The pitch depends on the level of these two kinds of feeling.

(Book XI)

Stress and pitch

As I have said, such is the variety of demands made during a plea that we must adapt our speech to the sense, and that is true, not always, but sometimes, of the words. 'Poor devil', 'little beggar' surely need to be spoken low and soft. 'Strong', 'vehement', 'thief' loudly and strongly. This agreement between sense and sound adds force and aptness to the subject. Without it mind and voice would be making different statements. The same words can also be made to suggest different things – suggestion, affirmation, reproach, denial, amazement, indignation, questioning, mockery, disparagement – according to the way they are spoken. There is a difference between

> *You* gave me this kingdom

and

> *You* outsang him

and

> Are *you* that Aeneas

and

> Do *you* Drances
> convict me of cowardice

If you take any word, *you* or something else, and think of it in a range of different emotions, you will see what I mean.

(Book XI)

Body and gesture

Gesture matches the voice and also obeys the mind. Gesture is important because it can convey meaning without the need for words. Nods as well as hands reveal our intentions. In the dumb they take the place of speech. A dance is often understood and moves us without words. Our state of mind can be perceived from our face or movement and dumb animals reveal their anger, joy and submission through their eyes and other physical signs. It is not surprising then if these things which require some motion should have such a powerful effect on our minds. But if our voice and gesture do not accord with what we say, if we look cheerful when expressing sorrow, or shake our heads when stating something positive, our words would not only lack authority but also credibility. Decorum [dignity] also comes from gesture and movement.

The head is most important when speaking [. . .] both as regards the decorum [dignity] of which I spoke and also meaning. For decorum [to be dignified] it must be upright and natural. If inclined, it suggests humility, if thrown back, pride, if leaning to one side, weakness, if stiff and rigid, a certain barbarity of mind. Also it should move in time with the nature of the plea itself, with the movements of the hands, the gestures. The eyes are always turned towards the gesture except when we wish to reject some point or other. In this case we appear to turn away our face and push something aside with our hands.

The head conveys meaning in many ways. Apart from agreeing, disagreeing and confirming there is also modesty, doubt, surprise and indignation. Teachers of acting consider it wrong to use the head alone. Nodding the head too often is also a fault and shaking it about is only fit for religious fanatics.

The face rules. It is the face that makes us appear humble, threatening, flattering, sad, happy, proud or submissive. This is what people look at, before we even say a word. The face is what makes us love some men and hate others. It makes us understand a great deal. It often replaces words altogether.

Its most important feature is the eyes. The mind shines through them. Even before they move they can sparkle with joy or cloud with sorrow. Nature has endowed them with tears as well, to show our feelings, which can either burst out in grief or overflow with happiness. When the eyes do move they can be intent, soft, proud, fierce, gentle or harsh and they should take on the colour of the plea. They must never be in a fixed stare, pop out, look weary, sleepy, seem amazed or pleasure-seeking, be shifting, swimming, or filled with desire, looking sideways, or, if I may say so, lascivious, or looking for or offering favours. Of course, no one but an oaf would keep his eyes closed or half shut when he is speaking.

The eyes also have the eyelids and the cheeks to help them be expressive. A great deal of work is also done by the eyebrows since these to a certain extent shape the eyes and control the forehead which they can contract, raise or lower. The only thing that has more power over it is the blood which moves according to our state of mind. It flows into our sensitive skin when we feel ashamed and makes us blush. It retreats when we are afraid and leaves an icy pallor, but is calm when we are calm and normal. The eyebrows should neither move too much nor too little nor move separately and in opposition or contradict what we are saying. They express anger when contracted, sorrow when lowered, happiness when at rest. They move up and down to express agreement or disagreement.

As to the nose and lips there is almost nothing proper that we can use them for, apart from derision, contempt and disgust. It is not at all seemly to 'wrinkle the nostrils', as Horace has it, nor to flare them, twitch them, scratch them, give a sudden snort, or push them up with the palm of your hand. And you should not blow your nose too often.

As to the lips, pouting them, half opening them, pursing them, opening them wide, baring your teeth, stretching them from ear to ear, curling them in scorn, dropping the corners, talking out of one side of the mouth are all bad. Licking them or biting them is also ugly because they should not move while shaping the words. We speak with the whole mouth not with the lips.

The nape of the neck must be upright, but not rigid or bent back. As to the front, tightening it or stretching it are both ugly, though in different ways. Stretching causes tension and tires and weakens the voice, which, if the chin is pushed down into the chest, is then blurred and diffuse [unfocused].

Shrugging the shoulders is rarely acceptable because it shortens the neck and produces an impression of humiliation and servility, almost hypocrisy, because that is what people do when they pretend to flatter, admire or fear. Partly spreading the arm, with the shoulders relaxed and fingers wide as the hand advances, is very becoming in long, smooth passages. And when we have something very special to say, if we sweep it out to one side, our speech is thus enriched.

As for the hands, without which our speech would be crippled and weak, it is almost impossible to define all their movements since they are almost as numerous as words themselves. Other parts help the words but the hands, I might almost say, speak for themselves. We use them, do we not, to ask and promise, summon and dismiss, threaten and beg, show horror and fear, enquire and deny, show joy, sorrow, doubt, guilt, remorse and also size, quantity and number. They rouse, restrain, beg, approve, admire, indicate shame. They replace adverbs and pronouns when we need to point to persons or places. They are the common language, it seems to me, among all the great diversity of tongues in the human race.

The gestures of which I have been speaking go naturally with words. There are others which mime, such as feeling someone's pulse like a doctor to suggest a sick man, or appearing to pluck strings to suggest a musician. This should be avoided in oratory. An orator is different from a dancer. His gestures should match the sense, not individual words. That, in fact, is what good actors do. I have no objection to his moving his hand towards himself when speaking about himself or pointing someone out, or such like, but I do not approve of his miming what he is talking about.

This applies not only to the hands but to all gestures and speech. It seems to me that comic actors make a great mistake when they are playing a young man and have to report the words of an old man when telling a story and deliver them in a quavering voice like a woman. This is a form of bad imitation in an art that consists entirely of imitation.

(Book XI)

Hands

The commonest gesture is to bend the middle finger to touch the thumb while extending the other three. This is useful in the opening section of a speech. The hand is moved forward a little with a slight movement from side to side while the head slowly follows in the direction of the hand. It is also good for narrative but the hand should move a little further forward. It shows energy and assertiveness when condemning or refuting, and the hand needs to be extended even further and move more freely.

The two middle fingers can be tucked under the thumb. This is an even more positive gesture than the last.

When three fingers are tucked under the thumb, the index is extended. This is important in condemnation or pointing something out. When bent downwards a little, with the hand raised and turned towards the shoulder, it is affirmative and when pointed towards the ground marks a point.

A gesture which is particularly suitable to the expression of modesty is to bring the thumb and first three fingers gently together in a point, and move the hand towards the mouth or breast, then to let it drop, palm downwards and slightly forwards.

The hand may also be brought towards the body with the fingers pointing downwards more freely, then opened wider in the opposite direction as though seeming to deliver our words.

A good gesture for surprise is to turn the hand slightly up and then close it by bending all the fingers inwards, starting with the little finger, suddenly opening them again as one and turning the hand over.

A common gesture for asking questions is to turn the hand towards the person being questioned with the fingers in any position you choose.

A good gesture for expressing approval, or in narrative or making a distinction, is to touch the middle of the right edge of the thumbnail with the first finger.

There is also a common everyday gesture to suggest emphasis which consists in rapidly opening and closing the hand.

The trembling hand really belongs to the stage.

We can also clench our fist and place it on our breast in remorse or anger.

Experts tell us never to raise our hand above eye level or drop it below the chest. It may be moved to the left as far as the shoulder. Anything else is not suitable. But when we push our hand out to the left to indicate revulsion, the left shoulder should come forward while the head moves to the right. The left hand should never make a gesture on its own. It often accompanies the right if we are counting off our arguments on our fingers, or turning our palms out to the left in horror, or thrusting them forward to express objection, or stretching both hands out sideways, or dropping them to express an apology or to beg, or, finally, raising them in prayer or extending them to point at something or in an invocation.

Walk and posture need attention. It is ugly to stand with the right foot forward and to advance the hand and foot at the same time. You may put the weight on the right foot but the torso must be straight. Again, when you put the weight on the left foot, it is bad to raise the right, or keep it on tiptoe. It is ugly to keep the feet too far apart when standing still and almost indecent when in motion. A step forward is allowed provided it is appropriate, short and moderate. So is a certain amount of walking up and down if there are long delays caused by applause. We are advised not to turn our backs on the judges when walking but move at an angle and keep looking at the tribunal. This is not possible in private trials with a single judge but distances are shorter and we do not have to turn our backs for long. Stamping the foot may be right when beginning a speech or for vehement argument but if it is overdone the speaker looks a fool and loses the judge's attention. Swaying left and right and shifting the weight from one foot to another are equally unseemly. Avoid effeminate movements and do not rock to and fro.

It is wrong to keep moving the shoulders.

(Book XI)

With the collapse of the Roman Empire, classical theatre and its theory disappeared. Medieval drama is an independent phenomenon, arising out of the liturgy and the need for Christian moral teaching. Its forms are episodic and narrative. The actors were ordinary citizens who took on roles at certain points in the year. They had no 'art'.

2 Shakespeare and His Contemporaries

No detailed discussion of the nature of rhetoric and acting took place between the fall of the Roman Empire and the Renaissance. Classical learning was lost. However, in the fourteenth century the Italian poet Petrarch discovered manuscripts of Cicero's letters and speeches. As the inventor of the sonnet, Petrarch's influence was considerable across Western Europe. A century later, Quintilian's complete works were discovered. These, once again, became key texts. The study of rhetoric flourished in Renaissance universities, and this included the performance of plays.

Acting was considered an effective means of teaching confidence and poise. But there was also a genuine interest in the drama itself, and, in England, a number of plays were written by the so-called university 'wits', who considered themselves superior to mere actors out for hire. By this they meant the new, permanent, professional theatres in London, offering a season of plays with a broad repertoire, which demanded a wide range and variety of skills from the performer. It was they who provided a focus for the discussion of the nature of acting.

Elizabethan dramatists were, in fact, generally men of good education and culture. Their writing is at a high level of sophistication. Ben Jonson might refer somewhat disparagingly to Shakespeare's 'small Latin and less Greek' but the latter's plays are full of allusions to and quotations from Seneca, Plutarch, Cicero and, nearer to his own time, Boccaccio, Rabelais and Montaigne. He had, and shared with his contemporaries, a classical and modern European culture. What the English did, in contrast to the rest of Europe, was to absorb classical learning into their own, native, partly Anglo-Saxon culture and the tradition of mystery and morality plays.

The Elizabethan audience, or at least the educated sections of it, enjoyed the play of language, the skilful use of rhetorical figures, puns and ambiguities. They constituted part of the pleasure of the performance. Wordplay could be effective even at the most dramatic moments. Thus, in *Macbeth*, after the murder of Duncan, when Lady Macbeth says she will smear the faces of the servants with blood, she makes a play on words:

> I'll gild the faces of the grooms withal,
> For it must seem their guilt.

This was not meant to be amusing. It shows Lady Macbeth's extreme, and chilling, presence of mind.

In *Romeo and Juliet* at one point, the two lovers speak a sonnet together, embedded in the dialogue.

Leading actors required considerable knowledge of language and skill of delivery if they were to please a critical audience. At the same time, they could not be so caught up in their own cleverness that they failed to move the less educated members of the public.

They also had to contend with an audience that did not hesitate to express its opinion either of the play or their performances. In *Hamlet* Polonius makes comments during the Player King's performance. In *A Midsummer Night's Dream*, Theseus, Hippolyta and the lovers comment loudly on the Mechanicals' acting.

It is not possible to speak of a theory of acting in this period. The English, in any case, have an innate mistrust of theory and of the 'intellectual'. There was no commentary on Aristotle, as in Italy and France. In Italy, the attempt to re-create Greek tragedy ended in the creation of opera. In France, the emphasis was also on classical imitation. Authors such as Robert Garnier established the tradition of tragedy based on classical Greek tragedy, in rhyming couplets. In pragmatic England, there were only traditions and sets of practices derived from late medieval drama. If there was any discussion of the theatre as such it usually took the form of a moral attack on its corrupting influence. The good burghers of the City of London, Puritans to a man, exiled the theatre to the south of the river, the district of bear-baiting and whorehouses, the 'stews'. Leading actors, nevertheless, enjoyed the favour of the court.

Elizabethan and Jacobean theatre dealt in outstanding individuals. This was the age of Elizabeth I, Lord Cecil, Burleigh, Raleigh, Drake, the merchant venturers, the great colonisers. The actors had to match personalities of this size. They had to portray outstanding individuals.

We have three main sources for Elizabethan notions of acting:

- Shakespeare's definitions

- descriptions of the acting of Richard Burbage, Shakespeare's leading man

- handbooks of rhetorical gesture

Shakespeare offers us two versions of the actor: the ideal performer he describes in *Hamlet*, and Bottom, the egotistical bombastic ranter, from *A Midsummer Night's Dream*.

In his advice to the players, Hamlet sets out his definition of the model actor. This is based entirely on classical precepts:

- clear, fast-moving diction

- harmony of voice and gesture

- recognisable human behaviour, within the 'bounds of nature'

By the 'bounds of nature' Shakespeare did not mean, of course, what would later be termed naturalism. The Elizabethan actor worked in the open air, in broad daylight, without the benefit of lighting or effects, mostly in front of a fixed structure, on an open acting area or stage that was thrust out into an audience of around two thousand, some of whom would be on the stage, and whom he had to dominate. But there is a difference between fullness of tone, variety of colour, broadness of gesture and rant and gesticulation. What is required is an *extension*, an *expansion* of normal behaviour so that the signals are clear and can be read and understood at a distance. The actor expands to fill the space until he dominates it. When court and social life required ease and sophistication of delivery and a capacity to persuade and dominate, the actor had to be superior to his models.

Equally, he needed to dominate by his emotional power, his capacity to feel and experience what he was saying. Hamlet expresses his admiration for the capacity of the Player King to transform himself into his character:

> Is it not monstrous that this player here,
> But in a fiction, in a dream of passion,
> Could force his soul so to his own conceit
> That from her working all his visage wan'd,

> Tears in his eyes, distraction in's aspect,
> A broken voice, and his whole function suiting
> With forms to his conceit? . . .

We need, at the same time, to be aware of what the Player King is called on to do. He has to

- deliver a speech without prior notice or preparation

- do so within a few feet of his audience

- control verse of great complexity and artificiality

- appear to be experiencing 'real' emotion

- draw his audience into the world of his experience

This suggests that leading actors had a repertoire of roles which they had mastered and could perform anywhere, any time. This proved to be the case well into the future, when actors who wanted to make a living had to be able to appear with almost no rehearsal and in performances which no modern audiences would recognise as a 'production'.

Shakespeare found his ideal model in Richard Burbage.

What impressed his contemporaries was Burbage's ability to transform himself into a range of characters, the absence of histrionics and the presence of genuine acting. In an anonymous elegy written on his death in 1619 he was described as England's Roscius:

> what Roscius
> Was unto Rome that Burbage was to us
> How did his speech become him and his face
> Suit with his speech, and every action grace
> Them both alike, while not a word did fall
> Without just weight to ballast it withal . . .
> He's gone, and with him what a world are dead,
> Which he reviv'd, to be revived so
> No more: young Hamlet, old Hieronimo,
> King Lear, the grieved Moor, and more beside,
> That liv'd in him, have now forever died.
> Oft have I seen him leap into the grave,
> Suiting the person, which he seem'd to have,
> Of a sad lover, with so true an eye
> That there I would have sworn he meant to die.

Oft have I seen him play this part in jest
So lively that spectators, and the rest
Of his sad crew, whilst he but seemed to bleed,
Amazed, thought that even then he died indeed.

'Elegy on the death of Burbage'

In 1664 Richard Flecknoe provided this account of his acting:

[He so wholly transformed] himself into his part, and putting off himself with his clothes as he never (not so much in the tiring house) assumed himself until the play was done, there being as much difference betwixt him and our common actors as between a ballad-singer who only mouths it and an excellent singer who knows all his graces and can artfully modulate his voice, even to know how much breath he is to give every syllable. He had all the parts of an excellent orator, animating his words with speaking, and speech with acting [gesture]; his auditors being never more delighted than when he spoke nor more sorry than when he held his peace; yet even then he was an excellent actor still, never falling in his part when he had done speaking but with his looks and gestures maintaining it still.

(The Acting of Richard Burbage)

This approach to performance, one of psychological truth and technical control, formed the bedrock of what was to become the tradition of English acting.

There was one further aspect to the study of acting in the sixteenth century: manuals of expression and gesture. Classical authors had been able to catalogue and describe the gestures that were appropriate for particular emotions. The advent of printing and the woodcut meant that these gestures could now be shown, studied and copied.

It is questionable whether major actors, except in a general sense, felt themselves constrained by these images. They used them as a shorthand guide for the audience but made them their own. You cannot characterise Hamlet, Romeo and Lear using the same stock gestures. These books were most probably intended for students studying rhetoric, and child actors who needed basic training.

The notion of codification and regulation did, however, become extremely important in the seventeenth century, with its neoclassical culture.

3 | Declamation

French neoclassical theatre dominated European theatre for much of the seventeenth and eighteenth centuries. The reasons were both artistic and political. No court could rival that of Louis XIV at Versailles. No state was as centralised as France and when the Sun King declared, 'I *am* the state,' it was not an idle boast. Every monarch and prince in Continental Europe wanted to be Louis, wanted to have their own Versailles.

The French state was built on three principles: control, formality and centralisation. Everything was regulated. Everything, including the arts, was 'official'. Louis created the Académie française to regulate the French language and the Comédie-Française to set the standard for the theatre.

In matters of taste, the court set the tone. Good speech, deportment, knowledge of etiquette were essential within a hierarchy that was absolutely fixed. Louis encouraged the arts, notably the theatre. He himself was a fine dancer and on occasion appeared in one of the *comédie-ballets* that were so popular – as Apollo, of course. His reign witnessed an almost unparalleled flourishing of theatre (Corneille, Racine, Molière), music (Lully, Charpentier, Marin Marais), painting (Poussin, Claude), philosophy and mathematics (Descartes, Pascal). It was also an age of moral reflection, of maxims on the nature of man and, following Theophrastus, of particular character types (La Bruyère, La Rochefoucauld). In their *salons* the leading female members of the aristocracy cultivated the art of civilised conversation, while writers would present their latest offering for criticism and enjoyment.

It was to this cultivated, sophisticated, critically demanding audience that dramatists and actors had to address themselves. In an extraordinary combination, court, church and stage came together to define an aesthetic that would dominate French theatre for two hundred years.

There was an important constraint on the actor. Leading actors played for the court. They represented a king to a king, nobles to the nobility. There could, therefore, be no hint of anything undignified, or unseemly, anything the idealised figure of the monarch would not do.

Aristocratic audiences and readers saw themselves in classical terms, as living by classical precepts and values. Even in comedy the characters never bore simple first names like Pierre or Marie. They were Philinte, Célimène. Alternatively, they had names taken from the *commedia dell'arte*, like Sganarelle.

In their attempts to re-create classical tragedy authors turned to Aristotle, or rather to a version of the *Poetics* that had come from Italy. During the sixteenth century, a number of commentators, notably Castelvetro, had produced critical works on Aristotle, in which they claimed to explain his ideas. What they did, in fact, was to replace Aristotle's forensic examination with a rigid set of 'rules'.

Primary among these 'rules' were the Three Unities – time, place and action.

A play must not cover more than twenty-four hours, must occur in a single setting and must have a single plot. As in classical drama there must be no violence on stage. All such events must be narrated by a messenger.

Any infringement of these rules provoked a furious debate, with attack and counter-attack in print at every level. Corneille's most well-known play *Le Cid* was heavily criticised because the events could not have taken place within twenty-four hours. Even Cardinal Richelieu became involved in the dispute as he was instrumental in laying down the 'rules'.

The chosen form of verse for the dialogue was the alexandrine and the couplet – a strict, controlled form.

French is a virtually unaccented language. If there is a stress, it is on the last syllable of a word. A line of poetry is, therefore, calculated not by the number of stresses but by the number of syllables it contains. The alexandrine is a line of twelve or thirteen syllables. They are joined in rhyming couplets which alternate between so-called masculine and feminine endings. The masculine ending is a single vowel, the feminine ending is an unstressed 'e'. The movement in the alexandrine is always towards the final word of the second line of the couplet.

In delivery, a line can be broken up in three ways:

- by a pause (caesura) after the sixth syllable

    1 2 3 4 5 6 / 7 8 9 10 11 12

- by two pauses, one after the fourth and one after the eighth syllable

    1 2 3 4 / 5 6 7 8 / 9 10 11 12

- or one after the third and one after the ninth syllable

    1 2 3 / 4 5 6 7 8 9 / 10 11 12

When there was a single caesura, the voice was supposed to rise and fall in the first half, pause, then rise and fall in the second half.

Like the Unities, the alexandrine became sacrosanct. When, two hundred years after the dispute over *Le Cid*, Victor Hugo attempted to experiment with the alexandrine in *Hernani*, and make it more flexible, he sparked off another 'battle'.

The rhymed alexandrine places enormous constraints on an actor. He is obliged to follow the structure of the verse almost as a musical score. This requires considerable technique and vocal skill if the delivery is not to become monotonous. The relentless drive towards the rhyme at the end of the second line of the couplet encourages repetitive inflections, with a 'clang' at the end of the alexandrine that effectively stops the action, which then has to start again with the following line. This makes it difficult to build a scene or a speech. All the actor's concentration and artistry have, therefore, to be on the words and this imposes a style of acting that leaves little room for physical movement. Emotion has to be conveyed through the voice, through declamation, with the appropriate supporting gestures.

The art of declamation

The word declamation requires some explanation. It now has a negative connotation – artificial, inflated, false. In the seventeenth century it meant what we would now call *projection*, the ability to be heard and understood in a large space such as a theatre, an assembly or a church. It requires greater volume, greater clarity of diction, greater energy than speech in a private room.

The danger of delivery of this kind is that it makes the act of speaking an end in itself, deforming sounds, vowels, consonants, using the same approach to every role whatever it might be, or tricks to attract a round of applause. Molière attacked this style of acting in much the same terms as Hamlet attacked the 'rant' school, insisting on pace, clarity and meaning, a 'natural' style, that is where vowels and consonants have the same values as in ordinary life and where delivery makes clear the author's meaning within the text he has written, respecting grammar and punctuation. It was vocal tricks that Molière detested.

Between 1657 and 1707 three major works appeared on declamation in tragedy, describing the tone of voice, the dynamic level and the pitch appropriate to the kind of writing (introduction, narration, exhortation, conclusion) or the emotion to be conveyed. In general, they are a reworking of the definitions provided by Cicero and Quintilian. They do, however, represent the kind of informed opinion of the period and the standards by which actors were judged.

At its worst, this could turn acting into a mere mechanical exercise. A script could be analysed in terms of its stylistic features and the emotions it described and the appropriate style of delivery would be produced in conformity with the rules. Great actors could, of course, make their own personality shine through the mechanics. The rules were a boon to the mediocre.

Gesture was little discussed, and then in terms close to Quintilian and only in terms of oratory. It was considered subordinate to the word.

Tragicomedy and comedy, free from the constraints of neoclassical tragedy, offered much more scope for stage action and byplay, particularly for plays written in prose. Molière, the only one of the three great dramatists to be a working professional, exploited these possibilities to the full and, while he was able in his more serious comedies, such as *Le Misanthrope*, to conform to notions of tragic form, in plays such as *Les fourberies de Scapin* he was able to draw on the improvised performances of the Italian companies so popular with Parisian audiences. While the works of Corneille and Racine can be spoken, the plays of Molière demand to be staged.

Just as there were typical forms (tragedy, comedy) and typical characters (hero, villain, old man, servant) so there were typical costumes and headdresses that enabled an audience to know what kind or category they were dealing with and, more important, what should be the category of their response. Actors in tragedy found themselves more and more constrained. Costumes became more and more elaborate, and wigs and helmets, so heavy, so tall, so stuffed with plumes they hardly dared move their heads.

Actors were, despite the many formal constraints, confronted with the task of creating fully rounded, individual characters. While Molière's comedies might deal in types, derived from classical drama – miser, misanthrope, hypochondriac – they were fully individualised and demanded individualised performances. This required great psychological depth, particularly for an audience greatly involved in the dissection of human behaviour and motives. In seventeenth-century literature, two works stand out: the *Maxims* of La Rochefoucauld and the *Characters* of La Bruyère. La Rochefoucauld's *Maxims* are mordant, merciless and savage. La Bruyère's *Characters* offer in eight sections an overview of society and of personal behaviour – the arts, the court, the town, the quirks and qualities of individuals.

Neoclassical drama might be 'Aristotelian' in form, but unlike Greek tragedy its primary focus was not on the action, as Aristotle had insisted, but on individual human dilemmas. It was the people, trapped in a dilemma, political, religious, emotional, that mattered. Tragedy dealt in the Passions, in intense feelings.

The nature of the Passions once again became a matter of concern and the discussion was taken up by Descartes but now in the context of new scientific discoveries, notably in anatomy. Where Aristotle had discussed feelings essentially within a social context, Descartes was concerned with the physiology of emotion and the relationship of mental to physical activity.

He held to two basic principles:

- The human organism was split between mind and body, so that the mind could both contemplate and analyse the activities of the body

- Man was a machine, so that fixed causes produced fixed effects

His seminal work was the *Traité des passions* (*Treatise on the Passions*) of 1649 in which he described and catalogued the major emotions. The externals, the physical expressions of the Passions were universals that could be studied and mastered and reproduced at will. Descartes' list of emotions does not differ substantially from Aristotle's and like him he assumed that they had an independent existence.

Like other writers before him, such as Thomas Wright in his *Passions of the Mind* (1601), Descartes, for both social and moral reasons, considered strong passions potentially dangerous since they were difficult to control. Aristotle had referred to 'ecstasy', being beside oneself. The most effective way to prevent the Passions from taking control was extreme physical tension.

Descartes divided emotions or passion into two categories – physical and mental. There were those that were produced by an external stimulus which excited the 'animal spirits' which were assumed to be situated in the 'gland' in the brain. It was the animal spirits that brought the nerves and muscles into play. There were others, however, that arose independently in the mind but which produced identical physical effects.

A treatise on the passions

I shall now list all the principal passions in the order in which they are to be found.

Astonishment
When we encounter an object for the first time and we judge it to be new or very different from anything we have known before, or we imagine it to be so, we are astonished and amazed. And because this happens before we know whether this object is agreeable to us or not, it seems to me that astonishment is the first of all the passions and it has no opposite since, if the object we encounter holds nothing strange to us, we are not moved, and we regard it without passion.

Respect and contempt
Respect and contempt are joined to astonishment according to whether we are surprised by the largeness or smallness of the object. And we can respect or despise ourselves; and that gives rise to the passions, and thereafter to the habit of generosity or pride, and of humility or baseness.

Veneration and despise
But when we respect or despise other objects that we consider as free causes, able to do good or ill, respect gives rise to veneration and mere contempt to despise.

Love and hate

Now all the preceding passions can be aroused in us without our in any way noticing if the object which causes them is good or ill. But when an object is presented to us as something good for us, that is agreeable to us, then we feel love for it; but when it is presented to us as evil or harmful, we are driven to hate.

Desire

All the other passions arise from this same consideration of good and evil, but so as to set them in order, I make a distinction of time, taking into consideration whether they carry us forward towards the future rather than the present or the past, I begin with desire. For not only when we wish to acquire something we do not yet possess, or to avoid an evil we think might arise, and also when we only wish to hold on to what we have or wish evil to stay away, all of which are included in this passion, it is clear that it is always forward-looking.

Hope and fear

All we need to do is think that the acquisition of some object or the retreat of some ill is possible for us to want it, but if we then consider if there is a great or little likelihood that we shall acquire what we want, the thought of a great likelihood makes us hope, while less likelihood makes us fear, and jealousy is a form of fear. When hope is very great, it changes its nature and is called certainty, while, on the other hand, great fear becomes despair.

Irresolution and courage

We can also hope and fear although the arrival of what we anticipate in no way depends on us; but when it is represented to us as being independent, we can experience difficulties in the choice of means and action. The first produces irresolution which encourages us to think and to seek advice. The opposite to this is courage, or boldness, of which the desire to surpass others is an example. Cowardice is the opposite of courage, as fear or terror are the opposite of boldness.

Remorse

If we decide on some course of action before irresolution has vanished, that brings remorse which does not look to the future as the preceding passions did, but rather to the present or the past.

Joy and sadness

The contemplation of present good provokes joy in us and that of present ill sadness when it is a good or an evil which is represented as being ours.

Mockery, envy, pity
But when it is presented to us as belonging to others, we may consider them worthy or unworthy, and when we consider them worthy we feel nothing but joy in that we find it good that things are as they should be. There is only this difference, that the joy that comes from good is genuine while that which comes from ill is accompanied by laughter and mockery. But if we consider these people unworthy, good provokes envy, and evil pity, which are forms of sadness. We should note that those passions which relate to present good or evil may often be associated with those to come, since the notion that they will occur presents them to us as being present.

Satisfaction and repentance
We may also consider the causes of good or evil both past and present. The good we do creates inward satisfaction, which is the sweetest of all the passions, whereas evil causes repentance, which is the most bitter.

Favour and gratitude
The good others do makes us feel favourable towards them, even when the good was not done to us. If it is to us, then to favour we add gratitude.

Indignation and anger
Similarly, the evil others do but not to us, merely results in our feeling indignation towards them, and when it is done to us, it moves us also to anger.

Glory and shame
Moreover, the good which is or has been in us, when considered in the light of the opinion others may have of us, causes feelings of glory, and the evil in us, shame.

Distaste, longing and happiness
At times the duration of things good causes staleness and distaste, while the duration of things evil reduces sadness. From goodness past comes longing, which is a kind of sadness, and from evil past comes happiness, which is a kind of joy.

The power of the passions
Perceptions which we attribute entirely to the soul are those whose effects are only felt in the soul and in general those of which we do not know any immediate cause. These are feelings of joy, anger and such like, which are sometimes roused in us by objects which stimulate our nerves and sometimes through other causes . . .

And as the soul, when it takes note of another object, is able not to hear a small sound or feel a small pain but cannot but hear thunder or feel fire burning that hand, so it can easily overcome the small passions but not the most intense and strongest until the heat of the blood and the animal spirits have subsided. All that the will can do while this emotion is at full strength is not to succumb to its effects and to hold back some of the movements it produces in the body. For example, if anger makes us raise our hand to strike someone, the will can ordinarily hold it back; if fear causes the legs to run away, the will can restrain them, and similarly with others . . .

When a dog sees a partridge, its natural inclination is to run after it; and when it hears a gunshot, the noise naturally presses it to run away, and yet we can ordinarily train gun dogs so that the sight of a partridge makes them stop and the sound they hear afterwards, when it is shot at, makes them run after it.

These things are useful to give each of us the courage to observe and study the passions, for, since we can with a little effort change the movements of the brain in animals who have no reason, it is evident that we can do even better with men, and that even those who are the weakest souls can achieve absolute command over all their passions, if they use sufficient effort to train and lead them.

The complex nature of expression in the eyes and face

There is not a single passion that some movement of the eyes does not reveal; and that is so obvious in some of them that even the most senseless servants can tell from his eye whether their master is angry with them or not. Yet while we can easily perceive these actions of the eyes and know what they mean, it is not easy to describe them since all of them consist of many changes both in the movement and the body of the eye, which are so particular and small that none of them can be seen separately, while their conjunction is easy to perceive. We can almost say the same thing of the actions of the face which accompany the passions, for while they are larger than the actions of the eyes, it is still difficult to separate them and they are so alike that some men have almost the same expression when they are weeping as when they are laughing. It is true there are some that we cannot miss, like the lines on the forehead when in anger and certain movements of the nose and the lips in indignation or mockery; but they seem to be not so much natural as designed. And generally all the actions both of the face and the eyes can be changed by the soul when, to hide its passion, it thinks hard about an opposite so that we can conceal our passions as well as reveal them.

Contradictory emotions

Our good or ill depend on those inner emotions that are caused in the soul by the soul itself, in which they differ from the passions which always depend on a movement of the animal spirits. And though the emotions of the soul are often joined to passions that are like them, they can encounter others and even some that are their opposite.

For example, when a husband mourns his wife (this often happens) whom he would not be best pleased to see alive again, it may be that his heart is gripped by sadness caused by the funeral service and the absence of one to whose conversation he had become accustomed, and it may be that some vestiges of love or pity in his imagination may draw real tears from his eyes, but none the less he may feel a secret joy in the depths of his soul, whose emotion has such power that the sadness and tears cannot diminish it. And when we read other people's adventures in a book, or we see them played in the theatre, we sometimes feel sadness, sometimes joy, or love, or hate and generally all the passions, according to the diversity of objects offered to our imagination; at the same time we feel pleasure to feel them rising in us, and this pleasure is an intellectual joy, which can equally arise from sadness as from other emotions.

It was control that mattered. Control through knowledge, study and reason. How was control in acting to be achieved?

Descartes had referred in his book to facial expressions being somehow 'designed'. Descartes' message was not lost, although it was first taken up in painting. In 1698, Le Brun's lecture, *Method for Learning how to Sketch the Universal Passions*, was published and was translated into English in 1702, gaining wide acceptance. In it he provides templates for six universal passions, which he accepts more or less in the terms Descartes provided. His drawings indicate a careful approach, based on observation and measurement. No more precise or scientific method was available in the period. His claim is that whatever the overall composition of a picture, the painter can use these templates to depict emotion in a particular figure since they are valid and rooted in nature.

This opened up a new range of possibilities for acting. The actor could design his performance through a mixture of set codes (body, hands, face) and the observation of daily behaviour. The externals of the passions could be studied and mastered and reproduced at will without involvement or loss of control (*ecstasy*).* Everything would be subject to the mind.

The classical notion that the actor/orator should experience the emotions he describes was now challenged.

* Aristotle.

4 | Acting

The question, feeling or not feeling, emotion or technique, now dominated the debate on the nature of acting and was to continue to do so for the next three hundred years. The battle lines were mainly drawn up between England and France.

With the Restoration, England had to reinvent its theatre and rediscover its Elizabethan and Jacobean roots. Under the Commonwealth, theatre was forbidden, as was dancing. When Charles II took the throne in 1660 he had spent most of his life in France under the influence of the French court, resident either in the Louvre or at Chaillot, his mother's palace. In his childhood and youth the preferred form of theatre at the court had been the masque – elaborate entertainment combining drama, dance and music with decor. This very much reflected the tastes of the French-born queen, Henrietta Maria, daughter of Henri IV and Marie de Médicis. It developed into the English operas of Purcell and Arne.

The richest plays in the repertoire were the comedies that derived from pre-Commonwealth England, from Ben Jonson and his contemporaries, which were not confined by the restrictions of the neoclassical aesthetic. They were plays for a limited and sophisticated audience, reflecting the manners of the court and London life and caricaturing the uncouth behaviour of country bumpkins. The performances relied on the observation of the received codes of social behaviour – the bow, the curtsy, the use of the snuffbox or the fan, the studied speech. This separated the admirable and the elegant from the buffoons.

Tragedy presented a different problem and here neoclassical taste dominated. Tragedy had to be dignified, stately. The difficulty for the late seventeenth century was Shakespeare. Everyone recognised him as the greatest English dramatist, but he was also a 'barbarian', with his obscene jokes, his mixture of tragedy, comedy and farce. But he had created great characters that were appealing to leading actors. So his works were simply reshaped and rewritten to conform to the conventions of the time. The major attempt to establish the neoclassical canons that should govern English theatre found its most complete expression in Dryden's *Essay on Dramatick Poesie*.

Tragedy became static: it consisted of noble sentiments expressed in dignified verse. The acting was necessarily mainly declamatory. It was still the voice that mattered.

The theatre buildings acquired a standard format. The acting area projected into the auditorium with on-stage boxes. At the beginning of the eighteenth century the acting area at Drury Lane was seventeen feet in front of the proscenium arch. Behind it was the scenic area, with flats and drops and sometimes elaborate stage machinery. Although working indoors, the Restoration actor was exposed, like his Elizabethan counterpart, on a bare platform from which he had to dominate his noisy, visible and fully-lit audience by his presence and his technique.

We can gain some idea of what was considered good acting from descriptions of Betterton, considered the greatest actor of his age.

> Mr Betterton (although a superlative good actor) laboured under an ill figure, being clumsily made, having a great head, a short thick neck, stooped in the shoulders, and had fat short arms which he rarely lifted higher than his stomach. His left hand frequently lodged in his breast between his coat and his waistcoat, while with his right hand he prepared his speech. His actions were few, but just. He had little eyes and a broad face, a little pock-fretten, a corpulent body and thick legs with large feet . . . His voice was low and grumbling, yet he could tune it by an artful climax which enforced universal attention, even from the fops and orange girls.
>
> (Aston, 'A Brief Supplement to Colley Cibber Esq.)

> When [verses] came from the mouth of a Betterton, the multitude no more desired sense to them than our musical connoisseurs think it essential in the celebrated arias of a Italian opera. Does this not prove that there is very near as much enchantment in the well-governed voice of an actor as in the sweet pipe of an eunuch?
>
> (Cibber, *An Apology for the Life of Mr Colley Cibber*)

He did possess, however, considerable emotional power which could be seen in the eyes.

His contemporaries admired the range and variety of his performances and his ability to stay in character.

> Betterton from the time he was dressed to the end of the play kept his mind in the same temperament and adaptness as the present character required.

(Aston, 'A Brief Supplement to Colley Cibber Esq.')

This recalls Flecknoe's description of Burbage.

A frequent point of reference was Horace's dictum, 'If you would have me weep . . .' It was applied to Betterton and to the leading actress of her time, Mrs Barry.

> Her action is always just and produced naturally by the sentiments of the part which she acts, and she everywhere observes those rules prescribed to the poets by Horace and which equally reach the actors.

(Gildon, *The Life of Mr Thomas Betterton*)

The study of rhetorical gesture had continued. Two major works by John Bulwer, *Chironomia or the Art of Manual Rhetoric* (1644) and *Chirologia or the Natural Language of the Hand* (1654), laid down strict rules, but it is questionable how far they were applied by professional actors.

Just as the seventeenth century had been the period of treatises on rhetoric, speech and formalised gesture, so the eighteenth century was the period of treatises on the actor or, rather, on the actor's process. It was, in fact, the century of the actor. The period could not match the richness and breadth of writing in Elizabethan and Jacobean England or the France of Louis XIV, or the Golden Age of Spain. Until the German Romantics appeared there were hardly any major dramatists. Only Marivaux provided a large body of work. For the rest – Goldsmith, Sheridan, Beaumarchais – they only produced one or at most two plays that have survived in the repertoire

In 1710, in the first modern textbook on acting, *The Rules of Oratory Applied to Acting*, Charles Gildon stated: 'we come now to the hands, which as they are the chief instrument of action, varying themselves as many ways as they are capable of expressing things, so it is a difficult matter *to give such rules as are without exception*'.

Gildon's recommendations as far as movement and gesture are concerned are, on the whole, extremely general but are made in terms that recall classical literature. He stipulates that

- the actor should rehearse in front of a mirror so that the body and the face should be harmonious and attractive

- the actor should experience emotion

He spoke of actors who, like Hamlet's Player King, were visibly and genuinely moved. He stressed, however, that the emotion must be grounded in nature, not in the dramatic situation. The actor should rely on his own personal experience. Artists of the first rank

> kept their own private afflictions in their mind and bent it perpetually on real objects and not on the fable or the fictitious passion of the play which they acted . . . When you are therefore to speak, you ought first with care to consider the nature of the thing of which you are to speak and fix a very deep impression of it in your own mind before you can be thoroughly touched with it yourself, or able by an agreeable sympathy to convey the same passion to another.

We know little of acting up to the 1730s except from later commentators who were critical of it. The major complaint was that it had become stilted and cliché-ridden. Male actors were cast because they were tall with booming voices and women because they were attractive. It is worth noting that neither Betterton nor Mrs Barry was in the conventional sense handsome or good-looking. In terms of subtlety and truth to nature, women seem to have come off better. Only recently allowed to perform, they came with less baggage, less 'tradition'. They could not strut. They could, however, flirt with their admirers in the audience, and they did.

Demands for reform came in the 1730s in England, notably from Aaron Hill, who was born in 1685 and had lived through the decline of Restoration acting. He was interested in training and suggested the creation of an acting academy. It was he who coached Mrs Susanna Cibber, the wife of Theophilus Cibber and one of Garrick's leading ladies. He was deeply dissatisfied with the state of acting represented by the theatrical establishment – Cibber, Quin, Ryan – and profoundly critical of contemporary costumes and staging. In 1734 he started publishing a twice-weekly magazine, *The Prompter*, in which until 1736 he ranged over every aspect of the theatre – acting, costume, decor, ethics.

At the heart of Hill's concerns is a desire for greater authenticity in acting and staging. An actor with a booming voice but no knowledge of the nature of human emotions and no capacity to feel them is inadequate. Equally, an actor who is content always to be himself, never to characterise and never to relate to the other characters is simply not doing his job.

The actor who assumes a character wherein he does not seem in earnest to be the person by whose name he calls himself, affronts instead of entertaining the audience . . . Have we not a right to the representation we have paid for? And is it possible to be deceived into a mistake of the player for the hero unless he *listens* as well as *speaks*? Unless his very silence is instructed to talk to the eye of the spectator by a thousand significant gestures, starts, changes and attitudes whereby the soul, at work, inwardly throws out marks of its sensations?

(*The Prompter*, 62, 13 June 1735)

. . . [T]he finest natural voice may be useless and insignificant to its possessor unless accompanied by a power to discover passions and express them; whereas a voice of much less depth and capacity, supposing it clear and articulate, being helped by those passionate changes which are the beauty and essentials of tragedy, shall outcharm any natural sweetness of tone and reach not the ear only, but the heart with its meaningly musical harmony.

(*The Prompter*, 64, 20 June 1735)

The bounds of probability, in the mean time, may be as openly transgressed in the appearance of an actor as in the sentiments which he utters. And the dress should always be *suited* to the person who takes it upon him. An old Roman could never with any propriety be made to look like a modern Frenchman, nor a Dutch burgomaster's wife like a Queen of Great Britain.

(*The Prompter*, 22, 24 January 1735)

Hill takes up some of the issues raised by Gildon in 1710. He agrees on the necessity for the actor to enter into the emotion of the character but he rejects a slavish adherence to Quintilian's precepts and rehearsal in front of a mirror.

Quintilian lays it down as a rule that the orator . . . is 'never to raise his hands above the height of his eyes'. Now who does not see and acknowledge the necessity of this caution in a pleader because, addressing himself to the superior power of his judges, he ought to govern his gesture by a conscious regard to his inferiority and dependence. In such a situation, no doubt, the hands raised higher than the head would form too bold and presuming an attitude. But what is all this to the player, who is sometimes to act a monarch who has no superior and in whom actions of menace or sudden transports of indignation carry neither indecorum nor impropriety? And how shall he express with proper gesture any passionate appeals to heaven, any strong postures of starting and astonishment, without throwing his hands to a height beyond the rule of Quintilian.

Some have formed tedious and laborious schemes of adjusting their gesture at looking-glasses but for want of conceiving the . . . dependence of the action on the idea, their imaginary graces forsook 'em, and in the very instant of their wanting them, were vanished quite out of their memory.

Nevertheless, the body needed to be trained:

Others, by experience of this insufficiency, have concluded all study of deportment to be useless, so abandoned themselves to a wild expectation that proper actions would spontaneously arise and present themselves in the moment of utterance. But here too they were mistaken because, adhering to no cause, they could depend upon no consequence.

(*The Prompter*, 118, 23 December 1735)

Equally, he felt that copying paintings merely led to face-pulling. He did, however, develop Gildon's notion that the actor uses his own experiences as raw material for his performance.

In discussing the Passions, Hill accepted the traditional classification but built also on Descartes' notion of how they operated, stemming from the mind to be expressed, by a natural process, in the body and the face. It is to the mind, to the imagination that the actor must first address himself.

For a new generation of actors for whom Aaron Hill essentially spoke, their art was based on two elements:

- the capacity to generate emotion through natural processes

- observation of behaviour

Certain conventional poses and gestures remained but we need to be cautious in judging the extent to which they were used, since the evidence we have is mostly contained in paintings and engravings, which themselves are subject to the conventions of pictorial composition.

The actor

[H]e whose trade is to represent human passion cannot be qualified for that trade without a knowledge of those passions and a power to put on, at will, the marks and colours which distinguish them . . . There are but six dramatic passions which are capable of being strongly expressed by the look and which, intermingling their differences on the visage, give us all the soul-moving variety of pain, pleasure or suspension which the heart can be strikingly touched by. These six passions are joy, sorrow, fear, scorn, anger and amazement. There are many other auxiliary passions which cannot be impressed upon the countenance yet may be well enough represented by a mixture of two or more of the six capital dramatics. Such are jealousy, revenge, love, pity . . . jealousy . . . requires a combination of three passions – fear, scorn and anger. Revenge requires only the two last. Love cannot be looked but with a joy that is tempered by fear. And pity, to express it on the face, must qualify that fear by a mixture of sorrow.

(*The Prompter*, 66, 27 June 1735)

The whole that is needful in order to impress any passion on the look is first, to conceive it by a strong and intent imagination. Let a man, for instance, recollect some idea of sorrow, his eye will, in a moment, catch the dimness of melancholy, his muscles will relax into languor and his whole body sympathetically unbend itself into a remiss and inanimate lassitude. In such a passive position of feature and nerves, let him attempt to speak haughtily and he will find it impossible. Let the sense of the words be the rashest and most violent anger, yet the tone of his voice shall sound nothing but tenderness. The modification of his muscles has affected the organs of speech, and before he can express sounds of anger in his voice he must, by conceiving some idea of anger, inflame his eye into earnestness and new-knit and brace up his fibres into impatience, adapted to violence – and then not only the voice will correspond with his visage but the step, air and movement, all, recovering from the languid and carrying the marks of the impetuous and the terrible, flash into a moving propriety from the actor to the audience, that, communicating immediately the sensation it expresses, chains and rivets our attention to the passions we are moved by.

Thus the happiest qualification which a player should desire to be master of is a plastic imagination.

Idea, then, is the great First Mover, and an actor, by that single principle, secures a consequent and necessary perfection in look, voice and action.

(*The Prompter*, 118, 23 December 1735)

By 1746, when he came to write his *Essay on Acting,* Hill had changed his mind. The dramatic Passions had been increased to ten – joy, grief, anger, fear, pity, scorn, hatred, jealousy, wonder and love. He relaxed his view of work with the mirror. It could now be used to check whether the inner experience had been correctly displayed in the body. It was a short cut, until an actor was master of his emotions. Until then, when trying to evoke a particular inner state, he could use the mirror to arrange his face and body so that they corresponded to the known characteristics of the emotion he was in the process of creating.

The new kind of actor was represented by Charles Macklin and David Garrick. Charles Macklin was born in County Donegal, Ireland, towards the end of the seventeenth century. In his early years in London he came up against the prevailing, bombastic style of speaking. He was not, as he put it, 'hoity-toity' and was entirely out of place with actors who could not order a cup of coffee without making it sound like a tragic declaration. He was advised to go out into the provinces and 'improve' his speech, which he did. He never, however, abandoned his allegiance to clear, simple speech which he taught to his students.

It was Macklin who first spoke of a 'scientific' method of acting. This was evident in his greatest performance as Shylock in *The Merchant of Venice.* Macklin transformed Shylock from a low-comedy figure to a character of almost tragic proportions. Moreover, he chose to perform Shakespeare's original text, rather than the adaptation, *The Jew of Venice,* by George Granville, which had first been performed in 1701 and had held the stage ever since. In 1741, few people had seen Shakespeare's play and saw Shylock only as a buffoon.

Macklin took his preparations very seriously. He researched the costume, discovering that Jews in the Venice ghetto wore red hats. He also visited the Jewish quarter of London to study their manners and behaviour. He read Josephus' *Jewish Antiquities.* In his diary he noted:

> Jews, their history. An instance of human incertainty – from the creation to the flood – in Egypt leaving it – robbing their masters, mutinying – Jericho – wilderness – murder of the Innocents – captivity – lion's den – Shadrach, Meshach, Abednigo, Babel. Go through the history of it – act the great characters.

He also insisted on a profound knowledge of the Passions.

Macklin

It is the duty of an actor always to know the passion and humour of each character so correctly, so intimately, and . . . to feel it so enthusiastically, as to be able to define it as a philosopher; to give its operations on the looks, tones, and gestures of general nature, as it is ranked in classes of character; and to mould all this knowledge, mental and corporeal, to the characteristic that the poet has given a particular character.

If the actor has not this philosophical knowledge of the passions, it is impossible for him to imitate them with fidelity . . .

Now, unless the actor knows the *genus, species,* and characteristic that he is about to imitate, he will fall short in his execution. The actor must restrict all his powers and convert them to the purpose of imitating the *looks, tones* and *gestures,* that can best describe the characteristic that the poet has drawn: for each passion and humour has its *genus* of *looks, tones* and *gestures,* its *species* and its individual characteristic . . .

Avarice, for instance, has its *genus, species* and individual characteristic. Molière has given the *genus.* [*L'Avare*]

As the poet hath drawn an individual characteristic, so ought it to be represented; the actor must take especial care not to mould and suit the character to his [own] looks, tones, gestures and manners; if he does so, it will then become the actor's character, not the poet's. No; he must suit his looks, tones, gestures and manners to the character; the suiting the character to the powers of the actor is imposture. I have seen King Lear, Hamlet and Richard III, acted without one look, tone or gesture, or manners of Shakespeare.

(*The Art and Duty of an Actor,* reconstructed in Kirkman's *Memoirs of the Life of Charles Macklin Esq.,* 1799, Vol. I, pp. 362–6.

Theatre had changed, audiences and the intellectual climate had changed. The aristocratic court of Versailles was one thing, the middle class another.

What eighteenth-century audiences looked for was an uplifting, transcendental experience, a moment of astonishment when they rose above the mundane. This came to be known as the Sublime, an idea formulated by the Greek writer Longinus in the first century AD.

[T]he sublime not only persuades, but even throws the audience into transport. The marvellous always works with more surprising force than that which barely persuades or delights. In most cases, it is wholly in our own power, either to resist or yield to persuasion. But the sublime, endued with strength irresistible, strikes home and triumphs over every hearer . . . the sublime . . . with the rapid force of lightning has borne down all before it, and shown at one stroke the compacted might of genius.

The true sublime, however, was to be distinguished from the false, which seems genuine but is no more than superficial sound. The real sublime passes the time test:

[W]hatever pierces no deeper than the ears can never be the true sublime. That, on the contrary, is grand and lofty, which the more we consider, the greater ideas we conceive of it; whose force we cannot possibly withstand; which immediately sinks deep, and makes such impressions on the mind as cannot easily be worn out or effaced. In a word, you may pronounce that sublime which always pleases and takes equally with all sorts of men.*

(*Dionysius Longinus on the Sublime*)

In his *Dictionary,* Johnson quotes Addison:

The *sublime* rises from the nobleness of thoughts, the magnificence of the words, or the harmonious and lively turn of the phrase; the perfect *sublime* arises from all three together.

The great actor responds to great writing; he embodies the noble ideas it contains, the high emotion, and in his performance balances the elements of the style through his voice and body.

Linked to the overwhelming experience of the sublime was the experience of irresistible weeping. There was a culture of tears throughout Europe, which were seen as a positive reaction. Whether reading alone or to one another, it was expected that tears would be shed as a sign of sensibility. The capacity to weep was also considered a sign of moral worth, of the capacity to repent and to forgive. The man who cannot weep has no genuine moral sense and is unredeemable. A man's duty was to control and contain his own feelings, while responding fully to the feelings and needs of others.

It was Boileau, the leading commentator and critic, who was responsible for reintroducing the idea of the Sublime. His *L'art poétique,*

* Trans., William Smith, 1743.

modelled on Horace's *Ars Poetica*, had been translated and adapted by Dryden. In the early 1670s he produced a translation of Longinus' text *On the Sublime* with a critical commentary to which he added, in 1693, a series of *Réflexions*. Following this, *On the Sublime* was translated into English and later retranslated many times. It became a seminal text in the eighteenth century.

Eighteenth-century England found its ideal actor in Garrick, the English Roscius. For thirty years Garrick ran Drury Lane, giving a series of great performances both in tragedy and comedy, introducing greater order into the rehearsal process and the beginnings of consistent direction.

Garrick wrote only one article on acting, in 1741, and that is part serious, part tongue-in-cheek. The only evidence we have of his ideas is a few comments in his letters and accounts by his colleagues and pupils. We do know, however, that, following Macklin's example, he based his performances on the observation of real behaviour which enabled him to break away from the standardised presentations of his contemporaries and their historic clichés. Garrick started with the dramatic situation and responded to it appropriately. He also trained continuously, honing his craft until he became a complete master of his means. His major preoccupation was with the rapid transition from one emotion to the other, so that he could, if necessary, do it in mid-line. He would practise running the whole gamut of emotions from delight to despair, from joy to sorrow, as a musician practises scales. This was a purely internal process. He felt the changes, however rapid they might be. Their physical expression was automatic. The many detailed accounts by con-temporaries of his performances bear witness to the extraordinary emotional range he possessed and the speed with which he changed.

We can gain some notion of what the ideal actor was in the late eighteenth century from articles by James Boswell. Boswell was the companion and biographer of Samuel Johnson, Garrick's oldest friend. He moved in Garrick's circle.

Boswell insists that an actor must be educated, that he must have the elegance of manner of a gentleman. Above all, he insists on the validity of Horace's principle, 'If you would have me weep . . .'

Significantly, he touches on the problem that began to preoccupy the eighteenth-century mind, that of what he called 'double being', split consciousness. How can the actor feel and at the same time be aware of what he is doing?

Remarks on the profession of a player

I

. . . in order to be a good player there is required a greater share of genius, knowledge and accomplishments than for any one profession whatever and for this reason, that the profession of a player comprehends the whole system of human life – *quicquid agunt homines.** When I talk thus, I talk of an universal player; and surely in order to be that to any degree of perfection, all that I have now mentioned is necessary. For any one of what are commonly called the three learned professions viz. Law, physic and divinity, there is, no doubt, required much knowledge and much address, or many accomplishments. But the player must have a share of the requisites of each of these classes of men, because he must alternately represent an individual characterstic of them. Mr Dryden's fine satirical lines on the Duke of Buckingham

> And in the space of one revolving moon
> Is poet, statesman, fiddler and buffoon

may with a little variation be seriously applied to the universal player: for he must in the space of a moon be lawyer, divine and physician, with all the other characters and dispositions of the human species, which have formed in society.

In Mr Samuel Johnson's noble Prologue at the opening of the Drury Lane theatre, it is said of Shakespeare

> Each change of many coloured life he drew.

The same may be said of a player, who animates the [paintings] of Shakespeare. We who live at present, have an opportunity of observing a wonderful example of what I have now set forth. Mr Garrick exhibits in his own person such a variety of characters with such propriety and excellence as not only to catch the multitude but to be the delight and admiration of the judicious, enlightened and philosophical spectators: as was said of Terence,

> *Primores populi arripuit populumque tributim.*†

When I maintain that learning is necessary to a player who is to represent a man of learning, I do not mean that is to be understood to have as much learning as may be annexed to the character he represents . . . yet it is necessary to have so much knowledge as to enter into the general scope of the character, and have a just perception of the different expressions: not to mention that without some knowledge of the science belonging to each character it is impossible fully to see

* Whatever men do.
† He captures hordes of r
both high and low.

the blunders and absurdities, arising from ignorance, petulance and conceit, which often constitute the ridicule of the part, and appear unmeaning and insipid, if not set off by the player with due intelligence and poignancy.

It may, therefore, be fairly maintained that the more knowledge a player has, the more will he excel in his profession . . .

But not only are learning and science necessary for an universal player; he must also have all the genteel accomplishments – he must be an *elegans formarum spectator** – he must have elevation and tenderness of sentiment, dignity and ease of deportment – he must even have a knowledge of the weaknesses, the follies, the awkwardness and rusticity of human life . . . I grant that to be an universal player a man must be born with extraordinary gifts and must employ unwearied pains; and even that these should have their effect a long course of practice is necessary, and every year will bring a greater degree of excellence. But the requisites for an universal player must be found in a greater or less degree in every player who would hope to excel in his profession; so that the more knowledge that he acquires in the department, or, to use the stage phrase, the *walk*, for which nature has intended him, the more will he be distinguished, and without a competent share of knowledge it will be vain for him to tread the stage.

We may indeed be told that we have had many players, whose names it would be invidious to mention, who though brought from the dregs of the populace, and grossly ignorant, have set the audience in a roar, and exhibited low comic characters, with much truth, as well as in a diverting manner. As to this it must be observed that knowledge is not to be circumscribed to what we learn in books and schools; a great variety of it is picked up in the practice of life; and however ignorant low comedians may have been in a relative sense, it may be affirmed that none of them who have excelled have been destitute in discernment and observation in the sphere in which they have moved; so that they cannot be said to have been ignorant of their *own subjects*, if that term may be here used. I would, however, beg leave to differ from the philosophers of old who, when treating of the duties of men in their several stations, and comparing them to players say that 'there is no matter what part is assigned to a performer, whether that of a king or a peasant'. The question is – has he done his part well? For though there is no doubt that he who performs the part of a peasant well is better than he who performs the part of a king ill, yet a player is entitled to a greater degree of praise in proportion as he presents a lesser or greater character, and also in proportion to the variety of characters which he represents.

ne observer of things
utiful.

II

Ut ridentibus adrident, ita flentibus adflent
Humani vultus. Si vis me flere, dolendum est
Primum ipsi tibi.* (Horace)

What is the nature of that peculiar faculty which makes one a good player? It is
something more than an imitative art. A painter can represent upon his canvas the
various appearances which the world affords, with such exactness of shape and
justness of colour as to be almost mistaken for the objects themselves. He can
even represent the affections and passions of the mind by representing their
external effects, which from habit instantaneously convey to us their ideas. The
poet can in the same manner give us descriptions of every thing, and by a choice
and arrangement of words, the signs of ideas, can instantaneously represent to our
imaginations whatever is the subject of his verse: but the player '*lives* o'er each
scene' and, in a certain sense, '*is* what we behold; and this constitutes the
mysterious difficulty of being a good player; for by what power is it that a man is
able at a certain hour to change himself into a different kind of being from what
he really is? How is it that a man, perfectly easy and happy, can make himself
wretched and sorrowful without the intervention of any cause whatever but a
voluntary operation of his own mind? And supposing him by intense meditation on
melancholy subjects to have at length effectuated so difficult an operation, how
does he regulate his sorrow so as to correspond exactly with the part assigned to
him in the play? How does he adapt his feelings to the vicissitudes of hope and
fear which are intermingled in the drama? I am persuaded that the better a part is
written the less difficulty will there be in playing it well. I say playing it well,
because to a bad player, to one who only mimics the character he represents, well
or ill written will be alike easy . . .

I take it for granted that my proposition is not denied that a good player is
indeed in a certain sense the character he represents during the time of his
performance. [Yet] I remember to have heard [Dr Johnson] exert his eloquence
against this proposition and with the luxuriance of humour for which he is
distinguished, render it exceedingly ridiculous: 'If, sir', said he, 'Garrick believes
himself to be every character he represents, he is a madman and ought to be
confined. Nay, sir, he is a villain, and ought to be hanged. If, for instance, he
believes himself to be Macbeth, he has committed murder, he is a vile assassin,
who, in violation of the laws of hospitality, as well as of other principles, has
imbrued his hands in the blood of his king, while he was sleeping under his roof.
If, sir, he has really been that person in his own mind, he has in his own mind
been as guilty as Macbeth.' But without staying to investigate the difference

* When someone laughs,
then other men laugh bac[k]
And when he weeps, the[n]
they weep in return. If yo[u]
would have me weep, you
first must suffer pain.

between a man in the full possession of his reason and a man mad or beside himself which a player in the sense now mentioned would certainly be* I beg leave to remind my readers that I qualified my proposition by saying that a player is the character he represents only *in a certain degree*, and therefore there is a distinction between his being what I have said and his being the character he represents in the full sense of the expression.

How to define my meaning with precision I am really at a loss. [. . .]

If I may be allowed to conjecture what is the nature of that mysterious power by which a player really is the character he represents, my notion is that he must have a kind of double feeling. He must assume in a strong degree the character which he represents while he at the same time retains the consciousness of his own character. The feelings and passions of the character which he represents must take full possession, as it were, of the antechamber of his mind, while his own character remains in the innermost recess. This is experienced in some measure by the barrister who enters warmly into the cause of his client,† while at the same time, when he examines himself coolly, he knows that he is much in the wrong and does not even wish to prevail. But during the time of his pleading the genuine colour of his mind is laid over with a temporary, glaring varnish, which flies off instantly when he has finished his harangue. The double feeling which I have mentioned is experienced by many men in the common intercourse of life . . . we insensibly, for our own ease, adopt feelings suitable to every occasion and so, like players, are to a certain degree a different character from our own.

A parallel, if much more theoretical, debate was taking place in France. There was an evident transition, as with Gildon, from the art of declamation to acting, from rules to 'nature'. The actor's practice and his art were being debated in terms of basic principles.

The question was, if, as Descartes asserted, the Passions operated through normal physiological processes, might we not assume that bodily and facial expression had been designed by nature to express every shade and nuance of feeling without our being able to express them at will? If the actor found the precise feeling, would that not express itself automatically in his body?

That was the viewpoint adopted by Luigi (or Louis) Riccoboni, a leading actor of his age, famous for his work both in Italy and France, equally at home in Italian comedy and the finely wrought plays of Marivaux. On his retirement he began writing a number of works,

ristotle.
uintilian.

including a comparative study of theatre in different European countries, an innovation for the time. Finally, in 1738, he published *Thoughts on the Art of Declamation*. His contention was that the voice would naturally respond to the nature of the emotion the actor conveyed. No mechanical technique could achieve the subtlety of nature. The human organism was designed to reflect the nature of the exact feeling experienced, not an abstraction. The secret was to define the precise nature of the feeling. The book marked a move away from the conventions of the seventeenth century towards a new concept of acting not so very different from the one that had developed in England.

Thoughts on the art of declamation

Under the title *The Art of Declamation* I include everything that stems from language which articulates and speaks. There is no speech so familiar, no conversation so simple and calm that does not have inflexions that are marked by nature herself.

I will not detail here the immense variety of inflexions of which the voice is capable and that we are obliged to use on different occasions to convey properly innumerable thoughts. If Quintilian when speaking of the orator says that he should not always follow given precepts but should heed his own nature, I believe I may rightfully say the same of the inflexions of the voice. I think indeed that it is useless to lay down rules because, generally speaking, these inflexions are infinite in number and can have no fixed rules if each man follows his own nature be it serious or light, gentle or forceful, and diversifies them accordingly.

Nature has never repeated herself when shaping men, not even in the tiniest parts of the body. No two voices are alike. So, how can we imagine we can prescribe certain tones, that are proper to so many millions of men, each of whom has a different voice and each of whom uses it according to his own nature? It is more than enough to indicate these tones in general, for sadness, joy, anger and the rest. There is no use, I believe, in setting them down in writing. They must be conveyed by the voice, the example of an able master brings out all their finesse.

If we could delve into our soul and examine it openly we would have no difficulty in finding these tones since it contains them all, since it needs them to communicate to us all the wonderful perfections that the Author of all things has placed in it. But as the matter that enfolds it is an obstacle to communication, it must be allowed to take flight and be free, as far as possible, from the matter that hinders it. We must free our minds from the slavery of the senses.

The exaltation of the poets and the profound reflexions of the scholars at the moment they are writing are the result of a profound concentration of mind that examines the origins of their inner feelings and the passions of the soul. It is at that moment that they see anger, compassion, vengeance, tenderness and other passions as they are, so that the picture they make of them is so vivid and truthful that the reader finds nothing to take away or add.*

When the poet in his exaltation manages to speak the language of the soul we hear something that takes us by surprise which we have to call divine.

How then can we perform or declaim such works except with the tones of the soul itself? It seems evident to me that the orator, the poet and the scholar are exalted as they declaim just as they did when writing. If the soul which inspired the thoughts dictates the way they are to be spoken, the tones will be truthful and infinitely varied. It is not by chance we often say, 'This orator does not breathe life into what he is saying'.

Words are not the only means the art of declamation uses to express the feelings of the soul. Nature has placed the appropriate expressions in the eyes so that they too can interpret those feelings and we can say that in the art of declamation the eyes have pride of place. Cicero and Quintilian did not forget them.

The eyes must be joined to an exalted declamation since it is clear that they express the tiniest feelings of the soul. We might even say that without the silent expression of our eyes, words would not be sufficient for the almost divine expressiveness our soul requires of us.

If the orator is steeped in his art, he will not be content merely to accompany his words with his eyes but will use the eyes first. In a passage that begins with an outburst of anger, if, before speaking, he gives an angry look, he will alert the audience to what he is going to say and will draw them in to his state of mind so that they will receive the more easily the rest of his speech.

Among the expressive acts of the eyes there is one of great importance. The orator should not provoke tears but he should not make the least effort to retain them if they come naturally.

We cannot believe that the rest of the face does not enjoy that glorious ability to express the feelings of the soul! The face speaks through its muscles and the blood that enlivens it. When the muscles and the blood are set in motion they express very effectively through colour and movement our inner feelings. The face can also speak alone.

We should take care however to distinguish between changes to the face that express the feelings of the soul and the grimaces of those who act with their faces. The first belongs to the orator, the second to Scaramouche. The speaker who

istotle.

achieves the requisite state of exaltation and declaims with the tones of the soul will cause his face to respond and accompany the meaning of the words with changes of colour which the blood will produce and the various movements of the muscles.

If the movements of the body do not occupy as honourable a place as the eyes and the face they are not without their uses and are not to be despised. A perfect orator who lacks a noble bearing and graceful gestures, loses much of his merit. The arms, too, have their own eloquence.

The first work on the actor proper was *The Actor* by Rémond de Sainte-Albine published in 1747. Sainte-Albine again took Horace as his point of departure. He, for the first time, stressed the notion of the *creative* actor who bring his own resources to enrich the script he is to play. Among these resources are

- feeling – to enter into the character

- intelligence – to control the performance

- fire, or energy or charisma – to inspire an audience

The new element was *fire.*

The actor

The power of painting is well understood. With its aid it seems that people we hold dear and who are far from us are still present. But however fine the works of this wonderful art may be they are no more than appearances and we soon realise that it offers us phantoms instead of real objects. Dramatic poetry however gives thoughts and feelings to the beings it creates and by means of stage action gives them words and movement. Painting only pleases the eye. The marvels of the theatre conquer the eyes, the ears, the mind and the heart. The painter can only represent events. The actor, in some sort, reproduces them.

Of all those arts that should only be practised by people endowed with rare advantages there are few for which this condition is so essential as for playing tragedy and comedy. An actor's duty is to deceive our minds and move our hearts. To fulfil these two duties he needs special help from nature.

Part one

There is a well-established view according to which it is possible to make a reputation in the theatre without being intelligent. But I am not disposed to believe that machines to which thought is unknown can practise an art in which thinking is of the highest importance. It is not enough for [an actor] to understand the fine details in his role. He must distinguish the proper manner in which each beauty should be played. It is not enough for him to raise a passion. The passion must be the right passion and with the degree of feeling the situation demands. It is not enough for his body to be right for the stage or that his face be expressive if his expression does not constantly match the movements he is supposed to show.

Not only is it essential that he lose nothing of the strength and delicacy of his speeches, but he must also lend them all the beauties that declamation and action can provide. He should not be content merely to follow the author, he must aid and support him, he must become an author himself, and not only be able to express all the subtleties of a role but add new ones, not just perform but create. A look or a gesture are often useful in comedy, or a feeling in a tragedy. Often an inflexion, a silence skilfully placed will make the fortune of a line that would have passed unnoticed when spoken by a mediocre actor or a commonplace actress.

There is a palette proper to poetry which, though different from painting, is subject to the same rules. We demand of both the same understanding of colours, the same good judgement in the distribution of light and shade, the same care to respect the fading of light, the same talent to bring objects to the fore or to distance them.

The actor also needs finesse and precision to do justice to a speech and express feelings. He has an equal need to respect the right appearance and behaviour that accompanies that expression; to compose not only his face but his entire exterior, according to rank, age and nature of the person he represents, and to match his tones and actions to the situation in which he is placed.

Intelligence is as necessary to the actor as the pilot is to a ship. It is the intelligence that guides the rudder, it is intelligence that navigates and works out the route. Experience of navigating can sometimes replace science. Long experience in the theatre can sometimes replace intelligence in an actor. He may, too, have received other qualities from nature to such a high degree, that in moments when his experience that he instinctively uses by chance accords with what he is saying, we will have no choice but to applaud him. But then a false tone, or gesture or expression in the face will remind us that the applause is due to his mechanics not himself.

Sentiment

The meaning of this word is very broad and refers in actors to that ability to go through in their soul the succession of passions of which man is capable. As soft wax in the hands of a skilful artist becomes either Medea or Sappho, the mind and heart of a man of the theatre must be able to receive all the changes the author wishes to make.

If you cannot accept these changes, do not go on stage. In the theatre, when you do not feel the emotions that you are supposed to show, you show an imperfect image of them and art [technique] can never replace *sentiment*. When an actor lacks this gift, all the other gifts of nature and study are wasted. He is as far from the character he plays as a mask is from a face.

There are actors who by shouting and gesticulating a great deal seek to replace the natural *fire* they lack with a kind of artificial heat. There are many who because of the weakness of their constitution cannot use this means. Not being able to dominate our senses they claim that *fire* in their colleagues is a weakness rather than a strength.

Let us not be the dupes of the artificiality of the first and the sophisms of the second. Let us not takes the yells and contortions of an actor for warmth and the coolness of the second for wisdom and let us say to men of theatre that they cannot have too much *fire*.

Let us state that many actors have the misfortune not to please the public because nature has denied them this ability, or because their natural timidity prevents them from using it and that on the contrary many actors who are applauded would enjoy an even greater reputation if they were quickened by this precious flame which gives life, in some manner to action on stage.

The notions will no longer be put in doubt when we cease to confuse vehemence of declamation and the actor *fire*.

Horace said, *If you would have me weep first weep yourself.*

Do tragic actors want us to believe them? They must first believe themselves. They must imagine they are, that they indeed might be what they represent and that a happy delirium persuades them that they are betrayed and persecuted. This error must go from their head to their heart and that sometimes a pretended misfortune draws real tears from them.

Then we no longer see cold actors who by studied tones and gestures wish to involve us in some imaginary adventure. Unless some insurmountable obstacle arises to prevent the effect they should produce, they are certain to work all the wonders they can expect of their art. They are kings with absolute command over our souls. They are magicians who can make the most unfeeling feel.

Part two

Since dramatic fictions please us all the more by their resemblance to real adventures, the perfection we most desire in the performance is what is called in the theatre *truth*.

By this word we mean the coming together of all the appearances that can deceive the audience. They are of two kinds. The playing of the actors produces one kind; the others have nothing to do with their acting but are the result of certain changes in the actor himself or are due to the costume he wears or the setting in which he appears.

The appearances of the first kind, that is, those that arise from the acting, are the most important for the illusion and they are also those which most closely concern my examination of the subject. They consist in the perfect respect of what is consistent in the character (*convenances*). Acting is true only when we see everything that is proper to the age, condition, personality and situation of the character. An actor who wishes to represent the effects of one of the passions must not, if he wishes to be truthful, be content to use the movements this passion excites in all men equally. It must have the particular distinguishing form it takes in the person he is to copy.

Expression, like movements, must vary according to the character. In a young man love bursts out in impetuous emotion. In an old man it is expressed with greater circumspection and moderation. A person of great rank has more decency, less excess in his regret, his complaints, his threats than a man of low birth and no breeding. The variety of expression depends on the truth of the action and the truth of the words spoken.

To be true in action is to present it in exact accordance with what the character would, or should, do in the circumstances in which the author successively places him.

Every scene produces a new situation for the actor and each change in the situation results in different, particular features appropriate to it (*convenances*). Certain situations dictate the action appropriate to them. A beautiful woman paints a picture of her lover from memory to soften the pain of separation.* A servant enables [his master] to witness how his mistress employs her free time. It is obvious that he must be able to observe what his lover is doing without being seen and that from time to time, in his desire to see her more closely, he involuntarily runs the risk of being discovered. He runs that risk with every movement she makes, he is afraid, and to prolong the wonder of what he sees, he quickly but regretfully returns to the position that can make his pleasure last the longer.

There are other situations that do not indicate what the actor should do so clearly. There are indeed some in which he easily can go wrong.

Le Médecin de l'Occasion by Boissy.

When Iphigenia ask Agamemnon if she might be present at the sacrifice he will make, he replies, *You shall be there, my child*. Many actors believe they can enhance the pathos of this situation by fixing their eyes on Iphigenia and that action will be contrary to truth because as he says this line Agamemnon would have averted his eyes so that she might not see the mortal pain that rends his heart.

This proves how true action is often very different from the one actors think of. Sometimes their silence must be as eloquent as their words and often they are more active when silent than when they have fine-sounding lines to speak. Some roles require even greater subtlety. They are those when the . . . actor must pursue one purpose with the audience and another with the other characters.

It was Louis Riccoboni's son François who rejected the idea of feeling and insisted that acting was a matter of technique. In 1750, he published *The Art of the Theatre*, which was simply a training manual intended for amateurs. It was not well received, perhaps for that reason. It was not sufficiently 'philosophical'. It did, however, represent a professional point of view held by many actors.

The art of the theatre

Letter to Madame

Paris is full of private theatres and everyone wants to be an actor. Since we should always do our best in everything we undertake, you thought you had need of advice on how to succeed in an art which you find difficult and you have done me the honour to address yourself to me to have a guide in your theatrical pleasures. But it is not enough to reflect on the few roles one has been offered and to learn to play them by mechanical means rather than knowledge. We must make ourselves capable of playing through reflexion and know the true principles of art. How is one to learn them since no one has taken the trouble to write them down? Actors themselves have to pass a lifetime to develop, through practice, rules that they should have known before they began and which they only learn when they are no longer capable of making use of them.

Gesture

I shall begin by speaking of gesture and that may appear strange to you. But if you but think that you have to present yourself on stage before you speak, you will agree that the first thing we have to learn is deportment and control. This part of acting appears to be the most troublesome for those who are not used to it. And so it is. We cannot speak our role as we would wish until we have overcome all the difficulties of our body. It is generally said that there are no rules for gesture but I believe that is wrong. By gesture I mean not only the movements of the arms but of all parts of the body. It is the harmony among them that makes an actor's grace.

To have a good appearance you must stand up straight but not too straight. Anything approaching excess becomes affectation and is unpleasing to the eye and causes constraint. Moreover, in standing up too straight you rob yourself of an advantage at important moments in tragedy and high comedy. It is when you need to show that you are superior to the other actors on stage with you and assume a commanding air that you need to pull yourself up to your full height and seem larger than they by your deportment. But if you have been at full height throughout the role, you have lost the ability to go further in moments when deportment should be grander.

There are times when you must bend forwards to show respect or affection. In these instances, some actors err by an excess of control. They tend to bend at the waist while holding their stomach and chest extremely rigid. As the body is off balance in this position if the feet are close together, they push one foot back and bend the knee of the other which is forward, they raise one arm very high, place the other on the hip and play whole passages like some ancient statue representing a gladiator in combat. As this unnatural position has become very fashionable, we have become so used to seeing it that we have lost sight of its ridiculousness.

We should bend the chest forward without fearing to enlarge the shoulders, which on this occasion can never look bad. You will say that the rigidity of a Roman breastplate and the billowing forms of the ladies contradict the rule I have given. I agree that all these adjustments are uncomfortable but it is better if the costume is a hindrance merely to incline the head which is always the most noteworthy and only bend the body slightly. In that position you are both agreeable to the eye and appropriate to the situation.

You should walk with equal, measured steps without jolts. Some tragic actors thinking to make themselves appear grander stamp the ground so that their whole body shakes and their tunic wobbles. Far from adding to nobility, this extraordinary walk destroys all illusion and reveals the artifice of the actor and not the freedom of the hero.

If we would but pay attention to the way in which a man is made, we would see that he is never more easy and more shapely than when standing equally on both feet, close together. He lets his arms and hands drop to the place their weight naturally takes them. In dance it is called the second position, hands on pockets. That is the most simple and natural position. And yet it is a position that is most difficult to impose on someone learning to dance. It seems that nature is perpetually at war with herself. The head always seeks to avoid simple beauty and in our times we see in every art how fashionable the extremely elaborate is.

When we speak our arms should move. I shall explain the mechanics of these movements in the minutest detail because bad habits once acquired cannot be eradicated.

Grace of the arms is only achieved through considerable work and study, and however good our natural gifts are perfection depends on art. For the arms to be soft the following rule must be observed. When we wish to raise one, the upper part, from the elbow to the shoulder, is first detached from the body and the other two parts should merely follow gently. The hand should be the last to move. It must be turned down until it reaches the height of the elbow when it is turned up while the arm continues its upward movement until it reaches the point where it is to stop. If all that is accomplished without effort, the movement is pleasing. To come down, the hand must drop first and the other parts of the arm follow in order. We must also take care for the arm never to be rigid, for the bend in the elbow and the wrist to be visible.

The fingers should never be fully extended, they must be gently curved and we should be able to see their natural gradation which is when the hand is only partly bent.

We should avoid as far as possible clenching the fist and, above all, presenting it directly to the actor one is addressing even in moments of the greatest fury. The gesture is in itself ignoble, discourteous in the presence of a lady and insulting towards a man.

You should not gesticulate quickly. The slower, the softer a gesture is, the more pleasing it is. If you disobey these rules and, for example, wave the hand and forearm first, the gesture is clumsy. Avoid extending the arms at equal length or raising them to the same height.

It is a commonplace rule that the hand should never be raised above the level of the eye.* But when an actor is carried away by a violent passion he can ignore all these rules. He can move swiftly and raise his arms above his head. However, if it is his custom to be gentle and graceful, his liveliest movements will always seem based on sound principles.

* Quintilian.

Voice

One of the most necessary studies in the theatre is the manner to produce a full, smooth, natural voice. When we speak we should become aware of sounds that can be sharp or long and thin, and see that there are others that are muted, or fade when we attempt to say them. Through exercises we can soften the first and give fullness to the others so as to make all the sounds within our range equal. Through constant hard work we can make our throat more flexible than it naturally is.

To avoid sharp, long and thin sounds, the chest must always be firm and the throat open to let sounds pass. We must control our breath and only let out what is needed. When the breath is too big it buries the sound, because it blocks the throat and produces what we call sepulchral tones. You must never overextend the chest to give strength to your expression, for, instead of making it stronger, you make it weaker and then we have to use those heavy intakes of breath which can be heard at the back of the hall and are painful for the audience to hear.

We must all use the voice nature has given us and never seek to replace it with something that is not our own. Equal damage is done in attempting to imitate the voice of another actor.

Declamation

The ancients took a poor view of the word declamation and its etymologies reveal that they only called declaimers those that shouted when they spoke. We should take care not to be mistaken about the true meaning of this word. It is not the strength of the voice that causes shouting but the way the sound is carried and the frequent drops in the voice at regular intervals. Actors and orators in ancient Rome were obliged to raise their voices so as to be heard by an enormous audience. Preachers are obliged to do the same thing. Actors in Italy speak more loudly than in France because their theatres are larger. Yet they do not declaim. It is vehemence and monotony combined that make up declamation. Begin low, speak with an affected slowness, drag out sounds without varying them, raise one suddenly at the half-pause in the sense and suddenly revert to the tone with which one started; in moments of passion express yourself with excessive force without changing the modulation of the voice, that is how you declaim.

Tragic verses should be spoken with the natural tones the thoughts they contain demand. When a hero speaks of things that do not move him, why should he affect a special voice? Why should a princess who is not shaken by passions weep? And yet it is a daily occurrence. To speak nobly, are we never to abandon a shocking monotony? Tragic verses in truth have a constant rhythm but they do not always flow in the same way. There is a change of thought and feeling in what we say at every moment. The tone should therefore change at every moment.

Erroneous ideas have been formed about declamation and turned into the most senseless principles. Here is one. It is believed that tragedy should always begin in a low voice, with subdued acting, so that the actor can manage his means and increase his powers of expression up until the end of the play. The only rule we should follow is the one laid down by the feeling we have to convey. If the author begins his tragedy with desperate lines spoken by a son who has lost his father, the son must, on his entrance, display the most vivid grief and express it with great strength. The actor must convey things as they are wherever they occur in the play. So much the worse for the writer if he is unable to take things further later.

Intelligence

At present, when we wish to praise an actor we affect to congratulate his intelligence. Indeed, great intelligence is needed not only to convey the variety in the characters he plays but also to bring out all the variety that exists in the same play. Yet we often see a crude manner of understanding of the lines honoured as intelligence. Such intelligence is but a small thing, and the least of the qualities an actor should have. But not all have it and we should be grateful to those who have. What truly merits the name intelligence in the theatre is the greatest of all talents. It alone makes great actors. Without it one can never be but one of those mediocre persons who sometimes shine through certain attractions in the voice and body but with whom the connoisseur is never truly satisfied. It is not enough to understand a speech the author has put in our mouth and to avoid mistaken meanings. We need to understand at every moment the possible relationship between what we say with the character and the dramatic situation and the effect it can produce as part of the whole.

In a scene we have to say *good day*. It is a simple word and everyone understands it. But it is not enough merely to understand that is a form of politeness offered to visitors or to people you meet. There are a thousand ways of saying *good day,* according to the person or the situation. A father says it tenderly to a son he loves and with coldness mixed with disappointment to one with whom he is discontent. A miser, even when saying good day to his friend, must show he is full of anxieties. The jealous man expresses an anger which good manners prevent him from venting when greeting a young man whom he is forced to receive against his will. A servant says good day in a flattering, insinuating tone to her mistress's lover and in an abrupt tone to an old man who seeks to obtain her against her will. The fop greets you with affected politeness mixed with pride which shows that if he greets you, it is out of the kindness of his heart but that, if necessary, he would feel no such obligation. A sad man says good day in afflicted tones. A valet who has taken advantage of his master greets him with apparent assurance but we should see fear behind it. A trickster greets the man he is going to dupe in a tone that inspires confidence in his victim. [One of the best actors] I have ever seen believed that there was not a single syllable that did not have its use in his role: a yes or a no in his mouth showed the situation and the character. I have seen the same roles played by actors who were considered perfectly intelligent but whose understanding was far less than his. It is by that intelligence that misses nothing that a good actor is superior to a reader or even a quick-witted man.

Those to whom nature has given quick wits and education would be able to play comedy if it necessarily entailed the intelligence I speak of. But we have too many cases to the contrary and have seen many actors never play more than the surface of their role.

Expression

We call expression the skill by which we make the audience feel all the emotions which we seem to be feeling. I say seem, not that we do. In that regard, Madame, I shall reveal to you one of those dazzling mistakes we have allowed ourselves to be deceived by, aided by a little charlatanism on the part of the actor.

When an actor expresses the feelings in his role with the necessary strength, the audience sees in him the perfect image of truth. A man, in such a situation, would not express himself differently and it is to that degree that illusion must be stretched to play well. Astonished by such a perfect imitation of the truth many have taken it for the truth itself and believed that the actor feels what he represents. They shower him with praise which he deserves, based on a false idea and the actor finding it to his advantage not to destroy that idea, confirms it and leaves them in a state of error.

Not only have I never shared this idea, widely accepted, but it has always seemed to me evident that if one has the misfortune truly to feel the things one must express, one would not be in a state to play. Sentiments follow each other in a scene with a swiftness that is not found in nature. The shortness of a play requires that speed, which by bringing objects close together affords dramatic action all the radiance it needs. If, in a love scene, you allow yourself to be carried away by your feeling, your heart will suddenly contract, your voice will fail. If one tear falls from your eye, involuntary sobs will fill your throat, you will be unable to utter a word without ridiculous hiccups. If you suddenly have to pass to great anger, will you be able to do it? Certainly not. You will try to recover from a state which prevents you from continuing, a deathly cold will fall upon your senses and for a few moments, you will only play mechanically. What happens then to the expression of a feeling which requires much more warmth and strength than the first? What horrible disorder will that produce in the order of subtle nuances that the actor must go through for his feelings to seem to be linked and be born from each other? Let us examine another occasion which will offer a more reasonable proof and which prejudice will find it difficult to counter. An actor makes his entrance. The first words he hears must cause him great surprise. He understands the situation, and suddenly his face, his body, his voice express a kind of astonishment which is striking to the audience. Is he really astonished? He knows what is going to be said to him by heart. He has come on precisely to hear it.

Classical times have preserved an extraordinary fact that would seem to prove the idea I seek to combat. A famous tragic actor, Aesopus, was playing the scene of Orestes' madness. He had his sword in his hand. At that moment a slave in the theatre's employ crossed the stage and unfortunately stood in his way. Aesopus did not hesitate for a moment to kill him. Here was a man apparently so steeped in his role that he felt it to the point of madness.* But why did he never kill one of the other actors playing with him? Because a slave's life meant nothing whereas he was obliged to respect the life of a citizen. His rage was not then quite so true since it allowed reason to choose. But as a clever actor he took the opportunity chance offered him. I do not say that an actor when playing passages of great passion does not feel strong emotion. Indeed, it is that which is most tiring in the theatre. But that state arises from the efforts one has to make to paint passion one does not feel, which so arouses the motion of the blood that the actor may himself be deceived if he has not studied its true cause.

We need perfect knowledge of the movements of the heart in other men and remain always the master of our own to make it seem at will like someone else's. That is the origin of that perfect illusion the audience must accept and which carries them away despite themselves.

Expression must be natural. Yet it is generally believed that we cannot be confined by nature's precise limits. They result in acting with little effect, and cold. My father used to say that to be striking we have to go just beyond what is natural but that if we overstep that line by a hair's breadth we are instantly unseemly and displeasing. This statement wonderfully explains the actor's danger of expressing too little or too much. Let us see, however, whether nature can provide examples, which, if exactly followed, would give extreme truth together with the necessary energy. Let us observe society; I do not just mean that select world that prides itself on elegance. I am speaking of society in general, and of the low rather than of the high. The high, accustomed to politeness, do not succumb to their first feelings in the presence of others, and may provide examples of lively expression. But lowlier men, who surrender more readily to the

* Aristotle.

impressions they receive, people who do not know how to restrain their feelings, are the true models of strong expression. Let us but add a veneer of politeness and everything will be perfect. In a word, we should feel like the people and present ourselves like the great.

We should never overdo expression. That is an incontrovertible rule. But we must understand that exaggeration never arises from too great a feeling. They are the accoutrements that spoil it, I mean the mechanisms of gesture and voice. If, in order to create a strong impression, we make a violent gesture having shown we are preparing so to do and then stop in an unnatural position, if we suddenly force and stretch out the voice, and if one sound bursts out louder than the rest, we have gone too far. The livelier a movement is the shorter it should be. In so doing we imitate nature which is not able to sustain the forces that govern it for very long.

Sentiment

The movements that arise in our heart the most readily, without the aid of reflection, and instantly govern us despite our will are the only ones that should bear the name of sentiments. There are two dominant kinds which can be regarded as the source of all the others, I mean love and hate.

All those that do not arise from these two sources are of another kind. For example, joy, sadness, fear are simple impressions. Ambition, avarice are considered passions. But pity is a sentiment that arises from love; hate and contempt are the children of anger.

This distinction is necessary for you to understand the reasons I have classified all feeling in two classes. The first are *gentle*, the others are *strong*. The first take their main character from love, the second are almost always accompanied by anger.

The pause

The pause is the moment prior to speaking, it is the interval that you must leave in your speech to allow the audience to rest, to receive new impressions and to differentiate among the sentiments. Those who play mechanically never observe these rests. Those who are mere imitators often use them wrongly while others overuse and misuse them, which gives their playing the most disagreeable kind of monotony. Here is the rule you should follow so as not to go astray. When you have to reply to someone, ask yourself whether what you have to say to him has come from a feeling his speech has aroused in you suddenly and without warning. The more sudden this feeling is, the more you need to precede your reply by a rest. For when we are surprised by an unexpected feeling, our mind is filled with a rush of ideas but does not distinguish among them with the same speed. For some moments it is confused as to which one should dominate. The idea that comes to dominate is the one that carries us away, while the rest fade, and we express that dominant feeling forcefully. It is on those occasions that the pause is of the greatest value, and is essential. There are other times when we need to use it, when the answer we have to give is only the fruit of reasoning. If we are suddenly taken over by feeling, we are at the same time held back by thought, which will only let us succumb to that first feeling by degrees, unless we overcome it entirely by a great effort. Let us take an example. Achilles in Act IV scene vi of [Racine's] *Iphigénie* provides one that is most striking. Agamemnon has delivered a speech to him so haughty that this young hero cannot but be revolted and be driven into violent anger. But he suppresses it as far as is possible for a man of his character. He does not answer straight away. He stops for quite some time; then he speaks these lines

> Give thanks to heaven for the ties that bind my anger.
> I still respect Iphigenia's father.
> Without that name, it might well be the last time
> That the chief of many kings would dare to brave me.
> I say just one word more, but hear it well!
> I have your daughter and my honour to defend.

His words are separated by pauses which express the inner conflict between anger and reason. Finally his anger carries him away. But actors are often mistaken in the appropriate form of expression for that moment. I have seen some speak the first two lines in a low voice, raise the voice little by little and round off blaring.

To render both the sentiment and the character of the man properly, the actor should play the scene in exactly the opposite way. In a man who is truly fearless great anger produces perfect calm. That is the true nature of courage; it adopts an extreme position that cannot be shaken by any form of fear. It is ice cold. Achilles then must speak the last two lines

> This is the path your blows must take
> To reach my heart and pierce it through.

with quiet assurance.

Let us note that by these words he is proposing single combat. Such a proposal is not made with uncouth cries from a man who merits our esteem. The outrageous head-waving that sometimes accompanies or follows these words is, in consequence, the most contrary to a sense of nobility and the truth of the situation. This is silent acting that is ludicrous and out of place. But it is the end of a great scene. The actors want to be applauded on their exit. However, if they play properly, in the manner I have indicated, that may not happen. For the audience, accustomed to seeing it played that other way, and to applaud it, are convinced it is good.

Let us return to the pause and examine the circumstances in which it is necessary. When we wish that the person we are speaking to to pay great attention to our speech, or we want him to be struck by our thoughts and that his heart should feel what we feel, we should separate the many and different ideas we present by evident moments of repose. In this way we give his reason time to weigh our words and we enable ourselves to increase our expressiveness, by degrees, so as to reach the point when we convince him or win him over.

It needs fine judgement for us to give a pause its proper length. Let the audience take in what we have said for them to be drawn in further by what follows. But do not allow them the time to lose the illusion. Above all, use the pause judiciously, lest the audience become used to it and no longer notice it.

Fire

What actors call fire is the exact opposite of the pause. It is no more than a liveliness, a swiftness of speech, a rapidity of gesture beyond the usual. This manner of playing is sometimes necessary and can be greatly moving when it is apposite. I will merely explain how fire is sometimes out of place and how what is sometimes taken for fire is a ludicrous kind of petulance.

If our heart is so moved as to leave no place for reason, and is no longer master of itself, we must speak quickly, move energetically, not leave other people time to reply, there is no order in our gestures. I think you see, Madame, the difference I make between what is called fire and what is called lively expression. This fire which, well used, can produce excellent effects is a fault which has long been in fashion: immoderate ranting. When we have a great speech to give, we believe we shall be admired if we speak it quickly, seeking to dazzle the audience by the speed of our tongue, which they often are. I have but rarely approved this method. If a long passage is full of matter worthy of attention, let us give those listening to us time to understand and feel. If it is nothing more than a collection of meaningless words, let us ask the author to cut it.

Novices often have too much fire, which makes them cold. They wish to be expressive but lack of craft leads them to take speed and vehemence for strength.

The culmination of this debate was Diderot's *Paradox*.

5 | Diderot

Denis Diderot (1713–1784) was an almost exact contemporary of Garrick (1717–1779), whom he called the English Roscius. He was both a theoretician, a *philosophe*, and a dramatist, and was probably the most outstanding intellect of the French Enlightenment.

He wrote extensively on the theatre. His own plays, which encountered considerable opposition, were often accompanied by commentaries (as later with Shaw's plays) in which he defined and defended the philosophy which lay behind them. Like Garrick, he believed that the theatre had a moral purpose. As a dramatist he was among the first to write in the new form the French called *le drame,* a new middle genre pitched between the classical forms of tragedy and comedy for the rising bourgeoisie. These were plays on domestic subjects, written in prose, precursors of the realist and 'problem' plays of the nineteenth century. His most significant innovation was to introduce detailed directions to the script, setting out the stage action as he saw it. Dealing with theatre as a whole, he set out a complete aesthetic in *De la Poésie Dramatique* (1758). His comments on acting are contained in his most famous work, *The Paradox on the Actor*.

In summing up his views on the debate on acting he had two objects in mind: as a *philosophe* he wanted, like Longinus, to introduce an element of rationality into what seemed a chaotic activity. In the *Paradox* he referred to English philosophers, empiricists like Hume, as a model:

> In our time, men of genius have brought the intelligible world* back to the real world. Can we not find someone who will do the same for lyric poetry and bring it down from the enchanted regions to the earth on which we live?

As a dramatist, he wanted to ensure the integrity, the consistency of performances, so that they did not vary from night to night.

*That is, the world of Platonic ideas.

The fundamental question was whether, as Louis Riccoboni had suggested, the actor should stimulate the mind (imagination) so as to produce the right physical effects, or whether, as his son François indicated, he should produce an exact replication of the physical effects of thought and feeling without ever feeling in performance.

For Diderot the great enemy of good acting and consistency of performance was sensibility in the sense that Jane Austen used it in her novel *Sense and Sensibility*. Sensibility is the ability to feel, the capacity to be swept away by sudden strong emotion.

At the time Diderot was writing, novels were full of characters who were in that sense 'sensible', and their sensibility, which was considered admirable, usually expressed itself in copious weeping.

In the *Paradox*, Diderot provided his own definition of the term. It is a kind of physical and mental illness:

> Sensibility, according to the only meaning given it until the present, is, and I agree, that disposition that accompanies a weakness of the organs, resulting from the mobility of the diaphragm, the vividness of the imagination and the delicacy of the nerves, which inclines us to be compassionate, to tremble, to admire, to fear, to be disturbed, to weep, to faint, to aid, to fly, to shout, to lose all reason, to exaggerate, to despise, to disdain, not to have an exact idea of the true, the good, the beautiful, to be unjust, to be mad. Multiply the number of sensitive souls and in the same proportion you will multiply good and bad actions of all kinds, exaggerated praise and blame.

In his *Elements of Physiology* of 1778 he is even stronger. Diderot and his contemporaries accepted the physiology of emotion, first outlined in Descartes' notion of the man-machine. In this article he attempted to explore current theories concerning the relationship of the body to states of feeling. He concluded that physiological factors were all-determining. Like Descartes he believed the passions to be inherently dangerous:

> Each passion has a different origin but there is none of them that may not end in frenzy, or the perturbation of one organ that sets all the others in motion. The eye darkens, the ears ring.

Not for him the 'ecstasy' that Aristotle had spoken of.

For Diderot the trouble with the actor of sensibility was that his sudden bursts of emotion distorted the shape of the production when the true task is to control and shape the total experience of the audience.

An actor who works on the inspiration of the moment, on instinct, is uneven, good one day bad the next in the same role, dependent on his own particular mood at that particular time.

The good actor, he concluded, is, therefore, always cool and in charge, as a good politician is in charge. It is the audience that does the weeping. Just as those who pretend to rule need cool heads, not strong feelings, so actors need cool heads to control audiences. Diderot is looking for a kind of rational art that Plato* might have approved of.

Diderot had three major artists as models: Mlle Clairon, Mlle Dumesnil and Garrick. The two actresses represented the two sides in the debate: Mlle Clairon who consciously created her performances, and Mlle Dumesnil who worked on the feeling of the moment. Garrick presented Diderot with a problem he never quite resolved, and which, perhaps, as someone with no direct, personal experience of the actor's process, he would not have been in a position to resolve.

Although his performances had been carefully worked out Garrick always left room for the unexpected, for the moment of the Sublime. In his copy of Hannetaire's *Observations sur l'Art du Comédien* which appeared in 1776 at the end of his career, he scribbled 'wrong' in the margin against the following statements:

> [A] real master, far from ever varying the different parts of a tragedy or a comedy, will always speak it in the same way, after ten years, just as after two years.

> There is only one way of speaking, of delivering.

In his *Essay on Acting* (1744), written at the beginning of his career, Garrick stated clearly that he was sometimes surprised by an upsurge of emotion in performance.

> I pronounce that the greatest strokes of Genius have been unknown to the Actor himself, 'till Circumstances and the warmth of the Scene has sprung the Mine as it were, as much to his own Surprize, as that of the Audience.

> (Letter to Helfrich Peter Sturtz, 3 January 1769)

Diderot had seen Garrick. He had made two triumphal visits to Paris and he had become a European icon. Garrick met all the leading artists and intellectuals of the time and, as was his custom, would play scenes for a small group. Again, the great complexity and ambiguity of his

*Diderot was familiar with Plato's works, although, it would appear, in Latin translation.

speaking seemed to defy definition. Diderot witnessed two examples. First, there was an example of his capacity to think himself into a situation. In his *Essay* he had said: 'An actor must be able to make love to a table.' He gave his French hosts a demonstration of this gift. He took a cushion and said:

> Gentlemen, I am this child's father. Thereupon he opened a window, took his cushion, tossed it in the air, kissed it, caressed it, and imitated all the fooleries of a father playing with his child. But then came a moment when the cushion, or rather, the child slipped from his hand and fell through the window. Then Garrick began to mime the father's despair . . . His audience were seized with such consternation and horror that most of them could not bear it and had to leave the room.
>
> (Diderot, letter to Madame Riccoboi, 27 November 1758)

Diderot and his companions did not know, nor did Garrick inform them, that this spontaneous scene was based on fact and the real observation of a man who had gone mad as a result of just such an accident. This had provided him with a model for King Lear.

On another occasion, Garrick went behind double doors and poked out of the gap from alternate sides, demonstrating, with a split second between them, some thirty different emotions.

How, Diderot and his contemporaries asked, could he actually feel *instantly*? Diderot assumed wrongly that Garrick had achieved his effects purely technically. He was unaware of Garrick's emotional virtuosity. He could play himself like a violin. In his art there was a perfect fusion of feeling and technique that bewildered his contemporaries, even those who were acting on stage with him. Was he genuinely feeling or not?

His pupil Thomas King recalled in 1807 that in the middle of a highly charged scene in *King Lear*, with the audience in tears, Garrick 'turned his head round to me, and putting his tongue in his cheek, whispered, "Damme, Tom, it'll do!" So much for stage feeling.'

Nevertheless, Garrick was convinced that the starting point for a characterisation was a detailed inner conception of the role, a character who was not the actor himself but a creation of the imagination that the actor embodied and communicated through his technique:

> There is for you, for me, for the spectator a possible, ideal* man who would be affected differently from you in the given position. That is the imaginary being who should be your model. The more strongly you

*'Ideal' in this context means 'conceptual', 'imaginary'. In his *Dictionary*, Dr Johnson gives '*Idea*: mental image'; '*Ideally*: intellectually, mentally'.

conceive him the greater, rarer, more wonderful and sublime you will be
. . . When I rend my innards and emit inhuman cries they are not my
innards, they are not my cries, they are the innards and the cries of
someone I have imagined and who does not exist.*

Diderot was driven to opt for the superiority of the rational Mlle
Clairon over the emotional Mlle Dumesnil. Only Clairon could supply
the kind of consistency he required.

Yet Garrick noted in his diary of his Paris visit that her playing was in
fact uneven. He felt that her rational approach was limiting:

> She has everything that Art and a good understanding, with great Natural
> Spirit can give her – But then I fear . . . the Heart has none of those
> instantaneous feelings, that keen Sensibility, that bursts at once from
> Genius, and like Electrical fire shoots thro' the Veins, Marrow, Bones and
> all, of every Spectator. – Mademoiselle Clairon is so conscious and certain
> of what she does, that she never (I believe) had the feelings of the instant
> come upon her unexpectedly.

The lengths to which Clairon would go rather than actually
experience an emotion are well illustrated in her *Memoirs*, where she
describes the extreme physical effort she employed to produce tears:

> Merely to wet my eyes, or to produce a tear, to a continuing tone of
> lament, I added a contraction of the stomach which made my nerves
> tremble, and a tightening of the throat which made it difficult to speak;
> my stifled, intermittent breath showed the agitation of my soul . . .

Garrick also had reservations about Dumesnil, whose acting was supposed to be 'natural' and spontaneous. He thought her a bag of tricks.

It was Garrick who was the indirect cause of the *Paradox*. Diderot was
led to formulate a consistent theory of acting by the publication of
Sticcoti's *Garrick or English Actors* in 1769. This was a translation of a book
by Dr John Hill *The Actor: a Treatise on the Art of Playing*, published in 1750
and later revised and expanded, to contain greater references to Garrick,
in 1755. Hill presented this as an original work. It was, in fact, an
unacknowledged translation of Sainte-Albine's book on the actor.
Neither Sticcoti nor Diderot was aware of this. Diderot claimed he only
knew of Sainte-Albine by hearsay. In his review of the book, Diderot
outlined the ideas that were later to form the basis of the *Paradox*.

The *Paradox* was not published in Diderot's lifetime. He had some

*Diderot reporting Garrick's
remarks to the Marquis de
Chastelux, Salon de 1767. As
Garrick was half-French and
spoke the language, we may
assume that Diderot reported
his words accurately.

twenty manuscript copies made which he distributed to friends and colleagues. Most were lost, however, and it was not until 1830 that a copy was discovered in St Petersburg and later published. Thus for sixty years Diderot's immediate successors used the review of Sticcoti's book as the source of their knowledge.

Observations on a book entitled:
Garrick or English actors

A work containing reflexions on dramatic art, on the art of representation and acting. With historical notes and criticisms of the different theatres in London and Paris. Translated from the English

This is an obscure, tortuous, overblown work, full of commonplace ideas. I guarantee that, once having read it, a great actor will be no greater and a mediocre actor will be no less mediocre.

It is for nature to provide those external qualities of face, voice, sensibility, judgement and subtlety; it is by the study of great masters, by working in the theatre, by application, by thought that the gifts of nature are perfected. An actor who merely imitates does everything passing well, there is nothing to praise or blame; the instinctive actor, the actor of genius is sometimes abominable, sometimes excellent. However harshly a beginner may be judged, sooner or later he will have the success he deserves in the theatre; boos only kill off the inept.

And how could nature shape a great actor without art, since nothing happens on stage as it does in nature, and all plays are constructed according to a certain system of conventions and principles? And how can any role be played in the same way by two different actors, since even the most energetic, clear and precise writer's words can never be the absolute signs of an idea, a feeling or a thought?

Listen to the comment which follows and understand how easy it is for people to use the same expressions and to say quite different things: the example I am going to give you is a kind of wonder, none other than the work here in question. Give it to a French actor to read and he will agree that it is entirely true; give it to an English actor to read and he will swear to you by God, that not a single word is to be rejected, that it is theatrical gospel. And yet, since there is nothing in common between the way of writing comedy and tragedy in England and the way in which we write these poems in France, and since, in Garrick's judgement a man who can play a scene from Shakespeare perfectly does not know the first thing about declaiming a scene from Racine and vice versa, it is evident that the French and the English actor who agree on the truth of the principles of the author under discussion, do not understand each other, and that there is sufficient vagueness, broadness in the technical language of their profession for two men of such diametrically opposed feeling to find them to be true. Hold more than ever to your maxim: nil explicate. Never explain if you wish to understand each other.

This work called Garrick has therefore two quite distinct meanings within the same signs, one for London, one for Paris. These signs clearly offer two distinct meanings, but the translator has managed to go astray, since by stuffing his translation from one end to the other with the names of our own French actors alongside those of English actors, he obviously believes that the things the original book said about one set of actors are applicable to another. I know no other work with as many misunderstandings as this. Words mean one thing in Paris, another in London.

Of course, I might be wrong, but my ideas on the essential qualities of a great actor differ from the author's. I would wish an actor to have great good judgement, to be a cool and calm observer of human nature, so that he might possess great subtlety of mind and not rely on emotion, or, which comes to the same thing, have the skill to imitate everything with equal aptitude in all kinds of characters and all kinds of roles. If he relied on feeling he could not play the same role ten times running with the same ardour and the same success. Passionate at the first performance, he would be exhausted, cold and marble by the third, whereas if he is a conscious imitator of nature when he comes on stage for the first time, he will imitate himself the tenth time; his acting, far from becoming weaker, will be strengthened by all the new thoughts he has had; and you will be all the happier.

I am encouraged in my opinion by the unevenness of actors who play from the heart. Do not expect consistency from them; their acting is alternately strong and weak, hot and cold, flat and sublime, they will fail tomorrow where they excelled today but will excel where they failed the previous evening. Whereas those who act out of thought, the study of human nature, imitation, imagination and memory, are consistent in all performances, which are all equally perfect. Everything is measured, everything is learned; passion has a beginning, a middle and an end.* There are the same accents, poses, movements; if there is a difference from one performance to another it is always to the advantage of the latter. They do not change: they are perfect mirrors always able to show objects and to show them with the same preciseness and truth; like the poet, they draw on the inexhaustible depths of nature whereas their own riches are quickly exhausted.

*Aristotle.

What acting is more perfect than Mlle Clairon's? Do but follow her, study her and you will soon see that she knows all the details of her actions as well as she knows all the words. No doubt but that she had a model in her head which she took pains to imitate; no doubt that she imagined the highest, greatest most perfect model she could: but if she herself had been her model how weak and paltry her imitation would have been! Once she had attained this ideal model through her endeavours, her work was complete. I do not doubt that she feels great torment within her during the early part of her work, but once this moment has passed, her heart is quiet; she is mistress of herself, she can repeat what she has done almost without inner emotion, her rehearsals have fixed everything in her head. Carelessly reclined upon her couch, eyes closed, she can silently go through her role in her memory, hear herself, see herself on stage, judge herself and the impressions she will produce. It is not thus with her rival, Mlle Dumesnil: she makes an entrance not knowing what she is going to say; three-quarters of the time indeed she does not know what it is she is saying, but the rest is sublime.

Why should the actor be different from the sculptor, the poet, the painter, the orator or the musician? They do not find the characteristic features of their works in the fury of their first creative outburst but in quiet, cool and quite unexpected moments: then, as though mid-way between human nature and the rough sketch they have made of it, they cast their eye first on one then on the other and the beauties with which they fill their works have a far more sure success that those they threw in at the first attempt. It is not the violent man, the man who is beside himself who captivates us,* no, that is the privilege of the man who is self-possessed. Great poets, dramatic poets above all, are dedicated observers of everything that happens around them: they seize on everything that strikes them, they record it, and it is from these records that many sublime moments in their works are drawn. Passionate, violent, emotional men make their entrance; they perform but they are not in control; it is these men that actors of genius copy. In my opinion, it is great poets, great actors and perhaps all great imitators of nature in every genre, of fine imagination, great judgement, tact, sound taste who are likely to be those least subject to feeling. They are too active, too busy observing and imitating to be strongly affected inside. Consider women: they certainly outstrip us, and by far, in their capacity to feel: what comparison can there be between them and us in the moment of passion! But just as we must grant superiority to them in action, they must be considered inferior to us in imitation. In that great drama, the drama to which I always return, the drama of life, the passionate hearts are on the stage, the men of genius are in the stalls: the first are called fools, the second, who take pleasure in copying their folly, are called wise. It is the fixed stare of the wise man that grasps what is ridiculous in so many

*Aristotle, *The Poetics*, 1

different people, and paints it, and then makes us laugh at the picture they make of the disagreeable originals of whom you have sometimes been the victim. You may try to demonstrate these truths but actors will never believe you; it is their secret. The ability to feel deeply is so admirable a quality they will not admit that one can, or should, dispense with it if you are to succeed in their profession. Do you mean, they will say, that those plaintive, painful tones this mother drags from her entrails, and shake my own so violently, are not inspired by actual feeling? Is it not pain that makes them? Not at all. And the proof is that they are timed, they are part of a system of declamation, they are subject to a law of unity, they contribute towards the solution of a given problem. They can only fulfil all that is needful after long study and, to be uttered correctly, have been rehearsed a hundred times. The actor has listened to himself and is still listening at the very moment he moves you and his talent does not consist in giving way to his feeling, as you suppose, but in imitating the outward signs of feeling so perfectly that you are deceived. The howls of pain are inscribed in his memory, his gestures of despair are planned; he knows precisely the moment when the tears will flow. The trembling voice, the halting, choked words, the quivering limbs, the shaking knees . . . pure imitation, a lesson learned, a sublime aping of which the actor is aware even as he does it, and which he remembers a long time after, but does not touch his heart but rather, like other activities, merely drains his physical strength. [His costume] removed, his voice is gone, he feels great weariness, he changes into his night shirt and goes to bed; but there is no more pain, no disturbance, no weakening of the soul; it is you, the audience, that bear all these impressions with you. The actor is tired and you are sad; he has done and not felt, you have felt and not done. If it were otherwise the actor would be in the most sorry state. Happily for us and for him, he is not the character, he plays it; otherwise how flat and gloomy he would be!

Different men of feeling who combine to produce the greatest possible effect – that makes me laugh! And so I say again: it is feeling that makes the horde of mediocre actors; it is feeling that makes minor actors; it is the lack of feeling that makes sublime actors. An actor's tears come from above, those of a man of feeling well up. The entrails make a man of feeling's head reel out of control; the actor's head creates a passing discomfort in his entrails.

Have you ever considered the difference between tears produced by a tragic event and those provoked by a sad speech? We hear something beautiful; slowly our heads are worried, our gut moves, tears flow: but when we see a tragic event the gut suddenly is stirred, we lose our head and tears flow; they are spontaneous. But in the first case, they are induced.

This is the advantage of a natural, real surprise in a theatre of words. It quickly produces the effect the stage leads us to expect. But it makes illusion much more difficult; a wrong move, badly done, destroys it; voice patterns are easier to imitate than actions but actions strike us with much more force.

Consider, please, what we mean by being true in the theatre: does it mean showing things as they are in nature? In no wise: a street beggar in the street would be poor, small, paltry there; truth in that case would merely be the commonplace. So what is truth? It is the consistency of outward signs, voice, face, movement, action, speech, in a word of all the aspects of acting after an ideal model either given by the poet or imagined in the actor's head. That is what is wonderful.

An unhappy, a truly unhappy woman weeps and yet you are not touched. Worse, something wrong about her makes you laugh, something in the way she speaks offends your ear, something natural to her in her sorrow makes her appear sullen, because genuine passions often produce ugly facial expressions which an actor with no taste copies but which a great actor avoids. We want a man at the height of his torments to protect his human dignity; we want this woman to fall with decorum and gentleness; we want a hero to die as an ancient gladiator died in the arena with grace, nobility, in an elegant picturesque pose to the applause of the amphitheatre. Who will best meet your expectations? An athlete confused by his own emotion, a victim to pain, or the trained athlete who practises the rigorous lessons of gymnastics until his dying breath? The ancient gladiator like a great actor, the great actor like an ancient gladiator does not die as though he were in bed, he must play out a different kind of death for our pleasure. And the discriminating spectator will feel that the truth of an action stripped of all beauty, is but a small thing and not in keeping with the rest. Not that nature does not have its sublime moments, but I am sure that if anyone can preserve what is sublime in them it is the man who knows them in advance and delivers them coolly.

I would not, however, deny that there is not some kind of factitious stirring of the entrails which can be learned; yet it is my view that this is almost as dangerous as natural feeling; in the end it will drive the actor into mannerism and monotony; only a head of ice can avoid that.

Yet you will say that when a crowd of men reveal each in their own way their feelings, it makes a marvellous spectacle although they did not deliberately come together: agreed; but it would have been even more marvellous had they done so. Moreover you are speaking of a fleeting moment, whereas I am speaking of a work of art which has a structure and a duration. Take each of these people and show them to me one by one, two by two, three by three, each freely making their own movements and you will see the cacophony that ensues; and if, to avoid this mistake, you make them rehearse together, then there is no more individuality, no more natural feeling, and so much the better. It is like a well-ordered society in which each sacrifices his primal rights for the good of the whole. And who will best judge the extent of this sacrifice? The just man in society, the man with a cool head in the theatre.

I now have to speak of the pernicious influence of a bad partner on a great actor who has conceived his role on the grand scale but is forced to abandon his ideal model to come down to the level of the poor devil on stage with him.

What are two actors who give each other mutual support? They are men whose models, more or less, are equal to or properly subservient to the circumstances in which the author has placed them; otherwise, one would be too strong and the other too weak; to prevent discord, the stronger will not raise the weaker to his own level but rather instinctively or deliberately go down to the other's.

At what age can one be a great actor? At the age when one is full of fire and the blood boils in one's veins, when the mind takes fire at the slightest spark, when the slightest shock makes the innards churn? Not at all. It is when one has acquired long experience, when the passions have calmed, when the heart is cold and the head rules . . . an old actor is only ridiculous when his strength is gone and his talent is not big enough to cover the contrast between his age and the youth of his character.

In our own time, as beginners, Mlle Clairon and Molé played like mechanical dolls; then they became great actors. How did that happen? Did they acquire heart, entrails, feeling?

If these two actors had been profoundly moved, as is supposed, would one have had the time to glance at the boxes or the other to give a smile at the wings?

Again I say, it is not someone who is beside himself, but someone who is cool, self-possessed, who is master of his face, his voice and his actions, his acting, who will make me his.

Garrick shows his head between two double doors and in two seconds I see his expression change rapidly from great joy to astonishment, from astonishment to sadness, from sadness to dejection, from dejection to despair and return with the same speed from the point where he is to the point where he started. Could he really have felt all these passions one after the other in his heart and play this kind of scale in concert with his face? I do not think so . . .

At the premiere of *Inès de Castro* (6 April 1723), when the children were brought on and the pit began to laugh, Mlle Duclos, who was playing Inès, was angered and cried: 'So you laugh, stupid people, at the finest moment in the play!' The pit heard and was silent, the actress took up her role once more and her tears with it. So! Can one pass from one deep feeling to another, from indignation to pain so quickly? I do not think so; her indignation was real, her pain a pretence.

Quinault Dufresne was playing the role of Sévère in *Polyeucte*. The character had been sent by the Emperor Decius to persecute the Christians. He confides to his friend his secret feelings on this vilified sect. This confidence could cost him his life and so had to be made quietly. The pit shouted, 'Speak up!' and he immediately answered, 'And you, sirs, shut up!' If he had really been Sévère, could he have so quickly become Dufresne? No, I tell you, only a man in control of himself, as doubtless he was, a rare, a complete actor, can take off his mask and put it on again.

In *Sémiramis* by Voltaire, Le Kain goes into his father's tomb and kills his mother and comes out, his hands covered in blood. He is filled with horror, his limbs shake, his eyes are wild, his hair seems to stand on end. You feel yourself shiver, terror grips you, you are as lost as he. Yet Le Kain kicks a diamond earring that had fallen from some actress's head into the wings. Did this actor feel? It cannot be. Are you going to tell me he is a bad actor? I think not. Who then is he? He is a cool-headed man who feels nothing, but who embodies feeling in a far superior manner. He may well cry, 'Where am I?' I answer, 'On stage, kicking an earring into the wings.'

An actor is passionately in love with an actress and they have to play a scene of jealousy together; the scene will gain if the man is a nonentity; it will lose if he is a man of stature; for then he will be himself, not the ideal, sublime model he has created of someone jealous. The proof that they bring themselves down to the ordinary level is that if they got on their high horse they would laugh in each other's face.

I will go further and say that the best way to give a poor performance is to play oneself. You are a Tartuffe, you are a misanthrope by nature and so you will play a Tartuffe, a misanthrope and you will do it well; but you will not match what the poet did, for he created the Tartuffe, the Misanthrope; you are no more than an individual and in general far inferior to the poetic model . . .

For every passage where the poet has felt more strongly than the actor, there are a hundred where the actor feels more strongly than the poet; and nothing is more true than Voltaire's exclamation, seeing Mlle Clairon in one of his plays, 'Did I do that?' How did that happen? Does Mlle Clairon know better than Voltaire? Indeed she does. Her ideal model as she declaimed was superior to the ideal model the poet conceived as he wrote. But this ideal model was not she. What did she do? What was her gift? To imagine a great phantom figure and copy it through the genius of her nature. She copied something greater; she imitated the movement, the actions, gestures, the entire nature of a being far superior to herself. She was acting and her acting was sublime.

Go to Mlle Clairon's house and see her in the full force of her anger; if she is theatrical in pose and speech and action you will laugh at her, though you would have admired her on stage. What are you doing, what does your laughter mean save that real feeling and simulated feeling are two different things? . . . the picture given in the theatre of passions is not a real picture; they are broader portraits, subject to rules and conventions. And so I ask, which is the actor who will confine himself the most closely in these rules? Who is he who will best understand the need to enlarge? Is it the man who is dominated by his own nature, or the man who sheds it to take on another, greater, nobler, more intense, higher? We are ourselves by nature, we are others by imitation. The heart we assume is not our own. What do we need in such a case? To acquire a knowledge of the exterior signs of the heart we have assumed, to be aware of the experience of the people watching us and deceive them by imitating those borrowed symptoms which necessarily form the basis of their judgements; for they have no other means of knowing what is going on inside us. The man who best knows and most perfectly copies these symptoms, after a finely conceived model is the greatest actor and the greatest author is he who leaves the least to the imagination of a great actor . . .

Here is an experience you have sometimes had. You have been invited to an actor's or an actress's home in a small group to judge their talent. You find the actress has soul and feeling; you shower her with praise. You left her with the conviction of a rousing success. The following day she is on stage and she is booed. How can that be? Has she lost her talent from one day to the next? Not at all. However, at her home you were on a level with her, you listened to her without thinking of the conventions, she was face to face with you, there were no other terms of comparison. You were happy with her heart, her feeling, her gestures, her pose; everything was in proportion with the small auditorium, the small space; there was no need to enlarge. On stage, everything disappeared. On stage she needed a model other than herself because everything around her was changed. In a small private theatre, an apartment, with you the audience on a level with the actress, the true dramatic model would have seemed overdone . . .

There is a dramatist in Naples whose name I once knew. Once his play is written, he scours the town for people whose faces, voices and character are best suited to the roles. As it is an entertainment for the sovereign, nobody refuses. Once the company is assembled, he works with them for six months, all together or separately. And when do you think they begin to understand one another, to act well, to move towards the perfection the author demands? When they are drained by endless rehearsals, when they are, as we say, blasés. From that moment on the results are amazing and it is after this painful effort that the performances take place. And those who have seen it agree that those who have not do not know what acting is. Performances continue for six months and the king and his court enjoy the greatest pleasure theatrical illusion can give. So, is it your opinion that this illusion which is as good, even better at the last performance than at the first, can result from feeling?

Diderot formulated the idea of split consciousness that Boswell had hinted at, the issue that has dominated discussions on acting ever since.

6 | Coquelin

Constant Coquelin (1841–1909) was the most famous actor of his age. After training at the Conservatoire, he entered the Comédie-Française. From there he went to the Théâtre de la Renaissance. Finally he took charge of the Théâtre de la Porte-Saint-Martin, where he created the role of Cyrano de Bergerac that Edmond Rostand had written especially for him. He wrote two short books, *Art and the Actor* (1880) and *The Art of the Actor* (1894).

Between the two, he published an article outlining his views in *Harper's Monthly* in 1887, which provoked a wide reaction, including a response from Sir Henry Irving, whom he had criticised.

The title of his article, 'The Dual Personality of the Actor', succinctly expresses his central concern: split consciousness. His starting point is Diderot whose theory he develops in terms of his own professional practice.

Coquelin's argument runs as follows:

- There are two aspects to the actor. The first, Number One, is the mind and imagination which create the image and nature of the character.

- The second, Number Two, is his expressive means of voice and body, his technique.

- Number One must always be in control and Number Two must follow its dictates.

- The actor first conceives an image of the character, as something outside him, that he can contemplate. He must then adapt himself to that image as though painting a portrait but he must also enter into the portrait and then control it. He does not belong to it.

- Acting is not identification but representation.

- In rehearsal the actor may experience feelings, but in performance, he must feel nothing but merely follow the cool-headed dictates of Number One. He is thus able to represent the character at will since he is in command.

- Not all actors, for physical reasons, can play all characters.

- It is the psychology of the character which is paramount. Physical characterisation will flow from that. There are actors who, even without make-up, seem to transform themselves *from within*.

- His expressive means, Number Two, must never take over, to embellish or produce picturesque effects for their own sake, or for a certain kind of theatricality.

- The danger is that the actor dominated by Number Two only plays one character and does not adapt to different plays.

- No attempt at natural, everyday speech should be made.

Art and the actor

One question divides the theatre into two camps: should the actor feel his role, weep to make others weep,* or should he remain in full self-control even when his character is at its most emotional, and is carried away, or should he feel none of the emotions he expresses so that, unmoved, he may move others more surely? That is Diderot's *paradox*.

Well now, I hold this paradox to be the truth and I am convinced that one can only be a great actor if one is in absolute control of oneself and can express, at will, feelings which one does not have, or ever will have, and which are not in one's nature.

The same ability which allows a dramatic author to produce, fully-fledged, out of his head, a character like Tarfuffe, or Macbeth, although he himself is a decent honest man, allows the actor to absorb this character, to wind it up and down as he wishes, while only ever being someone completely different, someone distinct and apart, as a painter is distinct from his picture.

The actor is inside what he creates, that is all.

He pulls the strings that make his characters run the gamut of human emotions   * Horace.

from within; these strings are his nerves and he must control them and use them as he thinks best.

The actor builds his character. He draws on the author, on tradition, on nature, on his own knowledge of men and matters, his experience and his imagination. In a word, he works, and once his work is done he has his role, he sees it, holds it, lives in it, but he does not belong to it.

That is why the real actor is always at the ready. He can pick up a role at any time and immediately summon up the feeling he wishes. Laughter, tears, terror are at his command. He does not need to wait to be caught in their grip or for grace to descend from on high.

The art of the actor

I

I define art, in general, as a composition in which poetry clothes and conveys an even greater measure of truth.

To create a work of art the painter has his brushes and his colours, the sculptor has clay, his modelling tools and his chisel, the poet has his words and his lyre, i.e., rhythm, metre and rime. The arts are different because their instruments are different. The actor, however, is his own instrument.

The raw material of his art, that he works on and shapes, is his face, his body, his life. It follows, therefore, that the actor is two people in one. There is his Number *One,* the instrumentalist; there is his Number *Two*, the instrument. *One* conceives the character, or rather since it is the author who conceives, he *sees* it as the author saw it. Hamlet, Tartuffe, Arnolphe, Romeo. *Two* then makes this model a reality.

This split consciousness is the hallmark of the actor.

It is certainly to be found elsewhere. [The writer] has his *One* and *Two*. The latter lives in the world, loves, hates, knows joy and sorrow. The other is on a higher plane, impassive, and in moments of high emotion observes, studies and makes notes for future reference.

But in the writer this split does not affect him personally as it does the actor. It cannot be seen. The writer's *One* observes his *Two* but does not change it. The actor's *One* on the other hand sets to work on his *Two* until it has transformed it, until it has drawn from it the character in his mind. In other words, until he has turned himself into his own work of art.

When the painter has to paint a portrait, he makes his model pose and with his brush puts all the characteristic features his seasoned eye can see onto the canvas through the magic of his art and then his picture is finished. The actor has one thing more to do: to get inside the portrait. For the portrait has to speak, move, walk within its frame, the stage, and that gives the audience the illusion he *is* the character.

When the actor has a portrait to paint, that is, a character to create, he needs first, by reading and re-reading the play, to get to the heart of the author's intentions, to be clear about the truth of his character, its degree of importance, its proper place in the action, *see* him as he ought to be. Then he has his model.

Then, like the painter, he captures all its features and fixes them not on canvas, but on himself. He endows his *Two* with every aspect of this person. He sees Tartuffe in a particular costume. He puts it on. He sees a certain way of walking and copies it. He forces his own face, and, as it were, like a tailor cuts and sews his own flesh until the critic inside his *One* is happy and says that this indeed looks like Tartuffe. But the matter does not end there, for there would only be a superficial resemblance, the outside of a character, not the character itself. He must make Tartuffe speak with the voice he thinks should be his and should make him walk and talk, think and listen with the very *soul* he believes to be Tartuffe's to shape the entire performance.

To sum up, first a deep study of the nature of the character; then *One* conceives the role which *Two* reproduces according to the nature of the character. That is the actor's work.

II

The two beings that live side by side in the actor are inseparable but it is *One*, the one who *sees* who has to be master. He is the soul, the other is the mind. He is reason. *Two* is to *One* what rime is to reason: a slave that must obey.

The more reason is master the better the artist one is.

Ideally *Two,* that poor body, should be no more than simple putty, that can be endlessly moulded, that takes all shapes according to the role to be played, that becomes Romeo for a delightful juvenile lead and a demonic hunchback for Richard III, who charms by his wit, and for Figaro, a wily valet with a saucy grin, bare-faced, sure of everything, etc.

The actor would then be universal and with a modicum of talent, fit for any kind of role. He could do what he wanted. Alas!

That would be too much to ask for. Nature will not allow it.

However flexible the body, however mobile the face, neither can respond to all the actor's ideas.

The fact is that the way they are built prevents them from taking on certain roles which they are well able to understand and teach.

Many are inevitably restricted to certain kinds of roles.

There are others whose *Two*, or rather their own self, is recalcitrant. Their individuality is so dominant that they cannot give it up and so, instead of adapting to the role and taking on its appearance, they adapt the role to themselves and make it take on *their* appearance.

The problem with this approach is that one can only play one role.

One other consequence is that it logically entails a failure to study roles *from the inside*, which to my mind is the most important, but rather to study the outside and picturesque details.

We should not mistrust the picturesque but we should not make it our sole concern. Above all, we must not take one particularly attractive detail, which we imagine is correct, as our starting point when creating a role. Everything stems from the *nature of the character.*

Latch on to the inside of your character. You will then understand its outside naturally and the picturesque effects, if any, will take care of themselves. It is the soul that makes the body.

III

Let us be clear. I am not against taking particular traits that reveal the inner man from nature. On the contrary, it is one of an actor's qualities to be able to capture those that are right for the stage. But we should only select those that are meaningful and use them with discretion. We should beware of those that are purely personal. When we are playing the miser, Harpagon, we should not reproduce this or that particular miser that *we* know but the audience does not. Harpagon is *all misers* and the audience will recognise him.

IV

But what about being natural? Should we not speak naturally?

Please do not talk to me about the natural speech of people who cannot be bothered to articulate properly, but who address an audience as they would if they were at table, stop, start, repeat themselves, chew their words like the end of a cigar, *babble*, that is the word, and turn the author's style into some kind of gibberish, make mince-meat of it.

The theatre is not a drawing-room. You do not address an audience of fifteen hundred people as you do a few friends at the fire-side.* If you do not speak up, you will not be heard; if you do not articulate, you will not be understood.

I know there are actors who earn an enormous reputation by appearing to be conversational. Not one word is louder than the others, the ends of sentences are

derot.

dropped, they mumble, cut, seem to look for words, say them two or three times over, hum and haw for ten minutes then rush towards the close for a final effect. And the sheep-like public cries, 'How natural . . . He could be at home . . . I didn't hear what he actually said, did you? . . . But how naturally he spoke!'

But if, as sometimes happens, people find the play more interesting than the actor, and they want to understand the action, one day, when they are tired of trying to follow, they will angrily shout, 'Speak up! Can't hear you!'

So: the actor's duty is to respect the words. However he speaks them, he must speak what the writer has written, no more, no less.

Coquelin's ideas provoked a general debate, summarised in a major critical work by William Archer, a leading drama critic and Ibsen's first English translator, *Masks or Faces*.

It was, however, from Stanislavski that the first, serious response came, and that response stemmed from an entirely different tradition.

7 Realism

Russia in the nineteenth century had to reinvent its theatre, a truly national theatre with a distinct identity. Medieval theatre had been very rich and a tradition of popular, fairground entertainment survived, but only the imperial theatres, controlled by a complex bureaucracy, were allowed to present serious drama. Commercial theatres were only permitted to do so towards the end of the nineteenth century. Moscow did not have its own imperial theatre, the Maly, until 1823, and this became the cradle of a new school of acting. However, private theatres could be created. Many nobles took their more talented serfs, male and female, educated them and created theatres on their estates – hence the term 'serf theatre'. Many actors, including the great Mikhail Shchepkin (1788–1863), artistic director of the Maly for thirty years, had been serfs.

The repertoire of the imperial theatres was mostly based on French models: stiff neoclassical tragedies and light comedies. There was scarcely a genuine Russian character in sight. This was not surprising since the aristocracy and the educated classes spoke French. Some only knew a few Russian words so as to be able to give orders to their servants.

The drive to create a new theatre was urgent, and partly caused by social and political as well as artistic factors. Censorship was so draconian that no public or published discussion of politics or philosophy was allowed. Literature and the theatre, therefore, became the media through which social, moral and ethical issues were discussed. The artist became a kind of mentor and guide and enjoyed a revered status which was unique to Russia.

The theatre existed not only to entertain but to educate, to broaden the mind and extend the audience's sensibilities. The audience should leave the theatre in a different frame of mind from when it came in. It was important for the actor to present recognisable human beings in situations with which the audience would be familiar and with which they would identify. The cool-headed technician, who represented a character, might evoke admiration and appeal to the head, but could not perform this essential task. Only the actor who could both think and feel or feel/think, think/feel could present a fully rounded character, a human being, and so provide the audience with a total experience which would give them both pleasure and food for thought.

The thesis of the *Paradox* was rejected.

The new approach to performance, generally known as Psychological Realism, was defined by two major authors, Pushkin and Gogol, and a great actor, Shchepkin.

A major catalyst to new thinking was Shakespeare. It was the discovery of Shakespeare by the Romantics that produced radical change. Pushkin (1799–1837) is credited with the creation of modern Russian literature and his one full-length play, *Boris Godunov*, was constructed on a Shakespearean model with a mixture of tragedy, comedy and near farce. Writing *Boris* led Pushkin to reflect on the nature of theatre and theatrical truth. What could be believed? What was probable? In the draft preface to *Boris Godunov* he wrote:

> When writing my *Boris Godunov* I thought a great deal about tragedy. Attempts have been made to base it on the appearance of truth, but the very nature of drama makes that impossible, not to mention [the rules of] time, place etc. What kind of truth is there in an auditorium, divided into two, one of which is full of 2,000 people who are not supposed to be seen by those on stage . . . *The true masters of tragedy have only ever been concerned with the truth of character and of situations.* [emphasis added]

He developed this notion in an unfinished article, published after his death. He maintained that it was the author's duty to ensure that the feelings experienced by the characters in the situation he had invented be truthful, that is, probable: 'Authenticity of the passions, sentiments that seem true in the proposed circumstances, that is what our intelligence requires of the writer.'

Gogol (1809–1852) wrote extensively on the poor state of the Russian theatre, the inferior repertoire and overblown, effect-seeking acting. He stressed the supremacy of the character's inner life, the need to discover the driving force behind his actions before turning to externals: the actor was to work from the inside out. Above all, it was essential not to try to be 'funny'. The actor simply had to present the character.

He set out his ideas in 1846 in an article describing how *The Government Inspector* should be played.

Advice to those who would play the government inspector as it should be played

Above all, be very careful not to fall into caricature. Nothing should be exaggerated or trite even in the smallest parts. On the contrary, the actor should do his utmost to be modest, more simple and dignified than the character he is playing. The less an actor thinks about being funny and comic the better the comic aspects of his role will emerge. The comic emerges of itself in the very seriousness with which the characters are busy with their own concerns. They are all busy, all hustle and bustle, all hot and bothered as though it were the most important thing in their lives. Only the audience can see, from a distance, the vanity of their concerns. But they are never a joke and never think that anyone is laughing at them. The intelligent actor, before seizing on tiny quirks and tiny external details of his role, must try to understand the aspects of the role that are common to all mankind. He should consider what is dominant in the role. He should consider the character's main concern, which consumes his life, the constant object of his thought, the 'bee in his bonnet'. Having understood that, the actor must make it his own to such an extent that the thoughts and efforts of his character become his own and are constantly in his mind throughout the performance. He should not be concerned about individual scenes or details. They come of themselves quite successfully and easily, provided he does not lose sight of the bee in his bonnet. All these details and petty incidentals, any actor can successfully use, if he can copy someone's walk and movements, but they cannot create a complete role. They are merely the colours that are applied when the picture has been composed and drawn faithfully.* They are the clothes, the body of a role, not its heart. So, first and foremost you must capture the heart of a role not its clothes.

Given the definitions provided by both Pushkin and Gogol, it is essential to distinguish realism from naturalism.

Realism depends entirely on authenticity of characterisation, on a revelation of underlying relationships, on authentic reactions to the dramatic situation.

Aristotle.

101

Realism is a question of belief, of the actor's conviction that what he is doing is genuine. He behaves as though the situation were true. It can take place on a bare stage.

The language of a realist play can be elaborate, complex and literary. The most famous comedy in Russian theatre, Griboedov's *Woe from Wit* (1825), modelled on Molière, is written in a complex stanza form, unknown elswhere. Shakespeare was considered a realist playwright.

Naturalism, on the other hand, depends on the exactness of externals – decor and costume and props – and on an approximation to daily speech. At its most basic, it is a facsimile, a replica of the surface, nothing more.

It fell to Shchepkin, a close friend of both writers, to develop these ideas in more practical form. Shchepkin is to Russian theatre what Garrick was to English, a seminal figure and a model. Just as Garrick had ruled Drury Lane, so for the last thirty years of his life Shchepkin led the Maly Theatre Company, raising the standard of performance, teaching younger actors who were to carry the tradition forward. The Maly was Stanislavski's 'university'.

Shchepkin had to find his own way to artistic perfection and the process was slow. He set out his progress and ideas in his *Memoirs*. Tradition has it that Pushkin was so concerned that Shchepkin should write his autobiography that he wrote the first sentence himself.

Like many other serfs, Shchepkin had the benefit of a good education. While at school, he acted in a number of plays for which he was warmly praised. But he had done no more than reproduce the worst excesses of bad provincial acting, as his father did not fail to point out.

Shchepkin recounts some of the absurd conventions current in the early nineteenth century. Words like 'love' or 'hate' had to be shouted at the top of the actor's voice. Any approach to normal speech was considered incompetence. Before making an exit, an actor had to raise his right hand. One unfortunate actor, who forgot, was almost off stage when he remembered his mistake, returned and raised his hand. Exits had to be made backwards, so as not to turn one's back on the audience. This caused much fumbling for the unseen doorknob. No one seems to have been aware of the absurdity of these conventions.

Revelation came when he saw a performance by Prince Meshcherski, an actor with a high reputation. Shchepkin was baffled by the simplicity and concentration of the prince's acting, which did not seem to be acting at all. Nevertheless, the performance made a deep impression.

However, when he attempted to deliver lines simply, he found it difficult and soon lapsed into the emphatic bombast to which he had become accustomed. It was only an accident at rehearsal that opened up the way to him.

Memoirs

I have to tell you that unfortunately for me my father had lived for some years in Moscow and Petersburg and had been a frequent visitor to the theatre, and, it seems, had seen the best actors of the time and had even attended performances at the Hermitage. When I began to gabble my lines at appalling speed my father burst out laughing, but my mother wept for joy to see her son being so clever. Realising that I was making such a effect I went on louder and faster and with great self-satisfaction I winked at my sister as much as to say let my father see what I'm made of and let me go on bellowing. All this was going through my head while my father was laughing. But imagine my surprise when he stopped me. 'All right,' he said, 'that's enough. Was that the way you all acted?' 'Yes, all of us,' I answered, 'and me more than the rest.' 'And you were applauded?' 'We were.' 'And was your teacher happy?' 'Very!' My father gave a sardonic laugh and said, 'Idiots, you are all idiots. You and your teacher should be birched, all of you, for acting in that way!'

Prince Meshcherski

I cannot tell you what went on in my head as I waited for the performance. I could already picture what his acting must be like and it seemed it must be colossal. 'Yes,' I thought, 'his acting must be beyond anything we can do, because he has not only lived in Moscow and Petersburg, but he has been to Vienna, Paris and London and, more than that, he has appeared at the court of Catherine the Great so what must his acting be like!' All this excited me tremendously until the performance itself. And there I was in the theatre, the orchestra played the overture, the curtain went up and there was my prince . . . but no it wasn't! It wasn't the prince but the miser, Salidar. The transformation in his appearance was frightening. The nobility of his face had disappeared and the meanness of the miser was sharply written on it instead. And yet! Despite this powerful impression it made it seemed to me the prince simply could not act. How triumphant I felt as I thought to myself, 'You see!, he's a nobleman, so he must be good! What kind of acting is this? He doesn't know what to do with his hands and he speaks – it's ridiculous – simply, the way everybody speaks. Is that acting? No, your highness is way behind us!'

All the other actors seemed better than he because they were acting, especially the man playing Scapino. He spoke very fast and waved his arms about like all the best, real actors. The prince went on as he had begun; yet it was strange, despite the simplicity of his acting, which I took for incompetence, throughout the performance, every time it came to money, it was clear to us that he was wounded to the heart and at that moment you forgot all the other actors. The fear of death and the dread of being parted from his money were astonishingly true and the simplicity of his diction was no hindrance to his acting. As the play went on the more I was carried away and, finally, even began to wonder whether it would not have been worse had he acted in our way. In short, I was overpowered by reality which did not let me go until the end of the performance. I saw no one but the prince. I, so to speak, became him. His pain, his cries found echoes in my soul. His every word, by its very naturalness, thrilled me and tore me apart, too.

The play ended. Everyone was in raptures and roaring with laughter but I shed the tears I always do when I have been deeply moved. It all seemed so different and my head was confused. 'The prince speaks poorly,' I thought, 'because he speaks simply.' And then it occurred to me that that was what was beautiful, that he spoke simply. He wasn't acting, he was living. A few words and phrases that he had spoken simply but with intense feeling stayed in my memory. I felt they were my own because I thought I could say them in the same way he had. How annoyed I was with myself for not having realised from the start that what is good is what is natural and simple! . . .

To become familiar with the naturalness of the prince's acting and not to let the impression fade, I asked to be allowed to copy out the play which I did in one sitting . . . I went to my own village and didn't let the play out of my sight. I knew it by heart in twenty-four hours. But what was my astonishment when I attempted to speak simply and couldn't say a single word naturally or easily? I tried to remember the prince and started to say the lines in the same way as he had but felt that though I was speaking like him I couldn't but recognise the falsity of my diction. But I could not understand why. For several days running I went into the woods and there, amid the trees, performed the whole play but realised that I was acting just as I had before and could not capture that simplicity and naturalness of which the prince was a master. I was driven to despair. It did not occur to me that to be natural I had to speak with my own voice, feel with my own feelings and not imitate the prince. After much effort I lost heart and came to the conclusion that I would never achieve simplicity in acting . . .

Then I had a happy accident. There was a rehearsal of Molière's *School for Husbands* in which I was playing Sganarelle. Because we had rehearsed a great deal and I was bored and had something quite trivial on my mind, I rehearsed in an off-hand manner.* I didn't act but just said the lines. I already knew my words by heart and I suddenly felt that I had said a few words simply, so simply they would not have been different had I spoken them in life. And every time I managed to speak that way I felt such pleasure that towards the end of the play I tried to maintain that conversational tone. Then everything went wrong. The harder I tried the worse it was because I reverted to my old way of acting which no longer satisfied me since, privately, I was looking at my art with new eyes. Yes, privately! Had I expressed the idea that was growing inside me I would have been laughed at. The idea was so contrary to current opinion that at the end of the play my fellow actors congratulated me for having made an effort to fall back into the usual rut and act like all the others, indeed, according to some, better than they.

I am trying to remember as best I can what was considered at the time to be fine acting: it was when nobody spoke in a natural voice, when acting consisted of excessive, ugly declamation, with the words spoken as loudly as possible, when almost every word was accompanied by a gesture. In love scenes in particular they declaimed so loudly it makes me laugh to remember it; the words love, passion, treachery were shouted as loud as was humanly possible. Yet there was no facial play to help the actor; the face remained in the same tense, unnatural expression it wore on the actor's first entrance. And again, when an actor finished a particularly powerful speech and had to make an exit, it was understood that he should raise his right hand in the air and thus quit the stage. I suddenly recall one of my colleagues who ended his speech and started to make his exit without raising his arm. What did he do? Half way out he decided to rectify his error and solemnly raised his precious arm. The audience loved it!

Shchepkin was the first actor to discuss in any depth the process of characterisation. He set out his ideas in a series of letters to fellow actors. Gogol had written to him an actor 'must not present but transmit', a principle which he adopted.

He was firmly opposed to Diderot's thesis. There was, he stated, an opposition between the theatre of reason and the theatre of feeling.

Shchepkin's principles were:

- An actor must get into the skin of the character, think like him, feel like him, walk, talk and behave like him. He must blot out his own personality so as to take on the characteristics of the person he is playing.

. Diderot's word 'blasé'.

- An actor must observe life around him, ask the why and wherefore of events. Why this way and not that?

- An actor must be able to feel and sympathise with all sorts and classes and behave in ways appropriate to different social groups.

- In comedy, an actor should not consciously attempt to be funny, comedy and tragedy both arise from truthful behaviour.

- This kind of playing might not always bring success, whereas technical playing might. But personal integrity is worth more than cheap applause.

These principles represent the first genuine, modern statement on acting; there are no references to rhetoric, declamation or rules of gesture. As such, they founded a new approach, one that would have long-term consequences.

Letters

To Sergei Shumski, 27 March 1848

Remember, perfection is not given to man save by conscientious application, you get somewhere near it insofar as your natural gifts allow. For God's sake don't think about amusing the audience. Both the humorous and the serious arise from a proper view of life . . . You must believe that personal satisfaction is worth more than applause. Mix with people, as far as time allows, study human beings in the mass, don't let one incident escape you, and you will always discover why something happened this way and not that. This living book replaces the kind of theory that, unfortunately, actors still lack. So, study all kinds and conditions of men without prejudice and you will see that there is good and evil everywhere. This will enable you, as an actor, to give to every class what is appropriate. So that when playing a peasant you will not be able to observe the social niceties when expressing great joy. When playing an aristocrat, you cannot shout and wave your arms about when you are angry. Don't imagine you are above hard work on the situations and details you meet in life. But remember they are only an aid, not an end in themselves and that they are only valuable when you know where you are going.

To Aleksandra Shubert, 27 March 1848

[O]ne actor does not cry on stage but by giving, so to speak, a semblance of tears, makes the audience cry; another actor is bathed in bitter tears but the audience does not share his feelings. Might one then conclude that real feelings are not needed in the theatre, merely cold artifice, the actor's craft? I may be wrong but no! How can I express my thoughts more clearly? For instance, one person has been endowed by nature with a soul that has a natural affinity with everything that is beautiful and good; all that is human is dear to him, he does not stand apart. No matter who he is with, whatever their station in life, he feels their joys and woes, he is passionate in his understanding as though he himself were concerned and so he will weep and laugh with them. Another man, much more bound up with himself, more self-centred, lives in the world, encountering sorrow and laughter at every step but will only participate in either insofar as he is linked socially to the people concerned, or because it is useful to express his sympathy . . . he will commiserate with someone who has been robbed of a thousand roubles but it would never enter his head how costly it is for a beggar to lose his last rouble; he will commiserate with some nobleman whose wife has been seduced but he will not raise an eyebrow if he is told that this nobleman has had his way with his coachman's wife. These people judge everything coldly but so as not to reveal themselves as the egoists they are, they make a show of concern as though it were real concern, and since they are always calm and collected express themselves with great clarity. It is the same in the theatre: it is much easier to convey everything mechanically, for that all you need is reason and, little by little, your reason will approximate to joy and sorrow to the extent that an imitation can approximate to the genuine article. But an open-hearted actor, that's another matter; indescribable labours await him: he must first begin by blotting himself, his own personality, his own individuality, out and become the character the author has given him; he must walk, talk, think, feel, weep, laugh in the way the author wants him – and you cannot do that if you have not blotted yourself out. You see how much more meaningful this kind of actor is! The first kind merely fakes, the second is the real thing . . . You may say that the perfection I seek is impossible; no, it is just difficult! You ask me why we should strive for some sort of perfection when there are easier ways of pleasing an audience? We might equally well ask: why have art? So, my dear friend, study it as something precise and exact not as a fake.

To Pavel Annenkov, 12 November 1853

Yes, real life and rousing passions should be shown artistically in shining colours, in all their truth, and real feeling should be allowed to the extent that the writer asks for it. However true a feeling may be, if it goes beyond the overall idea [of

the play], there will be no harmony, which is the universal law of all the arts . . .
Naturalness and truth are needed artistically only insofar as the overall idea
allows.

8

Stanislavski and the 'System'

The Stanislavski 'system' is the most comprehensive study of acting that we possess. It is not an abstract theory, but a theory of practice, based on Stanislavski's own experience and self-analysis. From the age of fourteen he kept a series of notebooks in which he recorded his ideas about his own acting, his failures, what he had learned from the great actors, both Russian and foreign. These notebooks form the basis for his books on acting, the first of which was drafted in 1906.

Just as Macklin had spoken of a 'science' of acting, so, in his twenties, Stanislavski wrote of a 'grammar' of acting, one that would enable him to combine truthfulness of behaviour with the demands of the stage and give him a measure of control to ensure the consistency of his performances.

Stanislavski's early career was similar in many respects to Shchepkin's. He too had acquired a series of tricks and clichés, drawn not only from Russian theatre but also from performances he had seen in Paris during his frequent visits. Fortunately, he was taught by two actors, Fedotov and his wife Glikeria, who had been pupils of Shchepkin and were thus able to pass on his methods. They taught him to rely on observation and not to copy other actors' performances.

Stanislavski based his approach on the ideas of Pushkin and Gogol and their definition of realism. His contemporaries believed that he would carry the realist tradition of the Maly during its golden period into the twentieth century.

Stanislavski is credited with the invention of the imaginary 'fourth wall' which divides actor from audience. It was in fact the culmination of a process that had been taking place since the middle of the eighteenth century. Both Garrick and Diderot agreed that they could not develop the kind of theatre they wanted while there were stage boxes flanking a thrust stage, or when the privileged actually sat on the stage. Then the stage boxes were removed, the thrust stage disappeared and the action took place behind the proscenium arch. The picture-frame stage had been created.

The coming of electricity offered the possibility of dimming the lights so that the auditorium could be darkened and all concentration focused on the action. This was the theatre structure that Stanislavski inherited. He insisted that the actor's concentration must be on the other actors, on the action, not on a direct relationship with the audience. Hence the fourth wall. It was he who encouraged, when necessary, actors to turn their backs on the audience, or to act in profile, which outraged the traditionalists who resolutely spoke their lines out front and placed their chairs to face out front. The dramatic action had to be self-contained, focused, but transparent to the audience watching.

Stanislavski, like the co-founder of the Moscow Art Theatre, Nemirovich-Danchenko, also reacted against the practice of throwing plays on with perhaps only four rehearsals, where actors had a repertoire of set moves which they always used. Very often they did not know their lines and so moved downstage to the prompter's box and repeated their speeches after him without any genuine sense or meaning.

Stanislavski was well aware of where he stood historically in relation to other schools of acting. Over a period of years he drafted a survey of the main schools of acting, entitled 'Various Trends in the Art of the Theatre', but never completed it. It was only published after his death although some of the material did find its way into the first part of *An Actor's Work*. He defined four main kinds of performance:

- hack-work, where the actor merely creates a string of clichés without any real thought

- representation, as advocated by Diderot and Coquelin

- experiencing, where the actor in some measure feels the emotions he is playing

- a combination of all three methods

*Various trends in the art of the theatre**

Hack-work

You can deliver a role, that is speak it in a loud voice in a manner that has been established once and for all.

That is not art, merely hack-work.

During the many centuries in which the art of acting has existed, fossilised and rarely challenged hack-work has become widely accepted as the norm. It has crushed true art, because talentless hack-actors constitute the overwhelming majority, whereas talented creative artists are desperately few in number . . . Quite often even great actors descend into hack-work and hack-actors rise to the level of art.

While the art of 'experiencing' is an attempt to feel a role every time it is played, and the art of 'representation' to experience the role at home at least once so that we can understand it and then create a form for it, to express its individual essence, the hack-actor forgets about experiencing and tries to work out ready-made forms for all feelings and all interpretations, for all roles and all genres once and for all. In other words, in the art of 'experiencing' and 'representation' experiencing is unavoidable while in hack-work it is unnecessary and only happens by chance.

Hack-actors are not able to create each role separately. They do not know how to feel and genuinely embody what they have felt. They just know how to say the lines, using theatrical means of expression worked out long ago in support.

They need technical tricks for delivering every kind of role, clichés to illustrate all human feelings, stereotypes for imitating all human characters. Technical tricks, clichés and stereotypes simplify a hack-actor's work greatly . . .

[W]hat is expressed in the language of gesture and words is not feeling, which the hack-actor does not have, nor the illusion of feeling as in the art of representation, but the mechanical aping of the physical manifestation of human feeling, that is, not feeling but the external result it produces, not the contents of the mind but merely its outward form. This theatrical mask of feeling, fixed once and for all, soon wears out, loses the tenuous connection it had to life and turns into a simple mechanical cliché . . .

There are technical tricks and clichés for everything: for delivering the line, that is voice and speech, for creating the body, that is walking, gestures, movements, posture, for expressing every kind of emotion and passion, for aping characters and types from every class of society, every period, every nationality, for specific plays and roles.

ited extracts.

Hack-actors want to substitute technical tricks for experience and creativity. These are taught in theatre schools by tutors in voice and movement.

They have to be examined, at least in general outline, if we are to understand how meaningless they are. Let us begin with vocal clichés.

To deliver their lines, hack-actors need a loud voice, which often rises to a shout, and diction which is obtrusively clean. Loud clear speech is needed not only so that they can be heard everywhere in the house or in the open spaces where they often play but mostly because it rouses an audience.

Remember the resonant actors' voices with oily vowels, rumbling, wheezing, whistling, cracking consonants, a shouted syllable here and there, often destroying the logical stress and even the sense.

Remember the way they stress every syllable and, without exception, round off each word with a flourish.

Remember their clear diction with the words like beads on a string.

All-purpose actors' speech, established for all time, is enlivened by a large number of tricks to copy the non-existent emotions hack-actors do not possess. For example, the strength or weakness of an emotion is conveyed by the strength or weakness of the voice, rising to a shriek, or dropping to a whisper. The level of emotional energy is shown literally by quickening the pace, and accelerating the rhythm.

Love is always expressed in a melodious voice; passion by rolling the consonants and chopping off the words; heroism prefers lilting vocal ornaments and an excess of shouting. When being lyrical speech almost turns into singing, especially in moments of rapture or despair.

Even individual words and expression have their own clichés which replace the real meaning of the words which are taken at face value. So with the hack-actor the line, 'the long, long days and slow nights' becomes 'the loooong, loooong days and slooow nights' in which he tries to illustrate the length of the days and nights musically.

In the sentence, 'suddenly there was a short sharp sound' the hack-actor will convey the suddenness with both voice and body and 'short, sharp' will be very short, sharp indeed.

Words like 'vengeance' and 'curse' are usually spoken in tragic tones, just as words like 'big', 'small', 'tall', 'short', 'long', 'wide' are drawn in the air, words like 'nice', 'nasty', 'good', 'evil', 'happy', 'sad', 'young', 'old', etc., are delivered literally, not according to the inner meaning of the sentence in which the words are spoken.

Hack-actors also want their voice to have character so they have worked out a whole collection of clichés.

Officers rap out their words like a command. Fops swallow half their words and drawl. Peasants always stumble over their words and speak in loud vulgar voices. Upper-class young people, especially when they are naive, speak in high-pitched voices, frequently squeaking. Mature, wise ladies and gentlemen speak in the bass register, with richer sounds etc.

Picturesque attitudes, studied gestures and 'effective' acting have been developed to match these resonant tones, this clear diction and solemn delivery.

Actors do not walk, they progress. They do not sit down, they ensconce themselves. They do not lie down, they recline. They do not stand, they pose.

Verbal and physical clichés complement each other. A gesture serves a word, a word serves a gesture.

The hack-actor approaches the complexity of inner feeling from the outside, imitating only the external result.

Love is expressed by blowing kisses, by pressing a hand to the heart, by rolling the eyes upwards where all the highest things are, by biting lips, flashing glances, flaring nostrils, panting, speaking in a passionate whisper, lisping.

Agitation is expressed by walking up and down rapidly, by trembling hands when opening a letter, knocking the water jug against the glass, and the glass against the teeth.

Calm is expressed by yawning, stretching, boredom.

Joy by clapping one's hands, jumping, humming waltzes, whirling round, peals of laughter, that are noisy rather than happy.

Grief – by black clothes, a powdered face, a sorrowful, nodding of the head, blowing the nose, wiping dry eyes.

An order by a downward pointing finger.

Prohibition by an upward pointing finger.

Death by clutching one's chest or ripping one's shirt collar open. Hack-actors only recognise two forms of death – heart-failure and asphyxia.

Pleasure is expressed by a smile, displeasure by a grimace.

It is as though each of these emotions were just one thing, not many diverse and often contradictory feelings. Hack-actors paint white on white and black on black.

Hack-actors have a gallery of ready-made characters, to represent all aristocrats, officials, officers, peasants, dandies, cuckolds, passionate lovers or anyone else in a play.

The material is taken from real life but it is reworked beyond all recognition.

Stage aristocrats are grander than real aristocrats, dandies far more dandified, beautiful women, even more beautiful, heroes more heroic, bumpkins more uncouth, soldiers more military and generals are generalissimos.

This often quite absurd exaggeration arises because, for example, the stereotype of an aristocrat takes no account of the noble traditions or class prejudices that are characteristic of the real thing. There is only his elegance and polish, externals, to suggest high birth. The actor is complete with top hat and monocle, he straightens his cuffs, plays with his gold watch and chain or gloves.

The stage peasant is not based on his real good nature, his naivety, his simplicity, only on the clumsiness of his speech and crude manners.

There are not just stereotypes for classes and people but for characters in plays. All the hack-actor has to do is follow the tradition established by his famous predecessors – the tone, the walk, the movements, the manners, the make-up, the costume.

There is an important question which hack-actors never ask. Do their stereotypes look anything like the originals they have been drawn from?

Can a coat that has been worn to shreds look like the coat the tailor first made?

There are few clichés that have come into being by accident. Say an actor takes a liking to someone else's way of moving, or walking or speaking. He copies it, uses it all the time. In due course it will become a tradition. I traced the origin of one such cliché.

A famous French actor bowed with a spectacular flourish at the end of a period play. A Russian actor who was with me, remembered how it was done and brought it back home. That bow is now taught in theatre schools and is considered indispensable for all costume plays whatever the period.

The hack-actor takes mere actor's excitement, mistakenly called emotion, for genuine creative experiencing. He confuses physical effort with inner energy, muscular tension with strength, muscular spasm with an expression of feeling, mechanical action with a mental process.

Actors' emotion is not experiencing. It is merely a bodily act, a mechanical excitement with the periphery of the body, i.e., of the network of nerves, muscles, etc.

Actors' emotion is self-standing, unconnected to inner feeling. It is a kind of theatrical hysteria, actors' hysterics. People of an hysterical disposition can work themselves into a fit, to order, without any inner cause, simply by exciting their peripheral nerves. Here is what the famous writer Theodor Lessing had to say on the subject:

In human psychology there is a law according to which a tired, listless mind, instead of discharging superfluous feelings externally by gestures, movements, excited words, tries to evoke an upsurge of feeling, using those very same gestures, movements and words it had previously used to express them. It is the opposite to what occurs in normal psychological life: muscular tension, rapid circulation of the blood etc., convey great artistic pleasure to the mind, which is found in a given situation. But after this artistic upsurge mental energy drops even lower and results in a further attempt at stimulation. This is called hysteria. This condition is extremely widespread in our cultural life. Contemporary man does what every actor does on stage when he begins to 'represent' passion and feeling, through facial expression, gesture etc., finally evoking a pallid, woolly, sometimes distorted approximation to these feelings and passions. In life as in art the men of our age 'present' themselves, they present themselves to themselves as men of sensitivity and feeling, which is characteristic of the hysteric. And the less they have living, inner strength, the more tense, exaggerated is the outward expression of these counterfeit, artificially inspired feelings. The less direct content there is in an artist's mind, of whatever kind, the more he tries to give clear, 'expressive' form to his creation and, in so doing, often loses all sense of proportion, takes refuge in effects which offend the ear and eye, as being artistically false . . .

[So] can we perhaps with justice describe actors' emotions as theatrical hysteria?

Hack-actors learn how to evoke it artificially both in school and on stage. This is encouraged by the tense atmosphere backstage which has the same effect on an actor as the call to battle on a warhorse.

In real art the effect on an audience is automatic. It is based on the fact that feelings are contagious and on their being experienced. In hack-work it is based on the fact that the audience has long been used to theatrical conventions which they expect and even love.

In art as in life feeling is evoked and demonstrated in two ways, going either from the heart to the body or the body to the heart. In other words from the centre to the periphery or the periphery to the centre.

Mostly an inner intention is first created and then revealed in action. But the opposite can happen: a familiar action can evoke a feeling associated with it.

Hack-actors are unable to arouse their creative feeling, except by accident and independent of their will.

The art of representation

In hack-work it is outward life and outward actions, the plot that is presented.

In the art of representation it is the character's thoughts and passions that are shown. These actors begin their creative work by a process of a living, human, so to speak, genuine experiencing of a role. That is indispensable. *There is no art without genuine creative experiencing.*

The second creative process – physical embodiment – is indissolubly linked to experiencing. It also occurs naturally, based on the laws of nature and the indissoluble link between mind and body.

These actors experience and naturally embody every role, *but not on stage, in front of an audience, but at home, alone or in private rehearsals.*

They experience the role once or several times so as *to note the outward bodily form when a feeling is genuinely expressed*. Thanks to the acuteness of motor (muscular) memory, characteristic of our profession, they remember the motor sensations of their body that accompany a feeling, its physical embodiment, not the feeling itself.

They do this because they maintain that genuine emotion can only be shown in private, when we are alone in our room. On the public stage living, genuine experiencing is *impossible*. Like hack-actors they blame the building and the poor acoustic, which disturb and distract, and other such obstacles which are supposed to kill live feeling.

They recognise that genuine experiencing and real embodiment are possible on stage during a performance but they consider it undesirable and even harmful to art, mainly because they are *untheatrical*. They are too subtle and elusive, they pass unnoticed.

The embodiment of inner thoughts and feelings must be distinct, clear, visible across the space that separates actor from audience. The means of conveying it have to be broadened, they have to be emphasised, presented for greater clarity. In a word, there has to be *a certain degree of theatricality*. It is only through clear theatrical forms that an actor can convey to an audience if not genuine feeling, its bodily appearance which he has noted in preparing his role. He creates at home and shows on stage. It is not what the actor is feeling at the moment that matters but what *the audience feels*. What the theatre needs is not the emotion itself but the appearance of the emotion. If this does not work, nature has to be corrected.

Art must be finer, more beautiful than mere nature, it must correct and enhance reality . . .

The theatre is conventional by its very nature and the stage lacks the means to convey the illusion of real life. So far from refusing conventions, the theatre should invent them. And since conventions are inescapable in the theatre, they should form the basis of art. Art is not real life, not even a reflection of it. It is its own creator. It creates its own art outside time and space, beautiful in its own conventions.

Conventions are not the same as clichés, which merely convey the plot. They convey the thoughts and passions for which the actor has found a form at home. They must be *emotionally meaningful*.

Pushkin said: 'The verity of the passions, verisimilitude of the sentiments in the proposed circumstances, that is what our intellect demands of a writer.'

The truth of the school of representation is not the verity of the passions, but the *verisimilitude* of feelings. It is a special truth, not the truth we know in life. Truth, or at least verisimilitude, is essential for an actor to be convinced by his creative work and to convince the audience. Art has to be *believed*. *Without belief there is no experiencing, no creative act, no effect.* The verisimilitude of the School of Representation doesn't create the belief we know in life, body and soul. It is merely *trust* in an actor's work, a coming to terms with theatrical lies and conventions, successful deceit, clever technique, the actor's own success and, through him, the author's talent. You cannot succumb fully to the half-truth and half-convention of this kind of acting. You believe it and half surrender not body and soul but with our intellect, eyesight, hearing and part of our aesthetic sense. In other words it does not create real, genuine truth but true-seeming stage emotions and our belief in them.

The inclination to beautiful artistic form is great. It is inherent in the actors themselves and leads them towards the *cult of theatrical forms*.

Once the actor has created in his imagination the best form of presenting the inner thoughts and passions of a role, he tries to embody it physically. He is the sculptor of his dreams, he shapes himself into the finest physical expression of his thoughts and passions.

According to Coquelin:

When the painter has to paint a portrait, he makes his model pose and with his brush puts all the characteristic features his seasoned eye can see onto the canvas through the magic of his art and then his picture is finished. The actor has one thing more to do: to get inside the portrait. For the portrait has to speak, move, walk within its frame, the stage, and that gives the audience the illusion he *is* the character.

When the actor has a portrait to paint, that is, a character to create, he needs first, by reading and re-reading the play, to get to the heart of the author's intentions, be clear about the truth of his character, its degree of importance, its proper place in the action, *see* him as he ought to be. Then he has his model. Then, like the painter, he captures all its features and fixes them not on canvas, but on himself. He sees [a character] in a particular costume. He puts it on. He sees a certain way of walking and copies it. He forces his own face, and, as it were, like a tailor cuts and sews his own flesh until the critic inside his *One* is happy and says that this indeed looks like Tartuffe. But the matter does not end there, for there would only be a superficial resemblance, the outside of a character, not the character itself. He must make Tartuffe speak with the voice he thinks should be his and should make him walk and talk, think and listen with the very *soul* he thinks to be Tartuffe's to shape the entire performance.

117

Now the best form has been created permanently the actor learns to express it technically, i.e. he learns to *represent* it.

The School of Representation is on the borderline of true and conventional experiencing, as on a knife edge. One step to the left and art will fall into the realm of real feeling, which it rejects. One step to the right and it falls into conventional lies and hack-work.

Only the living can create the living and so neither dazzling stage effects, nor beautiful theatrical conventions, nor even the very principle of representing the results of experience can create anything *live*.

As actors we cannot live just for ourselves, forgetting the audience, or constantly be aware of them and live just for show. In life we can respond to what our heart needs but we cannot weep and suffer for the pleasure of the audience. We cannot be divided at the moment we feel between ourselves and an audience. That is unusual for us. Our nature requires that on stage too we live a real life according to the laws it has laid down. It will not tolerate playacting by conventions.

The school of experiencing

The goal of the school of experiencing is to create the life of the human spirit on stage and to show it in an artistic theatrical form.

This life can never be created by skilful playacting, by truthful, sincere feeling and passion.

In general we ascribe far too much importance in life and on stage to everything conscious. The fact is that only one-tenth of our life is lived consciously. Professor Gots says that at least ninety percent of our life is subconscious and Maudsley asserts that consciousness does not even have a tenth of the functions attributed to it.*

In every role, at every performance, the actor must create not only the conscious but also the unconscious aspect of the human mind, the most important, profound, significant aspect both in life and on the stage.

However, it is not easy to deal with something beyond our conscious control. An ordinary actor's technique cannot cope. Only nature can do that, unconsciously creating living beings. That is why the art of experiencing is based on *the principle of the creativity of nature and natural law.*

Art is not a *game,* not *artifice,* not technical virtuosity *but a conscious physical and mental process.*

Each role has its own life, its story, its nature *with its so to speak natural elements of mind and body.* A role is a living, *natural creation,* modelled on man, not on a lifeless, worn-out theatrical cliché. It must be convincing, it has to instil

*Elmer Gots (1859–1923) American experimental psychologist; Henry Maud[...] (1835–1918), English psychologist and psychiatrist, after whom [...] Maudsley Hospital is nam[...]

a belief that it *is*. It has to *exist* in nature, *live in us and with us* and not just *appear to exist, remind us of, represent something living*.

All the feelings, sensations, thoughts of a role must become the actor's own vibrant feelings, sensations and thoughts. He must create the mind of the role out of his own mind and embody it with his own body. His artistic material is his own living feelings that the role has provoked, his memory of earlier impressions, sounds and pictures, emotions he has felt, joy, sorrow, grief, all his states of mind, ideas, knowing, facts and events. In a word, the memory of consciously experienced feelings, sensations, states of mind, moods, etc., relating to the character. *In creative work, pride of place is given to nature and its creative work is based on the intuition of feeling, to which we grant total freedom.*

Feeling does its creative work through the *normal process of a character's human experience and the natural embodiment of that experience.*

Why in a good play, well performed, however trite and worthless the characters may be, do we feel close to them, need them, feel interested in them, find them important for ourselves and our own lives? Why do they suddenly become symbolic? Why, when watching *The Government Inspector*, do we automatically think of our own ravaged, unattractive Russia? Why, when watching *The Cherry Orchard* and hearing the trees being chopped down, do we weep for the out-dated, useless yet beautiful life of the landed gentry? The reason is the same. The artistic life of the human mind, purified by poetry deeply felt and infused with the truth of life speaks not just of an individual but of a general event and acquires not just a personal but a social meaning.

The audience feels that the actor has not just come into a room because the writer has him do it to advance the plot, or his own ideas, not because he has to explain himself, show us what he is feeling, not just for their amusement, but because of something important to the character, with a definite aim, to put a question, carry out an errand, to make contact with other people.

There is nothing that can better produce a live human response from an audience than the live, human emotion of the actor. 'If you would have me weep, you yourself first must weep.'*

Combination

The art of experiencing, the art of representation and hack-work have fought each other from time immemorial. No sooner did the first dominate than the second came along to counter it and in the long run both degenerated into hack-work.

These three tendencies exist in their pure form in theory only. Reality is not concerned with categories and mixes theatrical conventions with true feeling, the true with the false, art with hack-work, etc. That is why all three tendencies can

race.

be detected in any performance, in every role. One moment the actor is really experiencing then he suddenly strays from the true path and represents the character or simply starts to gabble his lines and play-act like a hack. The question is the degree of genuine art, representation and hack-work in each individual case, in each theatre and in each production and performance.

Stanislavski, like Diderot, was fully aware of the fickleness, the unreliability of emotion. How can the actor be sure he will feel the right emotion at the right moment in the performance? How is he to assess and analyse what he has observed? How is he to gain control over the process of experiencing?

Stanislavski lived in a very different intellectual climate from his predecessors. The late nineteenth century saw the birth of the human sciences – clinical psychology, sociology, linguistics. The notion of the free-existing Passions was no longer valid. The emphasis was now on the process by which patterns of behaviour and emotion were produced. Wherever possible, Stanislavski always sought scientific confirmation of his ideas, which were the result of a careful analysis of his own process.

In an age where photography allowed an exact reproduction of the world, the question of the relationship of reality to art had to be examined once more.

In 1898 Tolstoi published *What is Art?* He reformulated Horace's dictum for his own time. Tolstoi pointed out that when we observe someone in the grip of strong emotion, we read the signs and are drawn into a sympathetic reaction. This is a normal human process, behaviour. When, however, we organise and arrange the signs so as deliberately to produce a reaction, that is art.

Art organises and structures this capacity to sympathise while, at the same time, producing an understanding of what is happening. But that understanding is not detached or analytical, it is rather the recognition of common human experiences. This defined the basis of Stanislavski's basic approach.

The fundamental principles of the Stanislavski 'system' are:

- that the actor must understand and make use artistically of the mechanisms of human behaviour

- that emotion is the result of an interaction with the world

Normal behaviour

In daily life our behaviour is, broadly speaking, based on necessity and intention. We feel certain needs and respond to them. If we are hungry, we eat. If we are thirsty, we drink. On the other hand, we create certain intentions, set ourselves certain goals which we then set about achieving. In either case there is the possibility of success or failure. Under certain circumstances I may die of hunger or thirst. I may be helped or hindered in realising my intention by the behaviour of other people. It is these actions and tensions that produce genuine, authentic emotion. In life there is no action that does not have a cause, even if that cause is not rational.

Dramatic behaviour

The real world is fact. We did not create it. In a play, the world is a fiction which we must transform into something resembling fact. A play is only marks on a page. It is not, like narrative prose, self-contained. It needs to be made 'real' by the actors, who must *assume* it is real or behave *as if* it were real. By believing in and engaging with the situations the writer has created, the actor calls into the play his own natural, organic mechanisms without needing to imitate externally. It is the fusion between the actor's self, his technique and the character the author has written that produces the performance. The character, as performed, is what Stanislavski called a Third Being – neither the actor's pure personality nor the author's pure concept but the child of both.

This fusion is achieved through the 'system'.

Stanislavski divided the 'system' into two parts:

- Personal preparation to provide the actor with full control over his resources, psychological and physical. He is at the same time raw material and an instrument.

- A rehearsal method to ensure consistency of performance. This came to be known after Stanislavski's death as the Method of Physical Action or Active Analysis.

The Method of Physical Action proceeds in three phases:

- Analysis, step by step, of the action and the events in the play, factually defined (the Given Circumstances). This is done without direct reference to emotion or feeling. The material of the play is explored without reference to the actual text through improvisation.

- Study of the text – its style, period and background.

- Shaping the insights gained in the first two stages into a coherent performance.

In the first phase, the actor works as himself, responds to the Given Circumstances in his own person. It is fundamental to the Stanislavski 'system' that the actor has no source other than his own experiences and emotions. These are the raw materials which he must transform into the experience of the character. The key question is: what would I do if I were in this situation? Thus the actor makes the problems of the character his own. He is engaged. He is involved. The play ceases to be something external.

This process of believing the fictitious circumstances to be true results in human, not theatrical, behaviour. The actor's performance conforms to the organic mechanisms of normal behaviour.

This process can take up to six months.

The first phase proceeds logically from a broad canvas to minute detail, from macro to micro.

The process is as follows:

- Steep oneself in the play. The impression the play makes on the actors will be the impression the performance makes on an audience. This, for Stanislavski, was the essential starting point. The actor needs to become enthusiastic about the play, so that his will to create is stimulated

- Define the subject, the meaning of the play, the *Supertask*.

- Begin to break the play down into manageable sections that can be improvised, first into large blocks or *Episodes*.

- For each *Episode* define the demands made on the character, what his response is to the situation, his *Basic Action*.

- Break down each *Episode* into smaller components, *Facts*.

- Define what the character has to do in order to respond to the situation in each *Fact*, his *Task*.

- Improvise the actions he performs to fulfil his *Task*.

- Ensure the logic and coherence of the individual *Tasks* and *Actions* to create the *Through-action*.

- Verify the definition of the *Supertask*.

There must be no direct attempt to create emotion, or to play emotions, such as love, hate, anger, pity. That can only lead to cliché. Emotion cannot be evoked at will. It is the product of action.

A logical Through-action produces a corresponding sequence of feelings, a Through-emotion.

The process can be summarised in the following diagram:

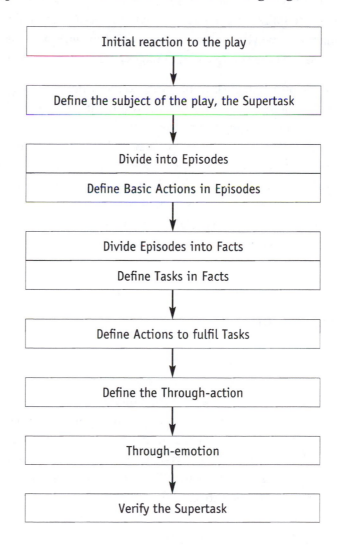

Initial reaction to the play

↓

Define the subject of the play, the Supertask

↓

Divide into Episodes
Define Basic Actions in Episodes

↓

Divide Episodes into Facts
Define Tasks in Facts

↓

Define Actions to fulfil Tasks

↓

Define the Through-action

↓

Through-emotion

↓

Verify the Supertask

In performance the actor should never attempt to reproduce earlier performances. He must engage with the tasks, re-create the intention that leads to action. In other words, he must play the cause and not the effect.

Two further processes remain:

- To create the situations and events the author has not included in the script. What happened to the character before the beginning of the play? What happens between scenes? This is the *Before-time*, the *Between-time*.

- To create the mental life of the character, the thoughts and images that occur while he is active, so that just as in life we are constantly active mentally, the character will be active mentally. Inner thoughts, however, can be in contradiction with what is openly expressed. These thoughts and images constitute the *Subtext*.

Stanislavski attached great importance to the Subtext, which gave the character depth and life, so that the actor was not merely saying lines but allowing the lines to spring from inner action.

It was important, too, for the Subtext to be communicated to the other actors. In rehearsal actors were asked to speak their Subtext aloud to each other. Equally, they should try to communicate it silently, radiate, or transmit it. An actor is seen as both transmitter and receiver, sending out waves and receiving them in a constant flow of communications with the other actors, so that what he says relates to what he has heard.

Emotion memory

A further strategy is the use of what was first called *Affective* and later *Emotion* memory. The human mind is a storehouse of memories of past experiences. Mostly they are hidden, but memory can be triggered by a trivial stimulus – a smell, a sound, a touch. This is random. However, an actor can enrich the level of emotion that has arisen organically in the process of rehearsal by recalling his own memory of an incident similar to an incident in the play. He can still re-experience his initial emotion and feed it into his performance.

Primary and recurring emotion

Stanislavski took a different view from his predecessors regarding emotion experienced both in life and on the stage. For him there were two kinds of emotion: primary and recurring. Primary emotions are those we feel for the first time, sometimes violently. We are carried away by them. Most of the emotions we experience, however, we have experienced before, they *recur* and do not have the overwhelming force of primary emotion. They are, in a sense, at one remove. This gives the actor a measure of control over his feelings. He is neither, in Aristotle's terms, 'beside himself' or, in Diderot's terms, in a state of 'delirium'.

Stanislavski often referred to 'multi-storey' consciousness, whereby someone can be engaged in an activity and at the same time be aware of other things going on around him somewhere else in the house or in the street outside. Thus, an individual can feel and at the same time be aware that he is feeling.

The 'I am being'

The careful, conscious step-by-step work done in early rehearsal brings the actor nearer to the character. He is in a creative state, called by Stanislavski the state of 'I am being', in which the mechanisms of behaviour and the creative subconscious come into operation, prompting unexpected discoveries. Stanislavski summarised the whole process as: *through the conscious to the unconscious.*

At this juncture the actor is ready to approach and analyse the text. During the course of improvisation the actual words of the script will mingle with the actor's own words, but this must be spontaneous and unforced. Now the text must be examined closely, its stylistic demands understood, its historical background respected. The actor can also begin to think about external, physical characterisation. As actor and author come together the Third Being is born.

In the final phase of rehearsal, the material is shaped into a coherent, artistic whole. Choices are made about the rhythm and tempo of individual scenes and the rhythmic pattern of the entire production, about the comparative importance of individual moments in the whole, what Stanislavski called the 'perspective'. Just as a painter places certain objects in the foreground, others in the mid-ground and yet others in the background, so an actor must learn which moments to emphasise, to highlight and which to play more lightly. The actor performs two functions. On the one hand there is the player, who acts from moment to moment. At the beginning of the play he does not know what the end will be. On the other hand, he is an artist, who controls and shapes and decides what he is going to do, decides just how each scene should be played, at what level of intensity. The artist knows, the player doesn't. This double process is essential when playing a major role such as Hamlet.

Let's say you are playing Hamlet, one of the most complex roles in its psychology. In it we find the bewilderment when faced with the sudden love of a mother who 'or e'er those shoes were old' has managed to forget her husband. There is the supernatural experience of a man who has a momentary glimpse of the life beyond where his father is in torment. When Hamlet understands the future's secrets everything in the real world loses all sense. We also have the desire to understand, and the awareness of an impossible mission that is needed to save his father in the hereafter. The role demands a son's feeling for his mother, love for a young woman, breaking with her, her death, a feeling of sorrow, and terror at his mother's death, and murder, and his own death after he has done his duty. Try to mix all these feelings into one, with no kind of order, and imagine what muddle results.

But if you put all these experiences logically, systematically into perspective, as the complexity of the character requires, with its ever more complex development throughout the play, then you achieve a firm structure, a harmonious line in which the leading role is played by all the dependent parts in the tragedy of a great soul as it deepens and grows.

Can you play any moment in such a role without giving it *perspective*? If you don't convey his disturbance and incomprehension at the sight of his frivolous mother at the beginning of the play properly, then the famous scene with her will not be sufficiently prepared. If he is not sufficiently shaken by his knowledge of the afterlife the impossibility of his earthly mission, his doubts, his urgent search for the meaning of life, his break-up with his beloved, his strange behaviour which seems abnormal would be incomprehensible.

It follows from what I have said that the more cautiously the actor playing Hamlet performs the opening scenes, the stronger the passions required of him will be as they develop throughout the play, doesn't it?

In our particular jargon we call that kind of performance *acting with perspective*.

(*An Actor's Work on Himself*, Part Two, pp. 154–5)

Stanislavski regarded this final process in rehearsal of planning, of refining and polishing as essential to a work of art. It has, unfortunately, been frequently ignored by those who seek to reduce the 'system' to a kind of naive subjectivity. However, Moscow Art Theatre productions were admired, and continue to be admired, not only for their psychological truth but for the precision, polish and refinement of the actor, of his craft.

Stanislavski planned two books on acting, *An Actor's Work on Himself*, which was subsequently divided into two parts, and *An Actor's Work on a Role*. Only one volume appeared in his lifetime, Part One of *An Actor's Work on Himself*, first in 1936 in a heavily cut and edited American translation and then in a revised, expanded Russian edition in 1938, which has never been translated into English. His drafts of the other books have never been translated but appeared, again in heavily cut and edited versions, as *Building a Character* and *Creating a Role*.

Stanislavski's style is often difficult and sometimes confusing, in contrast to his letters, notebooks and articles. His terminology was not always consistent. He used various sets of terms at different times and the standard English translations by Elizabeth Hapgood use a different set.*

The 'system' was substantially in place by the 1917 Revolution and the bases of Method of Physical Action had been laid. Three crucial documents are witness to the state of Stanislavski's thinking in the period 1910–20. They are clear in a way that Stanislavski is not. The first is a series of lectures by Vakhtangov, Stanislavski's favourite pupil, given in 1914, and endorsed by Stanislavski himself. The second is an article by Mikhaïl (Michael) Chekhov, one of the greatest actors of the Moscow Art Theatre. Finally, there is a short monograph by Vladimir Volkenstein, a scholar and specialist in dramaturgy, who was Stanislavski's secretary for a time and had daily contact with him.

Vakhtangov and Chekhov provide us with an overview of the actor's training as taught by Stanislavski before the Revolution and later enshrined in *An Actor's Work*.

* For a full discussion on the problem, see *Stanislavski and the Actor*, pp. 150–1.

Eight lectures on the Stanislavski 'system'

Vakhtangov

The basis of any classification of theatre work is to observe the different kinds of approach to a role in different theatres.

First, an actor can take on a role for his own selfish ends. This kind of theatre we call the theatre of exploitation. Second, we can take on a role so that once we have felt it and found the appropriate externals at home, we can demonstrate the results of our work to the audience (Coquelin, 'Weep at home and show the result to the audience'). That is the School of Representation.

In earlier times there was a kind of approach to a role in which once an actor had more or less learned his lines, he relied completely on inspiration, or as they said 'gut feeling'. The result was that once he had played a role a hundred times he managed to get it right and live the emotions in his role.

The fourth kind of acting is the theatre of *Experiencing* in which the actor tries to live the emotions in a role so as to convey them to an audience.

In the theatre of Representation the main purpose of the actor is to use external means (voice and body) to represent this or that experience. That means that for each emotion the actor produces a template or a cliché and uses them to represent that feeling. For any given passage in his role he has only to write 'joy', 'laughter', 'danger', 'contempt', etc., and he knows what he has to do. He knows – and there are books where this is explained – that anger is represented by frowning and clenching one's fists. For laughter, there is a sound in the throat which draws the muscles of the face into action in a particular way etc. He does not know that this is of no use to anybody, and that it is a shame to indulge in such stock-in-trade. He does not realise that it is all lies, that his anger frightens no one and his rowdy laughter will not draw a corresponding, happy laugh from anyone.*

We have come together to study the true art of the theatre – experiencing. There are no finished productions in a school. In the theatre they are creative moments. In school you must first acquire an external technique, learn to master your voice and body. You must second acquire an inner technique, the ability of the soul to repeat genuine experiences. Third, you must develop your imagination. The stage is not life. It is more beautiful than life. Imagination is an actor's second nature. So we have the human body, the human voice (outer technique), human feelings (inner technique), human imagination. Our task is not to teach you to act. That is not for us. Your task is to prepare the ground for the creative

* Horace.

process. And the art of the stage consists in the ability totally to transform yourself.

So, how do we get there?

Study programme

Part One

- muscular relaxation

- concentration

- belief, naivety, justification

- circle of attention

- task

- affective action, memory and feeling

- rhythm, high and low energy

Part Two

- relationship to the other actor

- public solitude

Part Three

- role and play analysis

Part Four

- external characteristics

Muscular relaxation

After Stanislavski had observed famous actors and spoken to them, and had compared himself with less famous or even quite obscure actors, he discovered that all eminent actors had things in common. One of these was relaxation, which all great actors or even minor ones, if they rise to the summit of their art, can achieve. An actor can only be creative when he is fully relaxed. Artistic creation is inconceivable in a state of tension. The more tense an actor is, the more clichés replace feeling. Lack of relaxation can arise from doing too much or doing little but with great energy. When an actor is tense, for example, he makes far too many unnecessary movements. He tugs at his cuffs or his hair. He examines his fingernails or closes the cigarette box. He wastes a great deal of energy or doesn't do what he should. There is nothing more difficult on stage than to light a lamp or pour a cup of tea. The matches break. The cup shakes in your hand which can't hold out till [the pot reaches the rim].

So how do we relax? We must create an inner *Monitor*, that constantly sees when we are not relaxed and gets rid of tension. Won't such a monitor get in the way? No, not when it is developed in such a way that it functions independently and automatically. You must exercise it continuously and activate it the moment tension is detected.

Concentration

The second essential for creative work is concentration. When we focus our attention on some object we have a central point for our concentration. It is obvious that we cannot focus on two central points at the same time. We can't read a book and listen to a conversation in another room at the same time. You can only be interested in one object at any given moment. We designate this object as the *Object of Attention*. This can be a sound, a thing, a thought, an action, one's own feeling or another actor's. *An actor must have an object of attention every moment he is on stage.* Otherwise he will not live the requisite emotion. It is a pleasure to have an object of attention on stage, be it a thing, a feeling or a thought – and to show an independent, personal life to an audience. An army of eyes are fixed on you, they follow you. You remember some purpose you have, and are unaware of the staring eyes, but rather listen to your own inner being. Your object of attention is your own emotions. You can also use concentration to get rid of the traces of tension which your monitor was not able to remove. Relaxation and concentration are strongly linked. When you concentrate, you are relaxed. But if you are not relaxed you will not be able to concentrate. And so you must release tension as much as possible. Then you must find your object of attention, so that the remaining tension disappears.

We must also learn to encourage our concentration. To concentrate we must cultivate the ability 1) to find an object of attention quickly, 2) to feel drawn towards it.

Belief, naivety, justification

For an audience to believe an actor is being genuine, he has to believe in the importance of everything that is happening on stage, in the importance and necessity of his words and actions. If he doubts even for a second it is damaging. He will be embarrassed at telling lies and everything he does on stage will become meaningless and false. What must we do to be able to believe? We must find a justification, that is, a reason for any given action, situation, circumstance. For example, adopt a completely meaningless position, raise an arm and a foot, sit down somewhere near and try to find a justification. Let's say you are sitting and have raised your right foot and your left hand. A very uncomfortable position, but when you justify it by the fact that someone has given you a very narrow boot to wear and you are leaning against a nearby post with your left hand so as not to be dragged out of your chair, you will feel better in that uncomfortable position. It now has a meaning. You believe in the necessity of a given posture when you have found a justification for it. When I feel that a given justification is right, then I am no longer embarrassed to adopt a given position. Justification is the way to truth.

You are playing an aristocrat and a stage manager has forgotten to remove a cigarette butt from your chair. That must be justified. Your partner is laughing in the wings. That must be justified. If your partner misses his entrance that does not mean he is asleep, [just imagine] that the person you are expecting has not arrived for some reason. That will oblige you to do something – something new. But you don't come out of character and it won't be damaging to you. Justification – that is the prerequisite for me to have no doubts. If you want to learn to find a justification quickly, you must develop your imagination. Even though we often find the justification in the writing, many times we also need to find our own. So we must develop our imagination through exercises to justify 1) a posture, 2) a place, 3) an action, 4) an object), 5) a series of linked situations, etc. But here I must issue a warning. You must not confuse justification with hallucination. You must know the difference between the two quite clearly.

My belief in my task results in naivety. This idea must be distinguished from what is normally understood by that word. I don't believe because I am naive. I am naive because I believe. Naivety is the result of belief achieved through justification.

Every actor needs this naivety. I am naive when I can genuinely relate to my colleagues as to my father, my uncle, my friend in the terms laid down by the play. When I am relaxed and have found an object of attention and reached a belief in the necessity of the stage action through justification, the right feeling will result.

The actor must believe in the necessity of the action every moment he is on stage.

Circle of attention

Everything we have discussed so far – relaxation, concentration, belief, naivety – we shall bring together in a single concept: the Circle of Attention. By that we mean a state of relaxed concentration and a belief in the necessity of the action.

This circle can be narrowed or widened. The ability to change the size of the circle quickly is a distinct advantage for an actor.

Exercises

Mime, using your imagination, the following activities: 1) sewing a cross stitch, 2) doing the washing, 3) dusting, 4) modelling clay, 5) making jam, 6) doing your hair, 7) wrapping up a box of chocolates, 8) repairing a hinge, 9) firing an oven, 10) getting dressed, 11) cutting out a sleeve, 12) cleaning a gun, 13) folding a box, 14) playing with dolls, etc. Of course you can choose any of these exercises that suit you best.

Task

Imagine a crowd scene, a fair for example. You see a painting. There are many people, buying, selling, haggling. You soon see that a scene like that can only be interesting for ten minutes. It needs something to make it exciting. It needs events, action. In the theatre there is never a still or a static moment. The stage needs action, then the actor comes on stage to do something. So, before he makes his entrance, he must have a task. First, he must know *what* he has to do, second, *why* he is doing it. What we mean is the purpose of the given action. Let's say my task is to ask my grandfather for money. Now the reasons I am asking for it can be very different. It can be for some charitable purpose, or for a new coat, or to pay my fees. Naturally my mood will change as my purpose in performing the action changes. So, on stage we need an action which arises from a sequence of tasks. We call the precise, logical and beautiful performance of a sequence of tasks the art of the theatre. What is ugly in life can be beautiful on stage in the crucible of creative art. There should be no real life on stage. Then the theatre ceases to be art and becomes crude naturalism.

A task contains three elements: 1) purpose (why I have come on stage), 2) will (why I fulfil the given purpose), 3) the expressive ways and means, or how I show it. The final element is the actor's talent.

The elements of purpose and will are, generally, conscious moments. Although, exceptionally, they can be unconscious. I know perfectly well why I am on stage (for what purpose) and why I do it (what I want). The ways and means of doing it, on the other hand, are unconscious and depend upon those accidents which occur as the task is performed on stage.

My goal is to comfort someone who has been offended. I comfort him, I achieve my goal. I have a feeling of pity. My eyes fill with tears. These tears are the means. What then is the nature of a task on stage? It must be action and can be nothing other than action. An action-free moment – feeling – is the result of action, of the fulfilment of a certain task. You cannot play feeling. It just comes to us of its own, independent of our will. [We have already said that we will not demonstrate it. That is the task of the theatre of representation. Our task is to *live* it.] You must play tasks. I comfort. That is action. I feel sympathy. That is feeling. I ask for money. That is action. I am angry because I don't get it. That is feeling. I escape from prison. That is action. Doubt over whether I can really escape. That is feeling. To suppress a laugh. That is action. Laughter itself is not an action. To hold back tears is an action. Weeping is not an action etc. [Feelings] occur independent of my will. Sometimes against my will. I do not wish to cry but I cry. Feeling is a fact of nature, not of my will.

Affective memory

Where do feelings come from and what is the essence of experiencing on stage?

In the same way that with the aid of our five senses we can store the smell, shape and colour of an object in our memory so we can store our feelings. When we have lived through a particular event, our mind will retain the feeling which we had when we reacted to that event. And when we often experience an event, the reaction we generally have will be [confirmed], when the same circumstances are repeated we are in a position to repeat the feelings that are lodged in our mind. But in life our feelings are always aroused by real causes. No such causes exist on stage. They always demand and we can do no more than accept them. The question then arises: can these conventions arouse real feeling in us? Under no circumstances. They not only cannot evoke real feelings, they should not, otherwise the stage would cease to be art. The origin of our stage feelings, which are not similar to our normal, real feelings, is not the conventions, but our capacity to repeat experiences I spoke of earlier. And this repeated experience is not the same as real-life experiencing. And so, in opposition to real-life emotions, we will define our stage emotion as *affective emotion*. They are governed by quite different laws from those that guide our emotions in life itself. Apart from affective (repeated) emotion we can also have real-life emotion on stage, most certainly. But these real-life emotions can only be of two kinds: either it is pleasant for me to experience affective emotions positively or it is not because I do not experience them properly. When I make my final exit and have completed my role, all my affective emotions leave me instantly. But when in life we have experienced great sorrow, is it over in a minute? Or are we able to succumb to true joy in five minutes? On stage an actor who has experienced great sorrow in one act has to start the following act with carefree happiness and vice versa. Actors take it for granted that they have to expend a great deal of energy on stage.

If we act the requisite emotions in a play as in life, after the performance we will be taken to the madhouse or the hospital, or worse still, they will say a mass for the dead on our behalf.

So, let us say, according to the play, an actor has to hit his partner and does it for real. The partner will feel pain and insult. And what will the audience feel? Doubtless it will feel sympathy for the actor who has been hit. But it will not feel sorry for the character the actor was playing but for the actor himself. Then there is not a trace of art. It is quite another thing when the actor uses the affective memory of pain and the affective emotion to arouse a sense of affront, and the first actor, who has not really hit his partner, experiences an affective feeling of shame. Then we are dealing with art. It is not great art to feel pain when we are hit, sorrow when our father dies, joy when we receive an inheritance, etc.

In the beginning then is the circle of attention, then comes the task, and then, as a result of the fulfilment or accomplishment of the task, comes affective emotion.

It is important to note that the emotions are the actor's own emotions, out of which he creates his character.

We may be asked: if an actor creates a character out of his own emotions, what does he do when there are some emotions he has never experienced – death, the barrel of a gun, forgery? The fact is there is no emotion that a grown man has not experienced. Possibly he has never experienced the situation in the play but he has lived all the emotions. Emotions that he has only lived five percent in life, he can live fifty percent on stage. That is the power of affective memory. Why that should be so, I do not know. The actor will not encounter any stimulus on stage that he has not met in life. If he has not experienced fear when the barrel of a gun is pointed at him, he has been frightened by a vicious dog, etc. There is not a man who has not experienced fear. And there is not a different kind of fear for every cause.

To experience happiness on stage, you must have experienced it in life. In life it undoubtedly felt as a result of unconsciously performing some task. On stage we must perform tasks consciously. The result, affective feeling, will arise unconsciously. The cause of my happiness is irrelevant. I don't care why I am happy. The important thing is that I can express my emotion to an audience. That is my creative pleasure.

Just as we can note our emotions, we can note our actions. Hence we have affective actions. We note our emotions with our psyche, actions with our muscles. But never with our intellect. No more than we note taste, smell, colour with our intellect.

Rhythm, high and low energy

There are a series of actions which we perform in a normal state or, as we say, in a usual rhythm. Each of us has his own usual rhythm in which we perform our tasks in life, having lunch, studying, making a telephone call. When a new element occurs while we are performing a task the rhythm can be broken. This new event alters the justification for my task and is the cause of the change in rhythm. Let us say I usually have lunch in a certain rhythm and I am suddenly told that in ten minutes I have to go to this place or that place. My rhythm changes. It will change because a new justification for my task has arisen. Let us take the following example: I have to go on a journey and am at the station. My rhythm after the first whistle will be different from what it was before and will change even more after the second whistle. When I perform my task in my usual manner I have my usual feelings. In another rhythm they depart somewhat from the norm and when the rhythm changes strongly they become heated. The same thing happens on stage. So we distinguished between high and low energy. Low energy is characteristic of sadness, boredom, grief. High energy is characteristic of happiness, joy, laughter, etc.

Any dramatic task can be performed in this or that rhythm. Say my task is to fry eggs. If I justify this task by saying that I am being forced to do it against my will, that I am being forced to fry eggs, although I don't want to, then I will fulfil my task slowly with low energy.

When I justify this task by saying that I want to give someone something to eat very quickly then I will fulfil it in a fast rhythm with high energy.

Relationship to the other actor

The audience is only interested in what the actor is interested in on stage. A conversation on stage is only interesting when the actors are interested in it. When two or more actors are on stage, their relationships change, they have different interests. We use our 'self' to influence our partner. Not only with words and with externals but with our whole being. The object of attention in this relationship is my partner, his inner life. I must treat my partner as someone who reacts to my words and actions. I shouldn't comfort him and say, 'Don't cry,' when he has no intention of crying and is not hurt. I must only react to what my partner actually does. When my partner is playing a king, I treat him like a king, and behave towards him as a person and not as the character of the king. Otherwise I will be using clichés. I must continuously adapt to a mind on the move.

This relationship is part of the immediate communication of feelings. My living 'self' influences my partner's living 'self' and vice versa. Only this relationship can arouse the audience's interest. So we should not study a role by working out gestures and inflections. When studying a role we should never just make noises. The moment the means of expression come to the fore the whole action of the play becomes empty and cold. In my relationship to the other actor I have a specific task. The object of my attention is a living soul and I adapt my means to it. If I live, but my partner does not, there is no relationship and there can be no acting. When my partner doesn't live, we have representation . . . In this relationship an actor must do everything for his own sake, not for the audience's. I must listen to my partner because I am interested to know what he is going to say. I must speak because I really am interested to tell him something.

Public solitude

When I am alone my behaviour is simple and natural. As soon as someone comes into the room, I become another. When I go to a ball I am completely different. But when I am on stage I must never change because an audience is present. When I am alone on stage I must be the same as when I am alone in life. That is public solitude. The difference between public solitude and the circle of attention is that the circle of attention can exist even when we are alone. Public solitude can only occur when there is an audience.

On the Stanislavski 'system'

Michael Chekhov

1

So then, what is the 'system' and how did it come into being?

Imagine an artist who not only creates but analyses at the same time and carefully studies his own creative process. In so doing he arrives at two sets of factors. One promotes creative strength, supports and nourishes it, the other, however, hinders it and slows it down. Armed with such knowledge he can already explain success or failure in any given case. He will not be stumped when confronted with failure and talk helplessly about his lack of inspiration on this occasion. He will know precisely why it did not come or what got in the way and killed it. And that is not all. Using this knowledge of what *hinders* and what *helps* the creative process, choosing among them, i.e. by freeing his mind of what *hinders* and strengthening what *helps*, he can arouse a creative state or get somewhere near it *whenever he wants* and will not have to wait for inspiration to happen . . .

The creative mind will not be forced. You all know that. You cannot order it to 'love', 'suffer', 'be joyful', or 'hate'. It is deaf to orders and does not surrender to force. It can only be enticed. And here the system is of irreplaceable help to the mind. It provides a *method* which can attract the mind and draw out the material the artist chooses. He now possesses magical power. He does not have to wait for a stroke of luck when the mind is carried away by this or that, a subject, an idea . . . if that is the case then there is no doubt that the artist's mind pushes back its borders and becomes infinitely deeper and varied. Think what becomes of all an artist's life experiences when they are refracted in his mind. What delight they give him. And what artist would refuse the pleasure of refracting the greater part of his life in his mind? The system provides him with that chance. Should the artist not be grateful to the system for giving him the key to his own mind?

But the system does more. It teaches the actor what he and all men lack and how to fight against it. One of the actor's toughest and strongest enemies is his own body. It is always treacherous, at every given moment, and exerts crude pressure on the actor's mind. It is always ready to exercise its power, its importance, always ready to alter a gesture, an expression and as soon as a feeling is born in the actor's mind . . .

That is what the actor must fight against and the system teaches him how to fight, how to set limits on the body and free the mind from force of any kind.

2

I divide the Stanislavski system into two halves: a) the actor's work on himself, b) the actor's work on a role.

a) Work on oneself should last a lifetime. It consists in developing the range and versatility of the mind. The actor must learn to control his mind, his power of concentration and his body. There are a whole range of exercises for this purpose, after which he develops a feeling of truth and the ability to find the right state of mind on stage both in general and for each role in particular.

b) Work on a role teaches him how to explore his material, how to find what is most valuable and essential, how to get into the role and find its key so that he can find a true interpretation for every role. How to be varied without in any way changing the essence of a role.

Then the student must learn to analyse his own wants and guess the wants of others. It is a good idea to try and guess someone's profession, character, life-style from his external appearance. He should do these exercises, like the exercises for developing the 'feeling of truth' daily. He can only understand their full meaning when he puts them into practice. He should understand that once he has acquired the skill to analyse his feelings, he acquires a certain insight which makes his work on a role and his relationship to other actors easier.

The task

A desire to do something, to get what we want, is a theatrical task. A task should be conscious, fulfilling it unconscious. I must know what I want so that I can carry out what the task requires truthfully, but I should not know how I am going to do it – that is for the unconscious. Generally speaking, the function of the intelligence is to clear the way for the unconscious creative process and then, following in its tracks, pin down the intention. A conscious task need not be defined in dry, logical terms. The definition should come through intuition and then be written down as conscious logic.

The following sequence of tasks should be complex. The student should learn how to create a special mood by means of 'affective memory' and fulfil his task in that mood.

Affective memory is the memory of certain feelings we have lived, which we re-experience.

There are three factors in every human, mental act: 1) intellect (intelligence), 2) emotion (feeling), 3) will (wants). No really strict definition of any of them is possible. All are indubitably present simultaneously in every mental act, but in different proportions.

'Affective life' can begin in different ways, either by remembering feeling as such, or by remembering the circumstances in which they occurred, or by arousing inner feelings, etc. The actor's technique consists in knowing what stimulates his affective life. Once he knows it he has the chance to use it. The teacher's task is to show the student in any given case what the origin of the feeling is.

Examples of tasks

- A sick man is waiting for the doctor at home. Guests arrive who need to be looked after.

- A poor relation comes to a rich relative and asks for help and finds the house full of visitors.

- A woman pianist is feeling nervous before going out on to the platform. Her friends calm her down.

- A doctor is called out when his wife is sick. He has to go.

- Meeting someone you think has been ruined.

- Visiting a couple who have fallen out badly.

- Relatives see someone off.

- An exhibition of paintings. People look at them and have divided impressions. They look at each other and are spiteful about their clothes, etc. The student must justify his task, that is, justify the circumstances in which he has to fulfil it. This can be done in the following manner.

Task

In the next room someone very close to me is ill. The doctor comes. I wait for the doctor to tell me about the patient's state of health. All my concentration is on that room. An unexpected guest arrives and I have to be polite and relaxed with him.

Let's imagine I have to fulfil this task on stage in the theatre. Then there is something strange because my close friend is in the theatre. Why should someone come to see me in the theatre and why am I on stage? This prevents me from believing in the task I have been given. I have to explain away all these inconsistencies. To do this the student has to imagine in detail all the attendant circumstances, he has to imagine the precise history of the given circumstances. This imaginary explanation can be very naive, simple or even stupid and in itself may not be able to be justified but that does not matter. Our imaginary explanation must help us justify the inconsistencies in a given task and, once we have filled in the blanks, make us believe that all the contradictory facts are possible.

I can justify the given task, for example, this way. I have come to the theatre with my sick friend because my landlord has managed to throw me out of my apartment for his own reasons and because I cannot find a new apartment for the moment and so I have been obliged to ask the director of the theatre to allow me to stay there for the time being, etc.

I am on stage because the manager has ordered all the floors in the theatre to be polished and has sent me on stage while it is being done, etc.

My visitor has come first because I have to be here for a while and second because he is leaving Moscow today, etc.

This justification is perfectly sufficient to remove all the unacceptable aspects of the task. Once he believes, the student feels very close to the situation in which the exercise takes place and achieves the state we call 'I am being'.

When he has justified the task in this way, the student should not tell anyone, for if he does, he loses his childlike belief, he reveals the silliness of his imaginary circumstances and, of course, loses credibility.

Preparing the ground:
  reading the play
  enthusiasm
  anatomy – (mechanics of bits)

Becoming enthusiastic should take as long as possible since the success of future work depends upon it . . . Teacher and student should live through it together. The student should not be aware of his growing 'enthusiasm'. *He should only know after it has happened.*

He needs to establish all the details of the character's life, his past, his present (off stage) and possible future.

Moving on to the affective emotions in the task, we need to explain the meaning of the 'object'. That is, when we perform a task we can play 1) for show, 2) for ourselves, 3) for our partner.

1) Playing 'for show' means you are trying to tell the audience by your gestures and expression what they are supposed to feel. In this case there can be no genuine experiencing or task. The actor not only is not aware of his partner, he does not even see them because he is tense.

2) Playing 'for oneself' means being absorbed by the content of one's actions, checking on one's inflections, being concerned with being simple, in small unnecessary details of movement, in a word, pleasure in the simplicity and elegance of one's acting. Most of the time the actor appears to be impeccable. But as with acting 'for show' there is no real 'object' (partner) and no task in relation to him.

3) The actor only achieves a true state of mind through a genuine relationship to his partner, through genuinely fulfilling a task in relation to him . . .

In fulfilling his tasks, the student should learn to use chance events. He needs to concentrate on that. Looking for them he schools himself to be more aware of place and people and that saves him from tightening up internally, which can to a very high degree even lead to blindness. However, we should not talk to a student about that.

Developing a feeling of enthusiasm immerses the student in the play and the role. He can start to divide the role into bits [facts]. Bits should initially be defined externally, i.e., as results. These definitions will be in nouns, for example: astonishment, servility, fear, etc.[*]

When the bits in a role have been found, we need to change nouns for verbs: 'I want . . .' Since we cannot play 'astonishment' (the result of some inner process) we have to define what that process is. Self-analysis begins and 'my wants' are created:

Nouns	'I Want' Verbs		Common 'I Want'
1) Astonishment	I want to understand		I want
2) Servility	I want them not to sack me	I WANT	I want
3) Fear	I want to escape danger		I want

[*] Stanislavski later insisted that bits [facts] should be defined in terms of an ever

So, from all these 'I wants' we can derive three which not only include all the previous 'I wants' but are more closely defined. Having combined them again we get a series of 'I wants' and we then need to find one, final 'I want' which will be the basic want of the character we are playing and will consequently be the 'through-action'.

The heart of a role exists but not yet its body. The process of embodiment begins, that is, creating an outer form. An actor may have a fine and profound understanding of the character he has created in his mind but that is not enough, he must convey it to an audience and that is only possible when his whole body and voice are so developed and flexible that he controls them fully and they can express and convey whatever he is living at any given moment . . .

The external form should not only match the inner but should, as far as possible, stem from it. When creating the inner character we can sometimes intuitively stumble across a means of expressing it, which is characteristic of the type we are playing . . . but our inner life does not always suggest outer forms of expression so obligingly. Most of the time we have to invent suitable characteristics. But when inventing them we must relate them to our inner life, we must justify them . . . the external characteristics must so become part of an actor that when he starts to live the emotions of his role they appear spontaneously and when he expresses the externals he should begin to live the feelings in the role . . .

Then there is the struggle against clichés. It is a lifelong battle to remove them and replace them with genuine tasks. Clichés most of the time emerge unnoticed. So the actor must always be on the alert and never think that because he has eradicated a cliché once he is free of it for ever . . .

Clichés are ready-made forms to express this or that feeling. When expressing unhappiness, for example, I can wring my hands irrespective of whether it is suitable or not for this part or the level of the emotion . . . clichés are harmful because they oblige feelings to express themselves in that particular form and destroy the natural path to experience and natural feeling is lost. Clichés are dead forms for living feelings . . .

Above all, the student must understand the outline of the system which is as follows:

progress of the system – a) work on oneself, b) work on a role
self-analysis
task
affective feeling
justification of the tasks
'I am being'
the object

ability to use chance events

process of planting the seeds – a) enthusiasm, b) anatomy (mechanics of bits and tasks)

through-action

the core

improvisations round the role

evaluating the facts

being active

external characteristics

clichés

what attracts today

concentration, imagination, belief and naivety

Volkenstein concentrates on the Through-action which he likens to Aristotle's unity of action. He also provides an early example when he describes the method of script analysis fundamental to the Method of Physical Action: breaking the play down into sections and determining the intentions and needs of each of the characters involved while at the same time being aware of the forward dynamic of the play, the coherence of its action, its Through-action and the core meaning, the theme of the play, the Supertask. His chosen play is *Woe from Wit*.

Crucially, Volkenstein rejects any connection between experiencing and Naturalism, which Stanislavski himself described as 'poison'.

Stanislavski

Volkenstein

You cannot understand Stanislavski as a director, as a man of the theatre, without some knowledge of the so-called 'system', if only in its broadest outlines.

The Stanislavski system is closely bound to his work as a director; it has a direct practical goal – to arouse inspiration in an actor.

Stanislavski tells us, 'Human nature is nine-tenths unconscious, one-tenth conscious. The one-tenth shows us how to create the nine-tenths'. He seeks conscious means to arouse unconscious creativity. Thus the Stanislavski system is above all practical. However, recognising the need for theoretical ideas in the theatre, in his relentless development of his thought, he did not shirk from using precise distinctions and analyses. He incorporated abstract ideas drawn from psychology and philosophy which were apparently totally unconnected with practical work, and that annoyed people who expected him to provide quick results. So, at one time, he lumbered his rehearsals with complex ideas taken from Ribot, from whom he often borrowed his terminology. Thus, actors working with Stanislavski had to come to terms with practical work expressed in academic terms.

Lost in the complexity and profusion of his ideas, and unable to find the right structure for them, Stanislavski chose to outline his system in a special form, that of a theoretical novel in which scenes of theatrical life alternated with matching ideas.

In his analysis of a drama – theatrical material – Stanislavski sketched the idea of 'through-action'.

'Through-action' is the basic purpose of the hero, his passion, his constant wish.*

Stanislavski's 'through-action' corresponds psychologically to Aristotle's logical and conjectural 'unity of action'.

'. . . Just as in the visual arts the thing imitated relates to a whole so the subject (of the play) which is the imitation of an action must relate to a single, purposeful action and the individual parts of an event must be closely linked in such a way that a change or damage to any one of them would result in harm and change to the whole. Nothing, either by its presence or absence, results in damage except in relation to the whole.' Thus Aristotle in the *Poetics*.

In other words, the wholeness, harmony and unity in drama are created by the unity of action.

Stanislavski's originality consists in his development of the idea of through-action or unity of action pyschologically, from the actor's point of view. 'Through-action' for Stanislavski must be *felt as spontaneous striving*, and for that you need to discover the 'core' of the play, its poetry and its ideas. Through-action can be made deeper by the actor, that is, the same role can be played with greater or lesser psychological depth . . . The through-action is difficult to define in words, especially at the beginning of rehearsals. The through-action in the actor's mind is the justification of the role, the needle of the compass pointing north. For example, to prove your innocence, to make someone leave the room, or to understand the mood of the person you are talking to, or simple physical tasks – to see, sense the nearness of your partner, etc. . . . Stanislavski distinguishes the through-action of the play and the lead role from the through-action of the other roles which moves either in accord with the through-action of the play or counter

ogol.

to it. In preparatory work the most important thing is to feel your way towards a productive line shared by all the characters.

The through-action is broken down into a logical chain of individual wants, directed to the fulfilment of precise, conscious tasks.

Stanislavski compared the through-action to arrows aimed at a target – the 'supertask' of a role, love, power, some ideal goal, etc. The actor's performance – the path of the arrows, is the fulfilment of individual, conscious tasks.

Tasks [at one time] took on a rather complex psychological character. Recently Stanislavski has tried to divide the role into simple physical tasks. Here is an example of an improvisation of the kind he used in 1912–1918.

I want to see a woman. I wait for her, looking at the woods, where she is supposed to appear. She comes out of the woods and I rush towards her. I want to look in her eyes . . . I want to know where she has been, why she did not come to our rendezvous three days ago. I want her to be frank, to sense her mood. My speech, questions, gestures, my entire conduct match my mood. She tells me ill health prevented her from seeing me. I want to know if this is true and express doubt. Suddenly she starts to cry. She is insulted by my lack of faith. I am convinced she is telling the truth. I want to comfort her, to show tenderness towards her, etc. The sum of these wants, of these conscious tasks, the logic of their links creates a whole love scene.

On the other hand, here is an example of how originally a role was divided into 'bits' and conscious tasks originally in the Art Theatre. Here is Act 1, scene vi of *Woe from Wit*, the meeting between Sophia and Chatski.

CHATSKI

It's dawn, and you're afoot, and I am at your feet. *(Passionately kisses her hand)*

Wants to restrain a violent desire to be kind to Sophia.

A kiss. I'm not expected? Say!

Wants to evoke an affectionate response – and further – in this line there are two small 'bits' – wants to understand why she is so unforthcoming.

Pleased to see me? No? But look at me!

Wants to understand why she is cold.

Surprise? Just that? Well, what a welcome!
As if it hadn't been a week
As if we'd met just yesterday
And bored each other half to death.
No hint of love. Oh, but you're too kind!

Wants to see her eyes. 'What has happened?' (Sometimes when dividing into 'bits' instead of defining them we write a sentence like that to express a character's wish.)

And yet, I can't get over it, I've come

Wants to elicit sympathy and comfort

Five hundred miles, without a soul,
Without a wink of sleep for near two days,
Excited, wild, through wind and storm
Disasters, and this is all my thanks!

and approaches Sophia.

SOPHIA
But Chatski, I am very glad to see you.

Wants to conceal her embarrassment (I want to hide – I want to restrain – basic wishes which contain many wishes).

LISA
O sir, you should have been outside the door
Five minutes since, and you'd have heard
All that we said about you in this very room.

Wants to calm him.
Wants to help Sophia in a difficult situation.

CHATSKI
You're glad. Well, that's more like it.
And yet, is that the way we look when we are pleased?
It seems to me that I
Have frozen all my men and horses
Just for my own pleasure.

Wants to be sorry for his sarcasm.
'How boring for you!'
Wants to evoke frankness.

SOPHIA
We've talked about you all the time
When people called or simply
Put their head inside the door
Coming from afar or foreign parts –
Sailors even – I always asked
If they had seen your carriage anywhere.

Wants to calm Chatski. 'I've done nothing wrong.'

Wants to hide her embarrassment. (Sometimes we note two wishes.)

CHATSKI
Well, let's have it so! Happy the man
Who trusts, his world is cosy.
Dear God! I'm here again. In Moscow!
In your home!

'Let's end this conversation.'

Conscious tasks are the colours in a role, their logic is the composition of the picture.*

When we select our tasks we must lay great stress on psychological contrasts. Only bad actors playing villains enter with bulging eyes. Villains can be relaxed, attentive, obliging, etc. These are the really interesting moments. What is interesting is the rage of a kindly, courteous evil man. A lover can blame, cause pain, etc. These are interesting colours.

Early rehearsal consists entirely in imaginative work on the colours of the tasks

ristotle.

145

whose logic combines them into one 'supertask' towards which the through-action is directed.

Stanislavski now concentrates much more attention on analysing the text. He teaches that intellect, feeling and will are inseparable . . .

Theatrical clichés are 'ready-made forms for expressing feeling and the interpretation of all roles and trends in the theatre'. They are 'the external form of feeling, the forever fixed mask of feeling' which are 'quickly worn out and lose their exact relation to life', in a word they are 'stock-in-trade'. . .

Stanislavski lists and vividly describes most of these clichés, 'glib delivery', 'vocal clichés' – a lover is always tongue-tied, passion always drags out the consonants and extends the words, a heroic stance procures fervent vocal decoration and excessive shouting, lyricism leads to singing, etc. Stanislavski observes the clichés for various words and phrases, for the way in which various people of different class and age speak. He ridicules clichéd gestures and movements, clichés in the depiciton of various feelings and passions, physical and mental states, etc . . .

Stanislavski distinguishes the art of 'experiencing' which attempts to have the feelings of a role at every performance from the art of 'representation' which attempts to feel the role once at home so as to understand and then to imitate the form which expresses 'the psychological essence of any given role', and also from 'stock-in-trade' which consists of clichés and ready-made 'tricks'.

There is nothing passive about 'experiencing', when it is concerned with the active selection of colours and images.

The doctrine of fully experiencing on stage is quite different from the trivial theory of naturalism which naively assumes that art is the exact reproduction of life, and reduces it to mere copying, to photography . . . Above all, he maintained that the most acute sense of artistic truth occurs when an actor believes with all his heart in the reality of the character he had created, however fantastic . . .

The play was divided into Bits – individual (actor's) conscious tasks. Initially rehearsals were carried out sitting, without words. They were trying to find the inner pattern of the role, carefully looking into each other's eyes ('looking for the object'). Then they began to speak, at first using their own words, then the script, getting to know each other, strengthening relationships, sometimes once again breaking off rehearsal for theoretical explanations . . .

Stanislavski and the Method

Stanislavski's reputation has been widespread, particularly in the United States where some of his pupils taught his ideas – or versions of his ideas, since most had left Russia in the 1920s when the 'system' had not been completely formulated. One of the most significant offshoots was the Method, as developed by Lee Strasberg at the Actors' Studio.

Strasberg was an expert in the history of acting and was originally engaged to teach theatre history. He was at loggerheads with the other members of the Studio – Robert Lewis, Stella Adler and Elia Kazan – who, broadly speaking, taught the Method of Physical Action. Lewis knew the 'system' and Stella Adler had worked with Stanislavski for six weeks in Paris in 1935. It was the departure of Kazan for Hollywood that left the way open to Strasberg, who then proceeded to re-create the Studio is his own image.

Strasberg placed the major emphasis on the release of emotion and the use of 'emotion memory'. Actors were encouraged to search for the relevant emotion in their own life experience for a particular moment in the play. Many of Strasberg's pupils sought total immersion in the character. Some would seek to experience in real life the emotion they were to perform in the play. Thus if they had to play a scene of exhaustion they would physically exhaust themselves so that they could transfer the experience directly into the performance. This is in direct contradiction to Stanislavski's own teachings. Stanislavski did not believe you could transfer life experiences directly on to the stage.

The problem was compounded by a mistranslation. The Russian original for 'experiencing' is *perezhivanie*, literally 'living through', 'undergoing' an experience. In the 1930s this was translated as 'emotional identification'. Nowhere does Stanislavski use the term 'identification'. He is on record as having stated that a man who actually believes he is someone else is a pathological case. Nor does he speak of 'empathy', a related concept. These terms have been mistakenly attributed to him and the result is widespread misunderstanding.

Critics of the Method complain of its excessive concentration on the actor and his emotional resources and a neglect of adequate textual study. This often leads to adapting the character to the personality of the actor, rather than the other way round. The various sections of the play are no more than hooks for a subjective series of emotions.

Stanislavski had spoken of 'Public Solitude', the actor's ability to focus his attention on where it should go dramatically without consciously appealing to an audience. One of Strasberg's most famous exercises was the 'private moment', in which an actor would play out a situation for an audience normally not seen by anyone else. The shift from 'public' to 'private' is significant. One adverse effect of the misapplication of this exercise is for actors to pause excessively while they search, privately, for the emotion.

This concentration on the subjective, on the inward, is, however, extremely useful in the cinema, where the camera comes in close and captures what is going on in the actor's mind. Moreover, once a scene has been finally shot, the actor has no need to feel that emotion again. The overall performance, its shape and rhythm are dependent on the director and the editor, the final cut. In the theatre, however, the actor is in overall control of his performance – pace, rhythm, timing, emotional level – and he has to be able to reproduce it night after night.

Strasberg was fully aware of the differences between himself and Stanislavski. Indeed, he claimed that Stanislavski had gone astray. The assumption at the time, carefully nurtured for political reasons by the Soviet authorities, was that Stanislavski had moved from a subjective approach based on Emotion Memory to a more objective approach, the Method of Physical Action, based on new Soviet science and psychology.

In the absence of any genuine knowledge of Stanislavski's work in his later years, many assumed, and still assume, that the Method and the 'system' are one and the same thing.

9 | Michael Chekhov

In recent years, the teachings of Michael Chekhov (1891–1955) have been revived in Russia and have obtained a wide influence both in the United States and Britain, where he worked after leaving the Soviet Union for good in 1928, on the eve of Stalin's rise to power.

The nephew of Anton, Michael Chekhov was, by common consent, one of the most talented actors ever to have worked at the Moscow Art Theatre and the First Studio. Trained by Stanislavski, he acquired a deep understanding of the 'system' and practised it until he developed a method of his own, into which he incorporated most of its basic elements. He did, however, harbour certain reservations about Stanislavski's methods, in particular that every action should be 'true' and performed as in life. What, Chekhov asked, is the 'truth' of a fantastical character like Don Quixote? Are his actions 'as in life'?

He did not concern himself with primary training. His teachings were mainly intended for those who already had some experience as professional actors but who needed guidance on how to work on a role.

Chekhov's approach is much more personal and subjective than Stanislavski's. Whereas Stanislavski's approach to characterisation was through the conscious, Chekhov's approach was more intuitive, global.

Both agreed that although actors wanted to achieve a state of 'inspiration', it was not a state that could be commanded at will.

> The 'system' doesn't manufacture inspiration. It just prepares the ground for it. Whether it comes or not, you'll have to ask the powers above, or your own nature, or luck about that. I'm no wizard I can only show you new lures, techniques for arousing feelings and for experiencing.
>
> I advise you in the future not to chase after the phantom called inspiration. Leave that to the enchantress, nature. You should concern yourself with what is accessible to human consciousness.
>
> (*An Actor's Work on Himself*, Part One)

Stanislavski created the character by consciously exploring the 'Given Circumstances' first in his own person, then gradually as the character. The raw material for the characterisation came from his own experience.

For Chekhov, the character was always *'out there'*. It was the product of pure imagination which had to be *visualised*. It did not grow from the actor – the actor had *to grow into it*, merge with the image. In this he was similar to Coquelin.

Michael Chekhov describes himself in his two autobiographical fragments as a highly intuitive actor who could make an imaginative leap into a role. As a young actor he was always aware of the wholeness of his characterisations. However, that sense suddenly deserted him and he felt bereft. The result was a breakdown. His reaction to his illness was typical. Just as he could not use Stanislavski's step-by-step, pragmatic approach to character creation, he could not respond to the scientific treatment he received from conventional psychiatry. He thought he could cure himself by reading the philosophy of Schopenhauer. Ultimately, he was saved by the teachings of Rudolf Steiner and anthroposophy. This appeared to restore his sense of the wholeness of the creative act.

Steiner's teachings are complex.

> Anthroposophical ideas are vessels fashioned by love, and man's being is spiritually summoned by the spiritual world to partake of their content. Anthroposophy must bring the light of true humanness to shine out in thoughts that bear love's imprint; knowledge is only the form in which man reflects the possibility of receiving in his heart the light of the world spirit that has come to dwell there and from that heart illumine human thought. Since Anthroposophy cannot really be grasped except by the power of love, it is love-engendering when human beings take it in a way true to its own nature . . . Words expressing Anthroposophical truths are not like words spoken elsewhere today; rightly conceived, they are all really reverential pleas that the spirit make itself known to men.
>
> ('Awakening to Community', lecture, 23 January 1923)

Anthroposophy is a path of knowledge, to guide the Spiritual in the human being to the Spiritual in the universe. It arises in man as a need of the heart, of the life of feeling; and it can be justified only inasmuch as it can satisfy this inner need. He alone can acknowledge Anthroposophy, who finds it in what he himself in his own inner life feels impelled to seek. Hence only they can be Anthroposophists who feel certain questions on the nature of man and the universe as an elemental need of life, just as one feels hunger and thirst.

('Anthroposophical Leading Thoughts', Letters to Members, 1924)

A key concept that Chekhov derived from Rudolf Steiner was a belief in the existence of 'Higher Ego', a 'Creative Individuality' above and beyond the normal everyday ego which the actor has to contact. He also believed that this Higher Ego was common to everyone and that within each individual there is a desire for transformation.

Thus the actor's desire to characterise is merely an extension of a normal human activity.

Chekhov also developed his own ideas on split or divided consciousness in the creative process. Unlike Coquelin, however, his One is not cold, rational and detached but, as the Higher Ego, works on a spiritual or transcendent plane, guiding and helping the ordinary ego, the actor's personality and expressive means.

He was mistrustful of conscious analysis, or of any intellectual activity that would impede the Higher Ego, on which the creation of the performance ultimately depended.

Chekhov's method, although intuitive, is rigorous and based, like the 'system', on a series of techniques and exercises. It demands full control of the expressive means.

In the initial stages of preparing a role Chekhov attached great importance to what he called 'Atmospheres', the instant, global impression made by an event, a situation or a person. We are all familiar with the situation in which we walk into a silent room where a violent quarrel has just taken place and feel we can 'cut the atmosphere with a knife'. This response is the result of a rapid, instantaneous appraisal of the situation arising from the facial expressions, body language and spatial relations of the people involved. No one single person is responsible for that atmosphere, it is everyone present.

A play can have an Atmosphere. As an actor reads through the play many times he gets the 'feel' of it. Like Stanislavski, Chekhov attached great importance to this initial impression. It serves both as the starting point and the end point of the performance.

A place, a setting can have an Atmosphere – a church, a busy restaurant, a sunny landscape, a bleak moor, a rowdy public meeting, all have a specific 'feel'. The same is true of individual scenes in a play.

People can also have an Atmosphere. They, too, give off a 'feel'. They have a particular quality that represents their individuality.

Work can now proceed in a more precise manner, although it is not in the strict sense 'intellectual'. It is exploratory, questioning. It is an examination of the character who is 'out there'. There are a number of precise strategies.

Defining differences

The first question concerning the character is: 'What is he or she like?' An actor will instinctively feel resemblances between himself and the character, but what about the differences? Defining them sharpens his knowledge of the person he is to play. He needs to ask:

- How does the character think? Better, faster, slower, more vaguely, etc., than I do?

- What is the emotional nature of the character? More passionate, colder, more bad-tempered, sweet-tempered, etc., than mine?

- What is the character's will (temperament) like?* Stronger, weaker, more dominant, indecisive, gentler than mine?

The centre

Chekhov believed each person, each character, worked from their own 'Centre'. There seemed to be a key point in their bodies from which their activities emanated. For example, an inquisitive person's Centre might be the tip of the nose, an arrogant person's Centre the back of his neck.

Equally, the Centre can be outside the body. An aggressive person's Centre will be in the person she or he wishes to attack. An affectionate person's Centre will be in the person for whom love is felt.

The location of the character's Centre is a key to its movements and posture. If the actor works from the Centre, the rest of the body will fall into shape.

* Chekhov used the term 'will' in a very personal way, to suggest a 'basic mindset'.

Will, feeling, intellect

Linked to the idea of the Centre are concepts drawn from the system of eurhythmy developed by Rudolf Steiner.

Steiner defined the functions of the mind as will, feeling and intellect. In the nineteenth century François Delsarte had taken the same three functions and tried to locate them within the arms and to classify the types of gesture accordingly. Steiner now attempted to locate them physically within the whole body.

First, Steiner distinguished man from the rest of the animal kingdom. Animals go on all fours, with the spine horizontal to the earth, and so are earthbound. Man is vertical, on two feet.

Man's head points heavenwards, towards the universe. It is the sphere of the 'Mind'.

The torso and arms are the domain of 'Feeling', of the heartbeat and breathing.

The legs and feet are bound to the earth and are the domain of the 'Will'.

The Psychological Gesture

This is the most widely known technique of the Michael Chekhov method and, in a sense, is a synthesis of everything we have discussed so far. It is a simple idea but difficult to implement.

Chekhov pointed out that we use physical words to express psychological states: we 'grasp' an idea, we 'seize' an opportunity. Similarly, there are physical equivalents for feelings, intentions, personality. Even in life we note how a person's posture can denote their character. In the theatre we may penetrate more deeply into a character by feeling and creating its body and encapsulating it into one shape or gesture. This gesture forms the basis for all future work and guarantees its unity and integrity.

In *On the Technique of Acting*, Michael Chekhov describes how he came to learn the nature and importance of the Psychological Gesture through his work with Stanislavski and later Vakhtangov.

While rehearsing the role of Khlestakov in *The Government Inspector*, with Stanislavski:

[He] suddenly made a lightning movement with his arms and hands, as if throwing them up and at the same time vibrating with his fingers, elbows and hands, and even his shoulders. 'That is the whole psychology of Khlestakov', he said laughingly.

And when working with Vakhtangov on Strindberg's *Erik XIV*:

One night at rehearsal he suddenly jumped up, exclaiming 'That is your Erik. Look! I am now within a magic circle and cannot break through it!' With his whole body he made one strong, painfully passionate movement, as though trying to break an invisible wall before him or to pierce a magic circle. The destiny, the endless suffering, the obstinacy and the weakness of Erik XIV's character became clear to me. From that night I could act the part with all its innumerable nuances, through all four acts of the play.

A third example was provided by the great Russian bass, Chaliapin, whom Stanislavski described as the greatest theatrical genius he had ever known. Chaliapin, a large man with a huge frame, astonished Chekhov by making himself appear small by the power of his imagination.

Working on the script: incorporating

Once the actor has achieved a total view of the character, he can then work on the script in greater detail. At this juncture, Chekhov's approach is similar to Stanislavski's, in that he emphasises the need for the actor to explore the play section by section.

When subdividing a play, however, Chekhov, unlike Stanislavski, defined his subdivisions in terms of mood, states of mind, rather than Tasks. This is consistent with his own account of the Stanislavski 'system'.

In this phase of rehearsal the actor's technique becomes of paramount importance: total, conscious technical control over all his expressive means. The object is to give all the imaginative work that has been done tangible, visible, theatrical form. The actor applies his early discoveries to the written text and its specific demands. Chekhov called this process 'incorporating'. By his own account, the actor's work is heavily director-led. The director poses what Chekhov calls a series of Leading Questions: how can the actor use his hands, arms and face to express a certain mood or feeling? What is the Psychological Gesture in a particular situation? At the same time the director can dictate certain specific moves, actions and gestures, such as the use of the walking cane or the hat. The major Psychological Gesture of the role is always at the back of the actor's mind, while the individual Psychological Gestures ensure the unity and integration of the performance at every moment. The total methodology is clear in the production plan for an American production of *The Government Inspector*.*

Finally, having removed all obstacles, physical and mental, to the creation of a character, having endowed it with all his qualities, what was once an external image has become part of himself and passes under the creative control of the Higher Ego. Thanks to Divided Consciousness, the actor becomes the observer of his own creation, enjoying all its joys and sorrows.

Of all Michael Chekhov's teachings it is the Psychological Gesture that has become best known and the most widely used in conjunction with other methods.

* Leonard, *Michael Chekhov's To the Director and Playwright.*

10 The New Actor in France
Antoine, Copeau and Jouvet

The French tradition of acting, essentially based on Diderot, Coquelin and the declamatory tradition, remained the strongest alternative, both practically and theoretically, to developments in England and Russia. But, at the end of the nineteenth century it had to face the challenge of a new kind of play, the four-act drama, less 'literary' more realistic in approach, with dialogue that approximated more to speech in real life – Ibsen, Strindberg, Turgenev, Chekhov, Tolstoi, Hauptmann. Where were the actors who could take on such plays?

Coquelin's most famous role was in *Cyrano de Bergerac*, the last play of any significance to be written in rhyming couplets, which demanded bravura delivery and which still retains its appeal.

Émile Zola's *Naturalism and the Theatre* was an attack on a moribund tradition. The emphatic, grandiose style of classical theatre matched the grandeur of the monarchy under the *ancien régime* and the splendours of Versailles. But that world had disappeared with the Revolution. The Romantics had essentially done nothing to modernise the theatre. They had merely replaced the tunic and the toga with doublet and hose and a great deal of overwrought emotion. Where was the theatre that reflected late-nineteenth-century society, the world of the poor that Zola had so savagely exposed in *Germinal* and *L'assommoir*?

He found an ally and a colleague in André Antoine, who founded the Théâtre Libre in 1887, the same year that Stanislavski created the Society of Art and Literature. He wrote two plays for the new theatre, and another production was based on one of his stories. All were slaughtered by the critics.

Antoine's mission was precisely to create a new kind of actor. He launched a fierce attack on French acting and the training methods of the Conservatoire, condemning its inability to produce actors capable of performing a modern repertoire in a modern theatre in a simple, unaffected style.

At the Conservatoire students received very few hours of genuine training. They were expected to prepare a scene and then perform for the 'Master' who would criticise it and then show the student how certain lines should be said, thus passing on either his own innovations or a 'tradition', a procedure not dissimilar to the treatises on diction of the seventeenth century.

Antoine cited the case of a young actor who had prepared a hundred lines of verse for his entrance audition, had spent his entire period of study working on those hundred lines, which he had then performed in his first job. He had learned nothing real about acting.

An extreme case, perhaps, but Antoine maintained that unemployed actors could be found on every street corner of Paris, unable to find work because they could not adapt to a modern repertoire. They only knew a traditional, declamatory style. Recordings made at the turn of the twentieth century show that leading actors almost sang their lines in classical tragedy, often with a rapid vibrato, a style that bore no relation to normal speech.

Thus when Antoine began to produce modern realist authors such as Ibsen, he was forced to rely on amateurs and semi-professionals. What was required was a theatre based not on declamation but on observation.

After the Théâtre Libre, Antoine moved on to the Odéon where he continued his pursuit of a contemporary style of performance. Ultimately, however, he abandoned the stage for the cinema. This was, perhaps, inevitable and, indeed, it was in the French cinema of the 1930s and 40s that a natural style of acting of great economy and subtlety was developed.

In general, French critics and commentators have not been sympathetic to Antoine, the term 'Antoine-style' theatre is somewhat pejorative, as though naturalism were by its very nature artistically inferior, unsatisfying to sophisticated tastes.

Reform finally came from a man of letters, a critic, Jacques Copeau (1879–1949).

It was Copeau who dominated the development of twentieth-century French drama. In 1913 he founded the Théâtre du Vieux Colombier where he worked until 1924. He then spent five years with his company in Burgundy, developing his ideas, before returning to Paris to become director of the Comédie-Française in 1936.

Copeau created a school attached to the theatre. The training he offered his young company was far removed from the traditional training of the Conservatoire, and included regular classes in voice, movement and dance. As a director, Copeau stripped away unnecessary scenery, all the clutter so beloved of nineteenth-century audiences, to return to Alexandre Dumas' principle of 'bare boards and a passion'. The emphasis was on the actor performing as far as possible in a bare space.

In 1940 he wrote:

> The stage is the instrument of the creative dramatic artist.
>
> It is the place for drama, not scenery and machines.
>
> It belongs to the actors, not to stagehands and painters.
>
> It must always be ready for the actor to use, for action . . .
>
> At the present time it is absolutely true to say that the creative dramatic artist is an *intruder* in the theatre, that everything works against his imagination, his efforts, his very existence. He should be master where he is now a slave. He is the sole master. Without him, the theatre today has no master.

> (*Registres* I, pp. 214–15)

It was the first example of what Grotowski later defined as 'poor' theatre.

Copeau was interested in Stanislavski's work and at one moment there was a question of setting up, with one or two others, an international studio, to see whether there were some basic, general principles, that all could apply. Unfortunately the plan came to nothing. When Stanislavski was in Paris at the end of 1922, Copeau was in the United States, so the two never met.

Above all, the Vieux Colombier was a theatre of text and that was what made it acceptable to audiences. It was simple but it was evidently 'art', not vulgar and sordid, like real life, not what in England in the 1950s came to be called 'kitchen-sink' drama.

In 1923 Copeau turned his attention to the issues raised in Diderot's *Paradox*. He rejected the simple opposition of feeling and technique. The actor could both feel and control, be both artist and raw material simultaneously.

In an article, 'To the Actors', Copeau analyses the complex process by which an actor creates a character both through private preparation and in rehearsal, the insights, the errors, the choices that have to be made, the constant transition from imaginative understanding to critical analysis and back, so that an interpretation can be both truthful and properly theatrical. Finally, he deals with the problem of maintaining a performance in the stress of an actual performance with all its potential accidents.

He begins with the particular status and dilemma of the actor, that he is at the same time a creator and an instrument, an artist and his own raw material. But his problems are far greater than those encountered by the sculptor who works in clay, or the painter who works in colours, since he has to deal with all the complexities of his own organism.

> The sculptor's battle with his clay is as nothing compared to the resistance the actor encounters from his body, his blood, his limbs, his lips and all his organs. Therein lies the mystery, that a human being can think of himself and treat himself as the raw material of his art, play upon an instrument with which he must identify and yet always feel the difference, to do, and, at the same time, to be what he does, a natural man and a marionette.

Of course, an actor can play purely technically but that is not true acting.

> That an actor does not always feel what he plays; that he can play the lines without playing the character or the situation, and can do so without apparent fault, that is more or less properly and correctly, and yet not be moved, is true. That is his failure. It is the slippery slope of the lazy and the mediocre.

Copeau describes the rehearsal process from first reading to first performance. He takes the case of an actor who is perfectly cast in a role that is ideal for him, that he feels instantly. He seems to have mastered it all at the first reading. But that is merely the beginning. His responses are all in his head. They have to be given theatrical expression. There is the process of transforming initial feelings and impressions into a performance that is firm and well structured. There is now a process of critical examination, of verification and selection, an interplay between technical judgement and an inner sense of truth.

> That is the moment when he starts to lose his character a little. He sees what he wants to do. He builds and develops. He establishes the sequence of events, the transitions from moment to moment. He works out his movements, selects his gestures, reviews his inflections. He watches himself, hears himself. He steps back. He is critical. He does not seem to

be giving anything of himself. Sometimes he stops in the middle of working and says, 'I don't feel that.' . . .

He is planning to capture something he has understood and sensed for a long time but which is still outside, still not part of him.

His colleagues, even the author himself, are bewildered. Why can't he go back to what he did at the beginning, why can't he just 'be himself'? But

> The actor is no longer himself. Yet he is not yet someone else. What he did on the first day disappeared as he prepared to play his part. He has had to say goodbye to freshness, naturalness, subtleties, all the pleasure of his enthusiasm to undertake the difficult, unrewarding, meticulous task of drawing theatrical reality out of literary and psychological reality. He has had to establish, master and assimilate all the transformatory elements which simultaneously separate him from his role and lead him towards it.

Technical control and mastery are essential to a professional. But control does not mean coldness, detachment. It means a capacity to contain feeling, to use it artistically.

> Are we to say that an actor feels nothing because he is able to use his feeling? That these tears and sobs are meaningless because they do not strangle his voice or affect his delivery? . . .
>
> To deny feeling to an actor because he has presence of mind is to deny it to any artist who respects the laws of his art and never allows the tumult of his emotions to paralyse his heart . . . The more emotion rises, the more his head is clear.

Copeau endorses Diderot's view that everything in a performance is planned, structured, but for him technique does not preclude feeling.

> The absurdity of the *paradox* is to oppose professional technique to liberty of feeling and deny that they exist simultaneously in an artist.

A solid technique is a licence to feel because the actor knows that he can pull back at moments when he could be carried away.

> The actor gives his all. But to give himself he must first be in possession of himself . . . Not only does technique not exclude feeling, it sanctions and frees it. It is its support and safeguard. It is thanks to our craft that we can let ourselves go, because it is our craft that enables us to recover. The study and observance of principles, an infallible instrument, a sound

memory, controlled diction, regular treating and relaxed nerves give us a sense of security that makes us bold . . . It lets us improvise.

Among the founder members of the Vieux Colombier was the young Louis Jouvet (1887–1951), destined to become one of the leading actors and directors of his time both in the theatre and cinema.

In 1927 he formed an association with three other directors, Charles Dullin, Gaston Baty and the Russian-born Georges Pitoëff. It was known as the Cartel. The intention was to create a group of art theatres, with a repertoire that was both classical and contemporary and that would steer a path between an ossified Théâtre Français and the commercial, Boulevard Theatre which they all despised.

All acknowledged their debt to André Antoine and Stanislavski. Jouvet had met Stanislavski when he was on tour in Paris in 1922, as did Antoine.

The Cartel sought to present a new repertoire. Jouvet championed, in particular, the plays of Jean Giraudoux, while Pitoëff introduced the works of Chekhov to a French audience.

Each member created his own company and engaged and trained talented young actors. None produced any formal theory of acting. Jouvet, however, spent the later years of his career reflecting on and writing about the nature of the theatre and the actor's art. While in exile in South America with his company during the Second World War and on his return to France he kept a series of notebooks, brief reflections, often written in his dressing room after a performance, on his own process and the actor's craft. At one level he would have liked to produce a general theory, but at another, he realised that his view of acting was such that such a theory was impossible. The actor's process is, as he put it, 'unstable'. But more than that, Jouvet had the sense of something secret, something private and mysterious at the centre of an actor's personality, which gives him his fascination. A character is a person, a *persona*. In Latin, *persona* means 'mask'. But what lies hidden behind the mask? Seeing Jouvet's screen performances, we are as aware of what he is not disclosing as of what he is. The stillness, the economy hide strange depths.

Jouvet was deeply marked by his time with Copeau whose influence is everywhere. But Copeau was not a working actor. Jouvet's notes are important in that they demonstrate a great actor, of high intelligence and considerable culture, battling to come to terms with his own art and resolutely refusing facile answers. Jouvet's range as an actor was enormous and he moved from Molière to the cinema screen with equal rigour, skill and subtlety. His ideas, therefore, spring from a wide range of experience.

Jouvet's prime concern is what he calls the necessary 'lie'. The theatre is a convention, fiction that has to become a kind of 'truth'. Everyone knows that the theatre is a convention, an accepted lie, actor and audience alike. But whose is the lie? The audience can choose to believe that what it is seeing is not a lie, but the actor must know that it is a lie and find a truth within that lie through his art which must be founded in some kind of reality. The theatre may be a matter of conventions, but acting must not be conventional in the sense of being a cliché: 'The art of acting is not to cheat where there is cheating by using another kind of cheating' (*Le Comédien Désincarné*, p. 44). But this is not the same thing as being 'sincere', a word Jouvet despised. There is no thought or planning in 'sincerity'. It is akin to what Aristotle called 'ecstasy' and Diderot 'delirium'. It is not theatre. The honesty Jouvet, like Copeau, is looking for is clear-headed, deliberate. An actor's initial responses to a script may be 'sincere', spontaneous, but they are personal, subjective, as Copeau pointed out, but that is not what the audience needs to see.

Jouvet makes a crucial distinction between the personality actor, the *acteur*, and the actor who transforms himself into someone else, the *comédien*.

The *comédien* must examine, test out his subjective feelings in relation to the text, with all its demands, its historical factors, so that what he offers becomes 'objective'. This means being clear about the nature of the action of the play, what happens, and playing that action, not personal feelings. Jouvet was perfectly aware that many young actors think of acting as an opportunity to give vent to their own personal feelings, however chaotic. The assumption is that they have meaning because they are 'sincere'. But the character exists. It has been created before the actor reads the script. He has to come to accept it, to come to terms with the facts, the events of the play, not to colour them with his own opinions and emotions.

Thus a performance is not a spontaneous outpouring of personal emotion, but a highly structured presentation which is both felt and organised according to the script, so that the audience can both feel and understand what the play is about.

Jouvet sums up his position in two statements. First, a quotation from

Rousseau: 'An actor puts his being in his seeming', and: 'Here is a good definition of a character: the character is not the individual that we are but the individual we wish to persuade others that we are.'

He was not overconcerned with the notion of split consciousness, which he saw as a natural occurrence that everyone experiences. If we are interested in it, it is because Diderot talked about it. But we should not, as he put it, 'make heavy weather of it'.

Jouvet, like Copeau, rejected entirely the notion that the actor must perform technically, coldly. Split consciousness must be used, exploited for artistic ends. It is the tensions between self and character, the awareness of playing a fiction that brings a role to life. This state of alertness also prevents the actor from falling into routine and acting mechanically.

He was much more interested in the complexity of the personality, its contrasts and contradictions. No one is ever just one thing. A man can fulfil a variety of roles and functions as he goes through life: son, brother, nephew, father, husband, lover, bank manager, gambler. Sometimes there is a conflict between certain aspects of the same life. A man can be an army officer and a Catholic with a conflict between the two. A character must be as many-layered as a normal human being. A characterisation based on one emotion, one ruling feature is unacceptable.

Jouvet also recognised that the scope of the actor's responsibilities depended on the quality of the writing. Classical texts, the great roles, are like a mountain to climb. They seem beyond any possibility of success. To be a 'great' actor, you need to play Hamlet, Lear, Macbeth, Othello, Cleopatra, Juliet, Lady Macbeth, Phèdre, Bérénice, in a single career. The text is dense, complex. At the minimum, if well and intelligently spoken, it can register almost independently of the actor's personality. But, as dialogue became less poetic, nearer to everyday speech, the words became less charged with meaning. The actor had to supply the subtext. In Shakespeare and the other classics, the subtext is in the text. For Jouvet, working within the French classical tradition, the cut-out point was Marivaux who died in 1767. Thereafter, plays ceased to have genuine literary value. It was perhaps for this reason that he championed the plays of Giraudoux with their finely wrought language. Despite his concern for the text and its style, Jouvet placed great emphasis on physical action, on finding what the character does, and on generating energy. The actor's presence is what counts, not his ideas about the role. The actor does not express an opinion on the character he is playing, does not judge it, he presents it in action.

Between 1949 and his death in 1951, he gave a series of masterclasses at the Conservatoire d'Art Dramatique, which seemed to encapsulate the ideas contained in his notebooks. The effort to communicate with students seemed to bring his ideas, which are still complex, together.

Classes at the conservatoire

We must be able to speak of 'lies' and not be afraid.

We need to understand the word 'lie' not in the religious or legal sense.

We should not attach any pejorative meaning to this word. What is important is to reconcile sincerity and lying within a professional context. Neither word is one we can use with any certainty in our profession or indeed in life. We cannot be limited to sincerity. Dramatic convention depends on a lie that is given, accepted and shared.

Isn't the actor's ideal to be sincere for two and a half hours? It is an ideal for someone overwrought or who wants to make a scene, but not for an actor. The actor's ideal is not to be sincere for two and a half hours. The audience's ideal is not to see someone giving vent to his feelings. Sincerity* is a twitch, a spasm, hysteria. It is not an activity.

Convention is an abstract word, the word lie is repugnant, but we have to use them if we wish to progress in our work. Words are only approximations to ideas, the means for exchanging ideas.

What we are after is a model for training which will enable you to understand the special gift you have for performing plays.

Rousseau said: 'The actor puts his being in his seeming.'

That is a definitive statement about which you can do nothing.

Secret

We need to find the actor's *secret*. At the centre of any given person, consciously or not, whether he knows it or not, there is a secret. Sometimes it is a feeling of inner silence or an inner contradiction.

There are actors who have a feeling of something secret and others who have not.

There are also actors who have a certain reserve, a certain shyness and those who have not. There are actors for whom expressing, showing, requires a great effort to overcome their shyness and others for whom self-expression is a special pleasure, an

*ncerity here is equivalent iderot's sensibility.

indulgence. There are the exhibitionists and there are the others. There are actors who have played their whole lives and never had an awareness of something secret. You do not have to possess it to be successful, but it might be better to be aware of that secret and introduce it into our lives and our work. You understand sincerity as a kind of authenticity, what English merchants call 'the genuine article'. The genuine article is not sincerity. It belongs to trade not to the theatre.

If you don't acknowledge the idea of the lie, you cannot acknowledge the idea of fiction. A mirage is a lie but there is nothing dishonest about it. There is convention, too, in painting. A picture has one dimension but represents three. It is no insult to the painter to call it a lie . . .

Lying, dissembling, pretending are at the root of all human activity. In our profession that activity is based on pretending. The actor's art is to become aware of pretending, to feel he is living that contradiction, that relative or provisional truth and not to fall victim to it, and above all never to believe in absolute sincerity which is a spasm, a congestion, a state we would like to justify but which is not normal or tolerable.

We have to choose between pretending half-heartedly or living that pretence fully and practising it with dignity. The actor's art is to know how to lie and pretend. It is not sincerity but a relative truth lived, accepted, offered, shared by the participants in which we can exercise that special belief which is ours with energy and confidence, so that dramatic convention becomes the nearest to religious convention.

When it comes to social conventions – good manners, marriage, negotiations with a lawyer – the reasons are obvious. They arise from needs which can be brought into the open. They are not lies.

Dramatic convention arises from a need that is inherent in nature herself – that you have an audience and you want to be actors. It is the dramatic need based on a feeling of solitude, a more or less conscious secret side to human beings.

The self

Henri Michaud said: 'I am only ever temporary, I am made out of everything. We are not perhaps made to be a single me and we are wrong to hold on to it. There is not one me, not ten mes, there is no me. I am a state of equilibrium.'

Sartre also says: 'I can only know myself through others.'

The self has many layers, divided among several kinds of reality.

It is not only actors who play dramatis personae. The idea of a person and a persona are part of social life. A man can be at the same time a good family man, a judge or an infantry officer, a Catholic, a Protestant or an atheist. That makes up a series of personae but not a single persona. You cannot draw a line and tot them all up. There are difficulties in passing from an infantry officer to a communist or liberal politician. This is a series of personae that do not follow one from the other and among whom there are even conflicts. The infantry officer may have difficulties with the Catholic.

Don't let's talk about sincerity. When a law officer puts on his judge's robes he does what you do when you act a play, but more unconsciously than you. What I would wish is that you do it more consciously. We are not the only ones who play characters but we have to know that we are playing.

The mask

The Latin word *persona* means mask. Person, persona are the same thing.

As well as the character there is the mask, the feeling of something secret in the man who wears it.

This conflict in our private lives, in which we feel we are a character while feeling ourselves, is the conflict of the actor, it is our profession.

The secret obliges the person to live his life in greater depth.

Yesterday I read a book by Edmund Gosse in which he says that when a boy he had told a lie. He loved his father, respected him greatly and considered him to be infallible, all-knowing and all-seeing. He father did not discover that he was the guilty person and he had no reason to confess and he suddenly realised:

> The strangest thought I had was that I had found a companion, a confidant inside me. There was a secret in the world and that secret belonged to me and to someone living in my body . . . There were two of us and we could talk to each other. It is difficult to define such rudimentary feelings but it is certain that it was in this form of dualism that my individuality suddenly became clear to me at that moment. It is equally certain that it was a huge consolation to find someone inside me who could understand me.

The secret is a source of power for the actor. It is the opposite of confession. What though is our profession? It is to bear witness, to confess, to battle with what is secret. Remember this: an actor without a secret is an actor without confession, superficial. He is not an actor.

Here is a good definition of a character: the character is not the individual that we are but the individual we wish to persuade others that we are.

The actor is not the one who lies. He is the intermediary between the author and the public. He does not lie, he simulates . . .

[A] character exists as a result of a series of complex operations, starting with the writing of the role, a script, and actors who exchange dialogue. It exists to the extent that if the actor is split in two, there is someone else acting in his place. It is the discovery of the character and oneself.

You will see how the more characters you play, you are able to differentiate between kinds of character. There are characters who exist, types that become characters, characters that become heroes. We end up with a hierarchy of characters which we need to study and understand.

Then we begin a genuine study of our behaviour towards the character, in which the actor is charged with representing it and has the right to do so, in which he must live with this character and perfect his abilities as an instrument and an instrumentalist when he plays it and when he must combine his personal life with his professional practice.

It is capital in our profession to see plays as action, and not to see anything outside the action. Feelings and ideas are not for us but for the audience. *We* have to perform an action. When we play *The Miser*, our job is not to play avarice or greed but a story.

What is difficult is to think about a play without all the ideas that have become attached to it. As soon as we mention the name Don Juan we evoke a whole series of ideas and theories.

I am going to ask you to do an exercise which requires you to be very clinical. You have to say strictly what happens.

You have to examine the play as evidence. If what you do is rigorous then you can go and perform the play. If there is anything murky about it, don't perform it.

There is no theme in a play, there is an action and it is for the audience to interpret that action, to see in it whatever it wants.

There is no consistency in a role any more than there is in a human being. We are in constant contradiction with ourselves. There is no consistency in the character either, which is infinitely superior to us. Critics try desperately to find the key to a character but their explanations are always personal. The character constantly contradicts himself. A consistent character is not alive. To behave truthfully he must not have a dominant feature, or obsession to his nature.

Every character, the Miser, the Misanthrope, Hamlet, is a series of contradictions throughout the action of the play, contradictions which are inherent in their activity.

A consistent character has no place on stage. He has nothing of interest to offer.

Of course it is normal to make a personal judgement about the character we are playing, but let me warn you by judging you deaden the character, the play, the action . . .

Difficulty is beneficial – you need to believe that. There's nothing to be gained by playing without any problems. That is not what our profession is about.

Problems, difficulties give you access to the resources you need to play the role.

If you are asked to make summaries, it is to give you an idea of the play as a whole. Our job is not to act roles but to act plays. If you know what the action is, if you take the action in which the character is involved rather than the character, you will see your role within a broader truth than the insipid, pretty-pretty ideas you might entertain about the character, which, on the whole, are purely egotistical. That is the problem.

The importance of action

The critic sits in the stalls, sees an action, judges it, criticises it, draws conclusions, then decides what was false, expounds his ideas about the production, the sets – what doesn't he do? He chills the warmth of the performance. He freezes it. For him what matters is not so much what is happening on the stage as what he is going to say about it.

The actor is another matter. He *does things* (*acts*) but before he does so he must find out what precedes and produces the act: the state of feeling, *the soul of the character*.

The character has a happy line. The audience hears it and says, Ah, a happy line. The actor must be happy before he says it. He must go back through the character. The approach to the line is long and arduous. The character is a difficult prey to catch, it gets away all the time. You need to build up a store of energy – the character's energy – to release it as you play. The character is *a store of energy*. That is the energy you must demonstrate and communicate to the audience, not give an exposé on a text or the intentions that surgical commentators discover.

There is neither explanation, reason or consistency in a character. Orestes, in his madness, cannot reason about it as we do. But he has a store of energy that drives him unconsciously and naturally – as it were – towards madness. There is a need for action for which the actor must substitute a need for speech. But here is neither inward contemplation nor narcissism in a character. And he questions, he does it without stopping, it occurs within the thrust of the action.

All the explanations we can give of a play or a character other than in terms of pure action are partial, subtle, clever, false, funny or contradictory. One after the other people find a truth that has been hidden from their predecessors and this truth changes every ten years quite happily. What good are these external controversies? None at all. Useless ideas merely bring on a headache.

What we need to see is action. Not ask whether Tartuffe is thin or fat. If Orgon is stupid or clever, if Elvire is coquettish or serious. There will always be someone who will tell you, and in print, too. We need to see the *situation* in which the characters are placed. The complexity of their behaviour becomes clear.

Physical states

It is the physical states, the physical feelings in a text that we have to find. And to do that you have to avoid the rapid reactions and judgements that spring to mind despite yourselves. You must let them go and return to the text with total detachment.

We are performers. We only participate in so far as our feelings and physical skill are required.

Split consciousness

This is a recent discovery, at least in the terms in which Diderot explains it . . .

There is normal split consciousness when we are aware of what we are doing at the same time as we are aware of ourselves and at the same time have sufficient awareness to be able to converse or listen.

Diderot only speaks of split consciousness to propose a paradoxical theory – but paradoxes can be fruitful – by which he declares that a great actor is one who remains cold with a cold heart; that second-rate actors are sensitive and emotional.

We should not make heavy weather of Diderot's *Paradox* – that leads nowhere. Dissociation exists in every human being but Diderot explains it to proclaim the advantage of thought over feeling. The difference between being moved by emotion or natural sensitivity and being moved intellectually is an interesting distinction but only a distinction.

We should draw one conclusion from Diderot's split consciousness; that if the actor uses his own emotion, he is no longer master of himself. His emotions rule him and so, when he is playing, he runs of risk of going wrong or drowning.

Diderot states that the best way of acting is coldly, clearly; that is an arbitrary definition. This distinction is only interesting in so far as Diderot was the first to discuss it.

It is clear that the actors of the Middle Ages or the seventeenth century were less intellectual than we – we live in another age – but they had their own kind of split consciousness.

I say this to make you understand that there are degrees, shades, of split consciousness, starting with the primary, basic awareness of being alive while at the same time of taking part in something outside ourselves.

We lead mechanical lives in which we are driven by our own wishes, our own sensations, but from time to time, there is a kind of shock, when we are aware of our own personal existence and an existence that is outside, of a sensation that comes from without and a sensation within. There are the people around us and there is us, there is the Me we discover inside and the sensations that impinge on us from outside and which constitute someone else, an other self, so to speak . . .

In one of his poems Racine says: 'Within myself I feel two men at war.' This duality exists at every level. Our task is to limit the problem to the kind of duality we wish to achieve. The important thing for you is to discover this duality and how to use it.

There are many people who live and never experience any kind of dissociation, or only feel it at a very low voltage. They spend their whole lives with mechanical responses, scarcely touched by any feeling of self.

We do not achieve knowledge of our self but of how to use our self through that duality which is an important undertaking in all our lives. The thinker, the intellectual achieves a certain level of split consciousness and seeks greater depth of self, greater self-knowledge through that split consciousness. There is a difference between the actor's trade and the grocery trade. The actor lives a life in which he has to split, not be himself. That is why we choose it. The principle of our profession is that we get away from ourselves and then try to come back to ourselves. What we should fear is that after a certain time we become mechanical again. The actor becomes a mechanical doll, unaware of split consciousness.

What draws people out of their automatic responses? An accident, something unusual. You work as actors because it takes you away from the usual, it puts you in special circumstances. But when you begin in our profession if you don't discover the beginnings of that double state you will exercise your craft in the same mechanical way as the grocer's boy. You take a role, you put it on and when it gets a little worn you take it off and put another on, like a suit. That is false.

But if you can reach the state of split consciousness, if you can use it – each in your own way – you can exercise your profession with full awareness of what you are doing. And you can perfect your professional skill and discover intellectual and emotional resources that mechanical acting will never give you, in particular for the study and performance of a role.

As beginners, you experience pleasure and delight. We call that the actor's first phase. We have seen that there are three phases: sincerity, the discovery of insincerity (phase two) and the use of that insincerity, that is split consciousness.

At first you act with pleasure for the delight it gives you then, after a while because of circumstances that hold you back – the constraints of our profession – you discover that this delight is not to be had daily, above all when you are playing to half-empty houses or unhappy audiences. At that moment pleasure stops and gives way to a feeling of a duty to be done, that it is a matter of professional honesty to act with awareness.

On the first night you experience a pleasure that is both painful and agreeable. When the play goes well, when it is a success you are happy to get to the theatre, to hear the house filling up, to see the curtain rise. It is an amusing, intoxicating feeling. You wallow in sincerity, in happiness.

But then something goes wrong. You are in a play that is not successful. You then realise that you are practising a craft, performing is no longer a pleasure but a duty.

You then realise the need to play, of insincerity. That is not yet split consciousness but the beginnings of it. That is phase two when you become aware of split consciousness, the special quality of an action which suddenly reveals who you are, your basic identity, your self and also someone else who is listening, understanding and participating in that action.

If actors were capable of describing what they feel, there are some who would tell you that they take advantage of that moment of danger on stage to find a freedom of spirit. There is a will to dissociate which comes primarily from a delight in 'being' inwardly, secretly, while being obliged to seem.

I believe that practising our profession without an awareness of split consciousness, without the sense of seeming and being at the same time, is futile. So I return to the three phases of acting: sincerity, insincerity, making use of insincerity.

---

11 | Meyerhold

Meyerhold (1874–1940) was one of the most profound, penetrating theorists of the art of the theatre of his time. His studies involved every aspect of performance. Trained by Nemirovich-Danchenko at the Philharmonic School in Moscow, he became a founder member of the Moscow Art Theatre and developed a devotion to Stanislavski which, despite their disagreements, lasted all his life.

Meyerhold represents a new phenomenon in twentieth-century theatre, the director who works from a specific aesthetic and ideology to which he subjects everything.

Meyerhold came to maturity in a period when the nature of art and, therefore, of the theatre was being redefined. There was a growing fear at the turn of the twentieth century that art was losing its identity as art, as artifice. The rise of naturalism and of photography seemed to blur the distinction between life and art. What was art? What was its purpose? Was it merely intended as a literal imitation of reality, a *mimesis*? Or was it an activity of its own, a language of image and metaphor, a *poesis*? Art had to reassert itself as art. It had to be freed from the dominance of social content, so favoured by the nineteenth-century intelligentsia.

An initial response came from Serge Diaghilev, creator of the Ballets Russes, and two designers, Bakst and Benois, who created a group known as the Mir Iskusstva (World of Art) which launched its own, highly influential magazine. The designs commissioned by Diaghilev and produced by Bakst and Benois tended towards the exotic and the pseudo-oriental and could never be confused with 'reality'.

At the same time Stanislavski was directing Andreev's *Life of Man*. He based the designs on the black-and-white drawings of Aubrey Beardsley, a far cry from the apparently naturalistic sets of *The Seagull* and Gorki's *Lower Depths*.

The World of Art, however, was soon overtaken by a much more radical, broader movement which spread across the whole of Europe. Art, particularly the visual arts, became the matter of its own study. The result was a series of movements or -isms: Post-Impressionism, Cubism, Fauvism, Futurism. Russia, at this time, was still part of mainstream European culture. Rich industrialists bought paintings by Picasso and Braque. Kandinsky exhibited in Odessa in 1910, while Russian painters and writers added one or two -isms of their own: Acmeism, Suprematism and, ultimately, Constructivism.

Common to all the various movements of the period is the notion of art as a 'made thing', an artefact. A major strategy was to make use of the *medium* of expression itself – paint, wood, metal – to explore its possibilities and to use those possibilities to create an art-object which would be essentially non-representational. In painting, the surface of life was broken down and reassembled. In his portraits, Picasso presented a composite image of the face made up of its features seen simultaneously from three angles. Attention was centred on planes, forms and surfaces. Sculpture was no longer solid. It was created out of tubes, metal, wire. It was an open construction, where internal spaces were as important as solid material.

In literature, the verbal surface was broken down just as the surface of the canvas had been broken down. Writers broke away from logical sequence and linear expression and experimented with sounds, hoping somehow to release long-forgotten meanings that lay in the roots of words, and to use sound as a means of creating an impression or an emotion.

In the period up to the 1917 Revolution, an artistic vocabulary was developed which was used by artists of varying and opposing ideological positions. This vocabulary was not the property of any one political programme but was shared by those who saw art as a self-sufficient activity and those whose concern was to create the art of the future, the art of the machine age, where what human beings produced was more important than the natural world. The director Tretyakov proclaimed this doctrine aggressively: 'The new kind of the artist-producer must abhor everything unorganised, inert, elemental . . . Repulsive is the virgin forest, unused waterfalls . . . rain or snow, avalanches, caves and mountains. Beautiful is everything that bears the trace of man's organising hand.'

In the period 1900 to the declaration of Socialist Realism as official Soviet art in 1934, Russia produced a wealth of original art in all fields –

painting, sculpture, architecture, ceramics, posters, plays, poetry – that was not equalled in its breadth and scope by any other country. The movement came generally to be known as Formalism, because of its emphasis on structure rather than content.

In the theatre Meyerhold began to break down the structure of classic plays, reshape them to reveal new meanings. Eisenstein developed the idea of montage before transferring to the cinema. Taïrov relied on heavy stylisation.

The age of actors' theatre was over. The age of directors' theatre had begun.

What was the actor's role and function in the new theatre?

In 1902, Valeri Bryusov published a seminal essay, 'Unnecessary Truth', essentially an attack on the 'naturalism' of the Moscow Art Theatre. This was followed in 1907 by a series of notes and drafts for a projected book on *realism* and *convention on stage*. In these works, Bryusov presents us with a series of dilemmas and paradoxes:

- Audiences cannot really believe that what they are seeing is real.

- Reality cannot be reproduced. If it could it would not be art.

- Art (Theatre) is convention. Artists must master specific conventions.

- If we attempt to turn theatre into pure convention, we run up against the irreducible reality of the actor's body, which is evident whatever the degree of stylisation. The alternative would be to replace living actors with puppets on wires with a phonograph inside.

- The actor is the sole creator. He is like a sculptor standing before a mound of clay.

The art of the theatre and the art of the actor are one and the same thing; in the theatre, the director and the stage hands are of no more importance than the editor and his subeditor in a magazine. The sets and props are the equivalent for actors of a frame for a picture and if the frame becomes all important it is a disaster.

At about the same time that Bryusov published his first essay, Adolphe Appia, the most influential and revolutionary designer of his period, who created sets out of non-representational geometric forms,

175

published an article, 'A New Art Material', and followed this two years later with 'How to Reform our Staging Practices'. His thesis was that only non-representational sets could give actors the expressive freedom they needed to convey the meaning of the play.

In 1907, as Bryusov was drafting his book, Edward Gordon Craig published an article expressing a diametrically opposed viewpoint. Although, like Appia, he was drawn towards abstract, geometric forms, far from wishing to liberate the actor, Craig wanted to get rid of them altogether. Art was order, organisation, the antithesis of human freedom. Actors were the extreme of that freedom and subject to the tyranny of their own emotions, which disrupted the harmony of the art-object. He welcomed Bryusov's ironically expressed notion of replacing them with puppets, the *Über-marionette*.

Craig's notion of the total subordination of the actor to the concept of the production was to have widespread repercussions in the 1920s.

Meyerhold accepted the idea of the primacy of the actor's physical presence but set it within a totally conceived production, where the actor moved as directed, as an element in the staging that was a construct.

The first artist to use the term 'construct' to describe her work was Aleksandra Exter, who produced a series of 'Dynamic Constructions' in 1916. Exter became one of the leading set designers at Taïrov's Chamber Theatre in the 1920s.

'Constructivism' in the theatre emerges in 1920–1. The idea of 'Construction' had many facets:

- constructing art works

- constructing/producing manufactured goods

- constructing a new society

- constructing new citizens for that society

'Making' and the consciousness of making were the dominant concepts. Making art and making new men were one and the same process. Men made themselves in making.

These concepts were enhanced by the ideas of Marxism-Leninism. Marx maintained that different societies were formed by the ways in which people transformed nature through industrial and agricultural production. By changing the mode and organisation of production in the interests of the masses, the consciousness and character of societies and people would be transformed. In Lenin's words, 'Soviets plus electrification equals communism.' Humanity would change itself.

Constructivism used and applied the theories current in the visual arts and poetry but went one stage further with the notion that producing art-objects and consumer-objects was one and the same process. The theatre became a 'machine-tool'.

This entailed not only removing the actor from the centre of things but also the script, the author's text. Theatre was no longer actors interpreting a given piece of writing, but a process by which meaning was produced out of a multiplicity of elements to a given end, usually a director's concept. Productions were meticulously organised, planned and all effects carefully calculated.

The audience became part of the process. No longer ignored, or apparently so, by the actors on stage, it became an overt part of the construction of meaning. The aim of performance was not to interpret (deconstruct) the text but, rather, to construct/organise the audience's responses. This entailed producing a certain kind of awareness in the audience during performance.

One major device for heightening audience awareness was the technique of *defamiliarisation*, a term coined by the formalist Viktor Shklovski, the most influential theorist of the formalist movement.

In 1917, he published his seminal essay *Iskusstvo kak Pryom*. This is usually translated as 'Art as Technique', but the Russian word *pryom* has many meanings, one of which is 'device'.

Shklovski advanced the radical notion that a work of literature can be considered as a series of devices or techniques which are received in a particular way. The secret is in the manipulation and articulation of the devices. One such device is defamiliarisation, *ostranenie*, derived from the Russian word for 'strange', *strany*. What major authors, like Tolstoi, do is to make the familiar unfamiliar, using defamiliarisation. This obliges the reader to see the world in a new way.

In a generally sympathetic portrait, Michael Chekhov refers to Meyerhold's enormous talent, and insight, but also to his arrogance – 'That's the way I want it and that's the way it's going to be.' The actors were there to give him what he wanted. Some members of his company left accounts of his extremely unsympathetic behaviour, his brutality towards actors who were auditioning for him, his repetition of the same comments and notes time after time since he would not allow any deviation from his direction, his indifference towards actors as human beings. One actor was so incensed at being systematically ignored that he assaulted Meyerhold at a reception.

Meyerhold showed almost no interest in the actor's creative process. He was like a conductor who expects the musicians to know their job. In 1936, he recalled how he had failed in his early career to understand the true significance of certain physical actions Stanislavski had given him in the rehearsals for *Three Sisters*.

In June 1922 he set out his ideas about acting in a lecture. Significantly, he defined his system of acting as 'Biomechanics', which was in direct opposition to what he supposed was Stanislavski's 'system'. He rejected the Aristotelian notion of ecstasy and, like Diderot, he was wary of 'sensibility' which caused the actor to lose control. What he wanted was a quick, automatic response to external stimuli – excitability in the strict sense of the word.

> Ecstasy is the notorious inner experience, the 'authentic emotion'; it is the system of my teacher Stanislavski . . . we need not ecstasy but excitation, based firmly on the physical premise.*
>
> (*Meyerhold on Theatre*, p. 200)

> The 'inspirational' method and the method of 'authentic emotions' (essentially they are the same, differing only in their means of realisation: the first employs narcotic stimulation, the second – hypnosis [the hypnotic conditioning of the imagination]) . . .
>
> Only a few great actors have succeeded instinctively in finding the correct method, that is, the method of building the role not from the inside outwards, but vice versa . . . I am speaking of artists like Duse, Sarah Bernhardt, Grasso, Chaliapin, Coquelin.
>
> (*Meyerhold on Theatre*, p. 199)

Meyerhold had not worked with Stanislavski since 1905 and he knew nothing of Stanislavski's notions of intentionality and action. His attribution of the notion of self-hypnosis to Stanislavski is entirely mistaken. Nevertheless, his version of Stanislavski's method gained wide credence among the avant-garde and later with Brecht.

Biomechanics is related to the notion that the production of a performance is the same as the production of consumer goods. The avowed basis of biomechanics is the teaching of Frederick Taylor, a

* Trans., E. Braun.

time-and-motion study expert who developed the notion of the production line.

Meyerhold wanted actors who could respond immediately and efficiently to direction, whose reflexes were razor-sharp. He pointed to the economy and effectiveness of skilled workers, who used no superfluous effort.

> *It is . . . essential to discover those movements which facilitate the maximum use of work time.* If we observe a skilled worker in action, we notice the following in his movements: 1) an absence of superfluous, unproductive movements; 2) rhythm; 3) the correct positioning of the body's centre of gravity; 4) stability. Movements based on these principles are distinguished by their dance-like quality; a skilled worker at work invariably reminds one of a dancer; thus work borders on art. The spectacle of a man working efficiently affords positive pleasure. This applies equally to the actor of the future.
>
> In art our constant concern is the organisation of raw material. Constructivism has forced the artist to become both artist and engineer. Art should be based on scientific principles; the entire creative act should be a conscious process. The art of the actor consists in organising his material; thus work borders on art; that is, in its capacity to utilise his body's means of expression.
>
> (*Meyerhold on Theatre*, p. 197–8)

Apart from the reference to Taylorism, there is an allusion to the ideas of William Morris, which were highly influential at the beginning of the century. Morris stated that in an ideal utopian society, which Meyerhold assumed the Soviet Union to be, where men were no longer required to perform menial tasks, work itself became art. Art = work + pleasure.

In his comparison of work with dance, Meyerhold anticipates the later research by Rudolf Laban with his system of 'efforts'.

Then he reformulates Coquelin's thesis:

> The actor embodies in himself both the organiser and that which is organised (i.e. the artist and his material). The formula for acting may be expressed as follows: $N = A_1 + A_2$ (where N = the actor; A_1 = the artist who conceives the idea and issues the instructions necessary for execution; A_2 = the executant who executes the concept of A_1).
>
> (*Meyerhold on Theatre*, pp. 198)

Meyerhold created a whole series of physical exercises to sharpen the actor's reflexes, his response to stimuli, his excitability, his ability to organise himself in space. Meyerhold himself was exceptionally agile and could easily demonstrate movements which other actors found difficult to perform. Typical is the Arrow exercise:

> The left hand appears to be holding a bow. The left shoulder is pushed forward. When the student sees the target his body stops, with the centre of gravity in the middle. The right hand moves back in an arc to reach the arrow which is held in imaginary belt on his back. The movement of the hand affects the entire body, transferring the weight to the back foot.
>
> The hand takes the arrow and charges it. The centre of gravity is transferred to the front foot. He takes aim. The imaginary bow is drawn so that the balance returns to the back foot. He shoots and completes the exercise with a leap and a cry.
>
> Even this very simple exercise teaches the pupil to think of himself in space, to understand the possibility of marshalling his forces, of developing flexibility and balance, to realise that even the smallest gesture, for example, of the hand, echoes throughout his whole body. The pre-gesture in this exercise, the 'sign of refusal' is the arm curving back for the arrow. The 'acting sequence' is a) intention, b) action, c) reaction.
>
> (*Bvstrechi c Meyerhol'dom*, pp. 322–3)

In a later article, 'The Profession of the Actor', Meyerhold explains the actor's process. A performance is a series of reflex responses to demands. No emotion is involved. Each response goes in a three-phase cycle:

- intention, whereby the actor accepts a task that may be given by the director, or the author, or at his own initiative

- realisation, which is the automatic response of the body and the voice

- reaction, which is the disappearance of the response to prepare the way for the next cycle

Closely related to the notion of successive cycles is the notion of 'pre-acting'. Pre-acting is linked to the notion of the 'pre-gesture', or the 'sign of refusal', which means allowing the audience to see what is coming in the moment before a line is said or an action performed. The audience sees the idea happen, sees it working its way through the character's mind. It is a moment when the action freezes and it serves to punctuate the performance.

> Pre-acting prepares the spectator's perception in such a way that he comprehends the scenic situation fully resolved in advance and so has no need to make any effort to grasp the underlying message of the scene. This was a favourite device in the old Japanese and Chinese theatre. Nowadays, when the theatre is once more being employed as a platform for agitation, an acting system in which special stress is laid on pre-acting is indispensable to the actor-tribune.
>
> (*Meyerhold on Theatre*, p. 205)

It was Gogol who had referred to the stage as a platform from which to address a whole nation.

Just as Stanislavski had dominated the theatre up to the Revolution, so Meyerhold dominated the theatre of the twenties and early thirties until he fell foul of the Soviet authorities who now condemned Formalism and instituted Socialist Realism, which was intended to help in the creation of the New Communist Man. Art was intended to be optimistic, void of conflict, socially positive. There was no place for aesthetic experiment for its own sake. Meyerhold's theatre was closed down in 1936 and he was arrested in 1939. After his execution in February 1940 his name was expunged from all encyclopaedias and histories of the theatre for nearly three decades. By then, almost no one was left alive who had actually practised Biomechanics.

12 | Brecht

No one recently has dominated the discussion on the nature of acting more than Bertolt Brecht (1898–1956). For over half a century his ideas have been examined and debated. Paradoxically he never trained actors and never produced a coherent training programme. His writings on acting extend over three decades, and vary greatly in tone and style, sometimes aggressive and belligerent, sometimes enquiring and reflective. It is generally the most aggressive passages that are remembered. Brecht was aware that he sometimes created a false impression because of the way he wrote.

We need to distinguish three periods in Brecht's discussion of acting:

- his early attempts to define the kind of acting he wanted for his plays, in opposition to the prevailing style or styles – the grand manner and naturalism

- the years of exile, 1933–1948, when he had no company of his own and little opportunity to stage his plays

- the return to Germany when he produced little theory since he was engaged with the Berliner Ensemble and was putting his ideas into practice rather than discussing them

Throughout, he had only one basic aim: to see his plays staged in the way he wanted. His views on acting, therefore, reflect the state of his thinking at various moments in his career.

There were four major influences on Brecht's development:

- the Russian avant-garde
- the Bauhaus
- Piscator
- Marxism

The Russian avant-garde

Brecht's arrival in Berlin in 1924 exposed him to a series of artistic experiences he could not have dreamed of his native Augsburg, not least that of the Russian avant-garde.

The leaders of the Bolshevik Revolution of October 1917 were convinced that it would unleash a series of similar revolutions across Europe, starting with Germany. They misread the complexities of German politics and history. Revolution failed. However, the Social Democrat government in Germany was sympathetic to the new regime in Russia, and Russian artists and intellectuals, including Viktor Shklovski, visited Berlin while German artists had free access to Russian society and the new artistic forms it was developing. There was a continuous flow of ideas along the Moscow/Berlin axis.

This was the world into which Brecht was plunged. Thanks to his friend Bernhard Reich who had moved to Russia with his lover, the actress Asja Lacis, he was kept continuously aware of developments in the newly created Soviet Union. It was Lacis who served as Brecht's assistant when he directed his adaptation of Marlowe's *Edward II* and who gave him his first experience of Constructivist techniques. The basis of Brecht's directorial vocabulary stems from Meyerhold, and writers like Sergei Tretyakov, who later translated three of his plays.

Berlin in the twenties was alive with every kind of artistic and sexual experiment. This was the period when new, exciting media came to maturity. The cinema, thanks to directors like D. W. Griffith and Abel Gance, achieved a complexity and a sophistication that had not existed before the war. Still photography developed techniques of montage and collage. Radio, too, became an art, not just a means of simple communication. The gramophone moved from acoustic to electrical recording and opened up the world of music to a wider public. There was political cabaret, a medium in which Brecht shone. This was, above all, the jazz age, music which seemed to have nothing to do with the prewar period and Prussian rigidity.

The Bauhaus

The most important artistic movement to emerge in the 1920s was the Bauhaus, under the architect Walter Gropius. The Bauhaus was a school of architecture but its principles spread through the decorative arts and even to the theatre. The name was significant. The word '*Architektur*' was replaced by '*Baukunst*' (building-art): the notion of building (construction) was not a million miles from Russian art of the period.

Bauhaus stripped away all decoration, all superfluous features, and replaced them with clean, straight-line, functional forms for buildings, furniture and household goods. It looked, above all, 'modern', efficient, fitted to the needs of the twentieth century, which seemed only to have begun in 1918.

Brecht wanted a stripped-down style of acting, not the usual display of histrionics by actors whose only thought was to please the audience, to give them what they wanted and so collect a round of applause. They were no more than peddlers of emotion, which the audience was all too happy to consume.

Piscator and political theatre

In Berlin, the leading innovative director was Erwin Piscator who defined the concept of 'Political Theatre' in 1928, a theatre deliberately designed to educate and inform the working class. It was Piscator who coined the term 'Epic Theatre', although it was substantially Brecht who worked out its theory. From 1923 to 1927, Piscator staged a series of productions at the Volksbühne (People's Theatre) which had been set up and generously financed by the Social Democrat government. The last of Piscator's productions, however, an updating of Schiller's *The Robbers*, so outraged the authorities – one of the characters, Spielenberg, was made to look like Trotski and 'The Internationale' was played at his death – that he was sacked. He then founded his own collective at the Theater am Nollendorfplatz. Walter Gropius of the Bauhaus designed a 'total theatre' for him, capable of being used in many shapes – proscenium, in the round or thrust. It was never built.

Piscator was seen by many of his contemporaries as what later came to be known in the cinema as an '*auteur*', a modernist director like the Russian Constructivists, who used the technical resources of the medium in which he was working to create a work of art. Piscator's method was to use multiple projections and film sequences, simultaneous sets and complex stage machinery to create the background, the historical and political context in which the action occurred. In a later, critical comment on *Mother Courage* he stated that whereas Brecht had staged an individual character, he would stage the Thirty Years' War itself.

Herein lies the difference between the two men. Brecht was never interested in experimental staging or innovative theatre shapes. His productions were always actor-centred. For him the essential relationship was between author and actor, the actor who could convey the author's meaning.

Brecht became part of a script-writing team at the Piscatorbühne, collaborating, notably, on an adaptation of *Adventures of the Good Soldier Schweik*, of which he was later to make his own version. Significantly, Piscator never staged, or offered to stage, any of Brecht's plays, although he frequently complained about the absence of good, contemporary scripts.

Brecht was also aware of other forms of political theatre, the workers' theatres, particularly those engaged in Agitprop. Most prominent among these groups were the Blue Blouses, who invented the notion of the 'living newspaper' and toured Russia. The Blue Blouses visited Germany in 1929 where there were scores of similar groups.

Marxism

The final element in Brecht's aesthetic was Marxism, or rather Marxism-Leninism, which transformed him from a simple anti-bourgeois rebel into a committed revolutionary.

The origins of Brecht's commitment to Marxism are significant. In 1926 he was attempting to write a play about the corn market. He realised, like Marx before him, that capitalists themselves had no idea how the system worked and discovered that the only coherent explanation of the functioning of capitalism was to be found in Marx. Although he had obviously been in contact with convinced communists for a considerable time, it was only at this point that he decided to make a serious study of their ideology and enrolled in a school which had been especially created to introduce artists to Marxist thinking.

Brecht's plays were never mere illustrations of Marxist theory. What Marxism provided was a *dialectical* method of thinking that enabled Brecht to analyse both real and dramatic situations and so structure his material.

Marx did not invent the dialectic; nor did Hegel from whom he derived it. It emerged in ancient Greece and is best summed up in Heraclitus' dictum, 'Everything is in a state of becoming.' The world is no longer a static object but a process of continual change arising out of interaction – contradictions which are resolved and lead to further contradictions and so on. History, therefore, is dynamic, the state of society at any given moment is not part of nature, it is susceptible to human action and therefore to change.

Dialectical analysis defines objects and events not only as what they are but as what they are not. Black is black but is also not white. It also allows, as the monk Abelard discovered in the twelfth century, for the answer to a question to be not only yes or no but yes *and* no (*sic et non*). A man is losing his hair. Is he bald or not? The answer is yes and no; he is in a process of balding. It was precisely this form of analysis which Brecht applied to dramatic situations.

Ideologically, therefore, Brecht's plays depend on two fundamental tenets: first, that society needs to be, and can be, changed and that theatre is one means of creating the consciousness that will produce that change. Perhaps the most relevant comment Marx made from Brecht's point of view was his statement in the *Theses on Feuerbach*: 'Philosophers have explained the world in various ways. The point is to change it.' This stance links him to the political theories of the Constructivists. Second, that there is no such thing as a fixed personality or human nature, that people, like society, can be changed. This view is presented as early as 1926 in *Mann ist Mann* in which a mild man, Galy Gay, is transformed into a killing machine by brutal conditioning. It was a view that was heavily endorsed by Soviet psychology and genetics. In Soviet political writings and in the literature of the 1930s the image of the factory where old metal is used and refounded into new products is a constant one.

It followed, therefore, that 'naturalistic' theatre which presented a static reproduction of reality was essentially a reactionary theatre, tacitly confirming the status quo, implying that things are as they are and cannot be otherwise. It did not challenge but merely provided an emotional experience, sending the audience away 'purged'. The audience was called on to empathise, not criticise.

This was a commonplace view on the left. At the Workers' Theatre Movement's First National Conference 25/26 held in London in June 1932 we find the following statement:

> The naturalistic form, namely that form which endeavours to show a picture on the stage as near to life as possible, is suitable for showing things as they appear on the surface, but does not lend itself to disclosing the reality which lies beneath. And it is just this reality existing beneath the polite surface of capitalist society that the Workers' Theatre must reveal.

What new kind of actor of actor, then, was needed?

The actor who provokes critical thought leading to social change.

What was inadmissible was a mere exchange of emotion, of empathy, whereby the actor 'suffered' to make the audience, who identified with him, 'suffer'. This was more than useless, it was socially regressive.

Brecht saw the kind of acting he wanted in a performance in 1929 by his future wife, Helene Weigel. She was playing a serving woman in *Oedipus* and had to deliver a messenger speech. These highly charged narratives were usually an excuse for an actor to pull out all the stops, to be 'dramatic'. Not so Weigel. She was an actress of a new sort:

> When an actress of this new sort was playing the servant in *Oedipus* she announced the death of her mistress by calling out her 'dead, dead' in a wholly unemotional and penetrating voice, her 'Jocasta has died' without any sorrow but so firmly and definitely that the bare fact of her mistress's death carried more weight at that precise moment than could have been generated by any grief of her own.
>
> *(Brecht on Theatre*, p. 28)

It was also the physical side of the performance that caught Brecht's attention.

> As she descended the few steps she took such huge paces that this slight figure seemed to be covering an immense distance from the scene of the tragedy to the people on the lower stage. And as she held up her arms in conventional lamentation she was begging at the same time for pity for herself who had seen the disaster, and with her loud 'now you may weep' she seemed to deny the justice of any previous and less well-founded regrets.
>
> *(Brecht on Theatre*, p. 28)

This, perhaps, was the first description of what Brecht was later to define as the *Gestus*.

The significance of Weigel's performance was that she demanded that the audience make decisions concerning the meaning of the events she had recounted.

A year later Brecht put the following question:

> Why should an actor give the audience an emotional experience when he could give them an opportunity to learn?
>
> Indeed, an actor can be 'understood' insofar as he feels sorrow and creates it in his turn but then all he does is unload the audience's imagination rather than adding to its knowledge, which is much more.
>
> *(Gesamte Berliner Frankfurter Ausgabe [GBFA], Vol. 21, p. 389)*

And again:

> When you demonstrate 'this is the case', do it in such a way that the audience asks, 'is it really so?'
>
> *(GBFA, p. 389)*

In building a character the actor must rely not on 'psychology' but on what the character does, how he interacts with the other characters and how they perceive him.

> Every character arises out of the knowledge of his behaviour towards other characters.
>
> This is crucial in any social group. The important thing for mankind is for each man to be judged by what he reveals about himself to the group, or by the way he behaves towards the group . . . It is not enough to be. *A man's character is the product of his function.* [emphasis added]
>
> *(GBFA, p. 390)*

Brecht always considered himself a realist and insisted that a performance should be concrete and rooted in everyday behaviour:

> The writer gives [the actor] abstractions which he must bring to life. He must not show anything metaphysical, anything 'hidden', anything 'between the lines', otherwise he is only half doing his job. If the writer has invented a 'struggle', or a 'fraud', the actor shows a specific struggle for a piece of bread, or a fraud that is 'once-only'.
>
> So he teaches us a point of view?
>
> No, he teaches behaviour, something that has method. He always has a specific goal. He does not give us a general view of human gestures, he does not show 'Man'.
>
> *(GBFA, p. 395)*

Just as Coquelin and Michael Chekhov had developed notions of split or divided consciousness, Brecht developed the idea of the divided actor, where character and the actor's own personality exist side by side and never merge. It is not merely that the actor is not emotionally involved but that he himself has a critical attitude towards the character and suggests that he could have behaved otherwise. That is 'epic acting'. The actor in some sense reports the person he is playing and forms an opinion of him. Brecht compares this to what happens in real life when someone with no theatrical talent or ambition recounts an incident or imitates a third person during a conversation.

> This representation of a third person happens every day innumerable times – the witnesses to an accident mime the behaviour of the victim for newcomers, a joker imitates a friend's funny walk without ever trying to plunge their audience into a state of illusion but that does not mean they do not get inside the character to acquire its special qualities.
>
> (*GBFA*, Vol. 22, p. 641)

In *The Horatians and the Curiatians* the lead character states his actions as he performs them:

THE HORATIAN

I climb the mountain. The spear
Is my stick. It is my third foot
The foot that never gets hurt
The foot that never grows tired.
One tool has many uses.
He reaches a crevasse in the mountain.
But how shall I go on? Here is a crevasse.
When I was a boy, I hung from an oak limb
And swung over a brook into a garden
Where there were apples. My spear was once
An oak limb.
In this way I shall cross the crevasse.
One tool has many uses.
He lays it over the crevasse and crosses hand over hand.
I have arrived. I lean
Over the cliff edge. Below me
Runs the road that my enemy shall march over.
I shall crush him beneath rock fragments.

With my spear I shall loosen them.

One tool has many uses.

He loosens rock fragments.

My spear is my crowbar.

It holds back the rockpile until my enemy is under it.

With a pressure from my fingers

I shall crush my enemy.

My spear has preserved me.

He prepares a small avalanche.

My enemy is not yet there.

And I am tired from running.

He sits down to wait.

And I lean back, knowing

I dare not sleep. And I am too exhausted

To act, but I am too exhausted to do nothing.

And I fall asleep.*

The character narrates himself without apparent emotion. But who is speaking? Not the actor himself in his own right, nor a fully individuated naturalistic character. The character is its function and purpose.

Brecht developed his theory of the divided actor largely under the influence of Chinese theatre, which Meyerhold had already referred to as a model. In 1935 he was in Moscow with Meyerhold and Tretyakov and was present at a number of demonstrations by the Chinese actor Mei Lan-fang. Lan-fang specialised in female roles, particularly young girls. There could, therefore, be no question of naturalism. Brecht took copious notes. One especially encapsulates the kind of acting he saw:

Chinese actors not only show how men behave but how actors behave. They show how, in their way, actors present human gestures. For actors translate the language of everyday life into their own language. So that when we look at a Chinese actor we see no less than three people simultaneously, one who shows and two who are shown.

Take a young girl preparing tea. The actor first shows preparing the tea, how it has to be prepared. These are precise gestures which are always repeated unchanged, and are perfect in every way. Then he shows the girl, how lively she is, or patient or in love. And he shows at the same time how the actor expresses that liveliness, that patience and that love with repeated gestures.

*Trans., H. R. Hays.

(*GBFA*, Vol. 22, p. 126)

Other things apart, it was the precision of the gestures that impressed Brecht. They both express and show, they reveal their meaning in the doing. As Vakhtangov had demanded, they showed the *how* as well as the *why*.

It was during the discussions with Meyerhold and Tretyakov that followed Mei Lan-fang's demonstrations that Brecht was reportedly introduced to the concept of *ostranenie* (making strange) which seemed perfectly to fit the Chinese actor's approach to his art. The term was eventually translated into German as *Verfremdung* or the *Verfremdungs-effekt* or *V-Effekt*, derived from *fremd* (distant) and *befremdlich* (unusual).

Thus, in writing about Mei Lan-fang, Brecht stated:

> The actor evidently wants to give the impression of something strange (*fremd*) even unusual (*befremdlich*). He succeeds by observing himself as though he were a stranger. That is how he makes the things that are represented surprising. This kind of acting drags daily things out of the world where everything is self-evident.
>
> (*GBFA*, Vol. 22, p. 155)

Translating *Verfremdung* into English has created a number of difficulties and confusions. The most common translation is alienation but this term has unfortunately negative and slightly aggressive overtones, as though the audience has, in some way, to be offended. This has led to a certain resistance to the technique. 'Distancing' has also been used. The more accurate 'defamiliarisation' is clumsy but gets to the heart of the matter.

How is a European actor to use this technique of the multiple self? Mainly he should see himself as he is seen. How do others define him? Where does he stand within the group? What are his interests within the group? How do his views differ from the writer's?

One simple procedure Brecht suggested was for the actor, rather as in *The Horatians*, to speak his moves out loud in the third person: he stands, he goes to the door, he opens it. Also to put his dialogue into the third person: he says that he is leaving.

Brecht constructed his performances on the same principles that governed his writing. He maintained that every sentence should be an independent, self-contained unit. The same was true of each individual speech and each individual scene. They were independent of what came before or after. The procedure was step by step.

Brecht rejected the notion of an all-embracing concept of the play and the character prior to beginning work on the play and which was to be worked out in rehearsal. For Brecht the actor had to arrive 'empty-handed'. When he was directing, Brecht treated his own plays as if he did not know them. There had to be a process of discovery where the material was explored step by step, bit by bit. He demanded of his actors a constant state of astonishment, of surprise at the events being acted out.

The actor built his performance moment by moment, learning who the character was, aware of what he was doing, remembering the process, discovering contradictions and various facets of the character. By building and performing his character in this way he could lead the audience through the same process, revealing the choices that had been made and the possibility that other choices could have been made.

Brecht also expected his actors to make a personal contribution. The author's world is not the only world. The actor also has his world and he needs to mark the contradiction between the writer's world and his own. Finally, once the broad outlines of the staging had been agreed he needed to introduce a fresh element:

> When the actor has forged all the relationships his character has with the other characters, when he can say his lines easily and perform the [actions] with the maximum enjoyment, he has created the author's world. The actor must then discover the difference with his own world and show it. How does he show the key contradiction? Every play makes a choice in the relationships the characters create among them. When the situations have been imagined merely to allow the character to show who he is, a choice has been made among the situations that allow him to do so. The actor is not obliged to follow that.
>
> If he has to play a situation which shows the hero as courageous, to that courage . . . he can easily introduce an incidental detail, a piece of by-play, a clever commentary on a line and thus show the cruelty the hero displays towards his servant. He can link greed to a man's loyalty, selfishness to apparent wisdom, a petty aspect to a love of liberty. This shows a contradiction in his characterisation which it must have.
>
> (*GBFA*, Vol. 22, p. 604)

One of the most important features of the rehearsal process is the discovery of the *Gestus*. The term *Gestus* had been used in neoclassical rhetoric to describe formalised positions of the hand denoting a feeling or a statement. It is in some sense a formalised gesture. Brecht developed the notion to cover any movement, grouping or attitude that revealed the meaning and essential structure of human relationships. Its nature is essentially social.

> Under the term *gestus* we need to understand a group of gestures, facial play and (more often) statements made by one or several people to one or several others. A person selling fish shows, among other things, the *gestus* of selling. A man drawing up his will, a woman who seduces a man, a policeman who beats up a man, a man who gives his wages to ten others – there we always find a social *gestus*. Following this definition the prayer a man offers up to God only becomes a *gestus* if the man prays while thinking of other people or in a context that includes relations of men to men (the king's prayer, *Hamlet*).
>
> (*GBFA*, Vol. 22, p. 616)

Or again:

> By [*Gestus*] we mean a complex of isolated and varied gestures connected to a statement, which is the basis of a human interchange that can be isolated and is concerned with the common attitude of all those taking part in the process (condemnation of a man by other men, a discussion, a fight, etc.), or a complex of gestures and statements which in an isolated individual sets certain processes in motion (the indecisive attitude of Hamlet, Galileo's confession of faith, etc.) or simply a basic attitude (like satisfaction or expectation). A *gestus* indicates human relations. For example working is not a *gestus* when it does not suggest a social relation such as exploitation or cooperation.
>
> The overall *gestus* of a play can only be vaguely defined but we can give the questions that need to be asked to define it. A writer's attitude towards his audience. Does he teach? Stimulate? Provoke? Warn? Does he want to be objective? Subjective? Will the audience be put into a good mood or a bad mood or does it just want to participate? Does he address our instincts? Understanding? Both? Etc., etc.
>
> (*GBFA*, Vol. 23, p. 188)

Once the *Gestus* had been found it was customary at the Berliner Ensemble to photograph key moments in the production. These photographs were not intended to be prescriptive but merely to indicate the best solution that could be found at the time.

One problem which Brecht found it difficult to resolve was the degree to which an actor identified with the character he was playing and the degree to which he wished to provoke empathy in the audience. At his most negative he rejected both. Just as Meyerhold had rejected self-hypnosis, he would speak of the actor in a state of trance and of the audience being mesmerised, resulting a kind of catharsis. Brecht understood the Aristotelian concept of catharsis in the same terms as most of his contemporaries, as a kind of emotional discharge, which was an end in itself. Modern scholarship tends to the opinion that catharsis is a kind of cure, a process that produces greater awareness and understanding, a willingness for more responsible behaviour.

The violence of Brecht's reaction can in part be explained by his horror at the mass hysteria that pervaded Hitler's Germany, the great rallies, the blind emotion. Never was reason more needed.

Nevertheless, Brecht recognised that identification was the hallmark of a professional actor, something which ordinary people, children and amateurs could not achieve. Total transformation into the character is a guarantee of a certain kind of authenticity.

> If we are to progress, we have to recognise total transformation as a positive act, as part of art, something difficult, a process that enables the audience to identify with the character. In its historical perspective, identification has enabled a new approach by man, has expressed a deeper knowledge of his nature. If we abandon this state, it is not absolute, you can't just erase a whole period because it went astray, you don't drop artistic means from your arsenal.
>
> (GBFA, Vol. 22, pp. 178–9)

Brecht began to realise that he was being seen as someone who was all intellect and no feeling and that a false polarisation was taking place. In 1951 he wrote in his journal:

> It becomes clear to me that the antagonistic configuration 'reason in this corner – emotion in that' has to go. The relationship of *ratio* and *emotion*, with all its contradictions, has to be examined minutely, and opponents cannot be allowed simply to present epic theatre as rational and counter-emotional. The 'instincts' – automated reactions to experience – which have become contrary to your interests. The bogged-down, one-track emotions which are no longer under the control of reason. Against that the emancipated *ratio* of the physicists with their mechanical formalism. Be that as it may, even if the interests of artists ought not to be expressed in especially emotional terms – probably they are – they do express themselves in an emotional form. The epic [principles] guarantee a

critical attitude on the part of the audience, but that attitude is highly emotional.

(*Journals*, p. 135)

Ultimately Brecht reached a position similar to that of Diderot and Coquelin. Identification could be used in rehearsal but not in performance where the actor should present his character objectively, as though from the outside.

Brecht summed up his attitude in 1951 in a 'Letter to an Actor':

I have been brought to realise that many of my remarks about the theatre are wrongly understood . . .

Most of the remarks, if not all, were written as notes to my plays, to allow them to be correctly performed. That gives them a rather dry and practical form . . .

This brings me to your question whether acting is not turned into something purely technical and more or less inhuman by my insistence that an actor oughtn't to be completely transformed into the character portrayed, but should, as it were, stand along side it, criticising and approving. In my view this is not the case. Such an impression must be due to my way of writing, which takes too much for granted. To hell with my way of writing. Of course the stage of a realistic theatre must be peopled by live, three-dimensional, self-contradictory people, with all their passions, unconsidered utterances and actions. The stage is not a hothouse or a zoological museum full of stuffed animals. The actor has to be able to create such people (and if you could attend our productions you would see them; and they succeed in being people because of our principles, not in spite of them!).

There is however a complete fusion of the actor with his role which leads to his making the character seem so natural, so impossible to conceive in any other way, that the audience has simply to accept it as it stands, with the result that a completely sterile atmosphere of 'tout comprendre c'est tout pardoner' is engendered, as happened most notably under Naturalism.

We who are concerned to change human as well as ordinary nature must find means of 'shedding light on' the human being at that point where he seems capable of being changed by society's intervention. This means quite a new attitude on the part of the actor.

(*Brecht on Theatre*, pp. 233–5)

He returned to the question of feeling and empathy once more in 1953 in a dialogue concerning a new translation by Gottsched of Horace's *Ars Poetica* and in particular his dictum, 'If you would have me weep . . .'

> In this well-known passage Gottsched cites Cicero writing on oratory, describing how the Roman actor Polus played Electra mourning her brother. His own son had just died, and so he brought the urn with his ashes on to the stage and spoke the relevant verses 'focusing them so painfully upon himself that his own loss made him weep real tears. Nor could any of those present have refrained from weeping at that point?'
> I must say there is only one word for such an operation: barbaric.
>
> (*Brecht on Theatre*, p. 270)

Brecht insisted that the audience must not be coerced or bludgeoned into feeling. A feeling must not be detached from its causes. It cannot be carted away and applied in other circumstances. There was a choice.

> Suppose a sister is mourning her brother's departure for the war; and it is a peasant war: and he is a peasant, off to joint the peasants. Are we to surrender to her sorrow completely? Or not at all? We must be able to surrender to her sorrow and at the same time not to. Our double emotion will come from recognising and feeling the incident's double aspect.
>
> (*Brecht on Theatre*, p. 271)

Brecht and Stanislavski

The polarisation between emotion and reason to which Brecht objected, dominated the discussion of acting in the second half of the twentieth century and now centred round the figures of Brecht and Stanislavski. It is true to say that Stanislavski was one of Brecht's constant preoccupations, the only major challenge to his concept of acting.

The debate these two major figures provoked has been clouded by two factors: first, lack of accurate information and published texts in translation; second, that it took place within the context of the Cold War. At its peak it amounted almost to ideological warfare.

Brecht's attitude to Stanislavski ranged from the openly hostile, to a sometimes grudging recognition and to respect.

In tracing the development of Brecht's views of the 'system', we need to ask what he could have known at any given moment about Stanislavski and how accurate the information he was given actually was.

If Brecht heard anything of Stanislavski early in his career it would have been from Soviet actors and directors he met in Berlin in 1924 and from his friends Bernhard Reich and Asja Lacis. Reich was closely connected with Tretyakov and Eisenstein, both of whom worked under the shadow of the all-dominant Meyerhold. Stanislavski at the time was under a shadow and on tour abroad, endlessly attacked by the hard left as a 'naturalist' and the 'standard-bearer of bourgeois theatre'.

A second source of his knowledge of Stanislavski was the USA.

In 1935, like so many refugees from the Nazis, Brecht turned to America as a possible new home. In New York, the Theatre Union, a so-called 'left-wing' group, was planning to present *Die Mutter*. Doubtless he expected to find people who would share his ideas on acting and staging. What he found was a group of actors who claimed to use the Stanislavski 'system', but saw his play merely as an excuse to explore their own feelings. His words, where necessary, had to be cut and changed to suit their 'personality'. Brecht fought hard to keep the text he had written and won, but was barred from the theatre. The play was a flop and Brecht's first apparent encounter with the 'system' left a bad taste in his mouth. He could not know, any more than the members of his cast, that Stanislavski detested, and in his writings condemned, a narcissistic concern with what he called 'actors' emotion'. Brecht's view of Stanislavski at the time was distinctly the American version and he assumed that Stanislavski advocated identification and empathy.

In 1936, Brecht attended a number of rehearsals at the Group Theatre with Lee Strasberg as director. They were working, according to Strasberg, on an unspecified *Lehrstück** (in fact *The Measures Taken*). Strasberg claimed that Brecht approved his explanation of 'alienation' as a question of the level of emotional intensity the actor uses.

After leaving the USA, Brecht asked his friend, the designer Mordecai (Max) Gorelik to bring him up to date with developments in the American theatre. Gorelik sent him copies of the magazine *Theatre Workshop*, which contained a number of articles, although none by Stanislavski himself, on the 'system'. Brecht's reaction was hostile. Writing to Gorelik in highly sarcastic terms he condemned the 'system' as quasi-religious in which the actor, without reference to the world and political and economic events, 'creates' like a god and is transformed like

* Didactic play.

the bread and wine in the Mass. He serves eternal 'truth'. The audience is, as it were, hypnotised by what it sees. It becomes a total victim of identification or empathy (*Einfühlung*). Where, Brecht asks, is there any discussion of class struggle? It was Meyerhold who first accused Stanislavski's theatre of being based on hypnosis. Brecht also took issue with the term 'justification', which he misunderstood. He assumed that actors were invited to justify the actions of their characters morally. In fact, all Stanislavski meant was that actions should have a concrete, specific reason behind them, that they should not be done 'in general'. It was a question of probability not morality.

Brecht's English was very elementary and remained so. How much would he have really understood of the *Theatre Workshop* articles? The likelihood is that he read such as he could with Formalist eyes, seizing on an offending word here and there. Brecht was constant in his view that Stanislavski ignored the social, the critical aspect of the drama. He did not understand that given the strict censorship that existed in Russia no overt criticism could be expressed. Russian artists made their criticism implicit and the evidence is that Russian readers and audiences were adept at reading between the lines. In fact, the idea that social and political criticism should be implicit was endorsed by Marx and Engels.

The years of exile were a period in which Brecht could only speculate and theorise on paper. He had almost no opportunity to stage his plays although he was now at the height of his powers as a writer. He never produced a general theory of acting. He made individual statements from time to time His views were formed over the years, slowly, tentatively. He debated with himself and others in many hundreds of pages of articles and scattered fragments. *The Messingkauf Dialogues*, of which only fragments have been translated into English, were drafted over a period of sixteen years (1939–55) and were never presented as a complete work. In his best-known theoretical work 'A Short Organum' (1948), his views on acting are incorporated within his general view of theatre.

With the creation of the German Democratic Republic Brecht for the first time had a permanent home. The Berliner Ensemble became, with the Moscow Art Theatre, the most pampered theatre in the world with almost unlimited money and resources. Brecht had the perfect instrument with which to stage his plays just as he wanted them. His days were spent making theatre. He wrote, translated and directed. The one thing he did not do was train actors. His company learned and mastered their craft elsewhere. They adapted to Brechtian methods. Problems were mostly resolved on the rehearsal floor and it is there, in a working theatre space, that the real encounter between Brecht and Stanislavski finally took place.

The government, to some extent, engineered this event. Famous as the Ensemble was, heavily subsidised as it was, it did not enjoy full government favour. Indeed, the hardline Stalinist, Walter Ullbricht, First Secretary of the Socialist Unity Party, had initially opposed its creation. In 1953, the GDR organised a Stanislavski conference in Berlin. Brecht knew that he was being targeted. The conference was intended to bring everyone, himself included, into line. Formalism was out. The party line was Stanislavski, official Soviet style. A special production of *Egmont* was mounted at the Deutsches Theater to demonstrate the right approach. It was remarkable only for its mediocrity.

Brecht prepared his response. In 1953, he had read a translation of Gorchakov's *Stanislavski Directs* in typescript. It revealed a Stanislavski he had not found in the German-language texts he had read so far. The first, ominously titled *The Secret of an Actor's Success*, had been published in Zurich in 1938. The second was the 1939 translation of *An Actor's Work on Himself Part One*, the third, the *Deutsches Stanislawskibuch*, appeared in Berlin in 1946. Brecht read it while still in Los Angeles and his reaction was the same as to his earlier reading. He inveighed against the 'loyolaesque exercises', the 'justification' and the 'homespun moral tone'.

Gorchakov's book, however, revealed Stanislavski's emphasis on *action* not *emotion*, his insistence that everything should serve the Supertask (the reason why the play was written). The actor's task was not to unleash a flood of highly personal emotions for his own benefit, but to use his own human resources to transmit the author's ideas; the 'system' helped the actor serve the writer. Brecht discovered the 'system' was *useful*.

He began to explore the Method of Physical Action. He was particularly drawn to the notion of 'the line of the day', 'the line of life', whereby the actor knows in detail what happens when he is not on stage.

Another fundamental principle of the 'system' would have interested him: that actors should base their characterisation on contradictions, looking for the light side of a dark character and vice versa. This would have gone some way at least to meeting his objection that Stanislavski was 'undialectical'.

He was now convinced that his knowledge of Stanislavski's thinking was totally inadequate. He decided, first, to create a workshop during the rehearsals for *Katzgraben*, and second, to refuse to enter into any useless polemic.

Accordingly, he only attended the conference once, and spoke very briefly. What he said was not recorded verbatim but his notes have now been published. It was Weigel who was the spokeswoman for the Ensemble. She, too, was very guarded, refusing to take up any fixed theoretical position, on the grounds that insufficient hard facts were available. Meanwhile, Brecht demanded that Stanislavski's complete works be published. He used the *Katzgraben* rehearsals to test out some of the techniques of the 'system' and kept a careful record of the results, sometimes imitating the dialogue form which Stanislavski preferred. The recently published material in Volume 23 of the new critical edition* confirms the seriousness of Brecht's intentions and calls into serious question the assertion made by some commentators that his notes 'What We Can Learn from Stanislavski' were a kind of lip-service. Brecht adopted a position of scientific agnosticism.

In 1955, Brecht read Toporkov's *Stanislavski in Rehearsal*, which made such an impression on him that he wrote a letter of thanks to the author.

In the same year Brecht paid his last visit to Moscow. Although rarely performed in the Soviet Union, and still under a Formalist cloud, he had been awarded the Stalin Peace Prize. During his stay he attended a performance of Ostrovsky's *Burning Heart* in Stanislavski's production. He noted in his journal, 'all Stanislavski's greatness made apparent'.

Talking to his old friend Bernhard Reich after seeing performances at the Moscow Art Theatre, he stated that Stanislavski's work must be studied 'closely and without prejudice'. Brecht's attitude, Reich notes, was truly 'scientific'.

Brecht at work

Angelika Hurwicz, one of the leading actresses of the Berliner Ensemble, wrote that it is more rewarding and revealing to look at Brecht's work as a director than to try to decipher the minutiae of his writings, most of which were composed when he was in exile and not

* *GBFA.*

theatrically active. Many of his colleagues were witness to the fact that once he was working at the Berliner Ensemble, Brecht rarely discussed theory. Indeed, having written 'A Short Organum' in 1948 he never discussed it formally with anyone. In rehearsal his constant cry was, 'Don't talk about it, show me!' According to his collaborator Kaethe Ruelicke, he took it for granted that an actor would empathise with his character. Ekkehard Schall, his son-in-law, is clear that the *V-effekt* is a secondary technique, a working tool, not the centre of the epic style. There is a level of relaxation that is in marked contrast to the kind of polemical discussion that took place in the West, based mainly on an imperfect knowledge of Brecht's writings.

We are fortunate in having four accounts of Brecht in rehearsal: his own account of his work with Charles Laughton, notes by Angelika Hurwicz on rehearsal style, and articles by Kaethe Ruelicke and Hans Bunge on *Galileo* and *The Caucasian Chalk Circle*.

Brecht's personal account is of his collaboration with Laughton on the translation and staging of *Galileo*.

Hurwicz provides a picture of Brecht as a director, applying his principles. She also deals significantly with the relationship between Brecht and Stanislavski.

Ruelicke describes Brecht's approach to the final scene of *Galileo*, the way in which he approached it from different angles at different rehearsals, trying to find the right balance between the two lead characters, working on their subtext.

Bunge describes Brecht working on the scene in *The Caucasian Chalk Circle* in which Grusha buys milk, his insistence that the actors work in response to the economic circumstances created by the war, not from preconceived, traditional stereotypes.

Laughton's Galileo

Of all the work Brecht did in the United States perhaps the most rewarding was his collaboration with Charles Laughton on *The Life of Galileo*. For the first time he was working with an actor of outstanding talent, not to say genius, capable both of subtle ideas and strong emotion and a power to find physical expression for his interpretation. On the surface it was a strange combination. Laughton was an actor in the British 'classical' tradition, and had played a series of major

Shakespearean roles before turning to cinema and ultimately Hollywood, while Brecht had the reputation of a communist 'intellectual'.

What Brecht shared with Laughton was an ability to think theatrically, concretely, not in the abstract. Laughton appreciated the nature and power of language and he had the ability to find the right *Gestus* at any given moment, while his immense technical control enabled him to do whatever he wanted.

The translation they produced was achieved by acting out a scene line by line, almost word by word, even sound by sound.

> [H]e spoke no German whatsoever and we had to decide the gest of dialogue by my acting it all in bad English or even in German and then his acting it back in proper English in a variety of ways until I could say: that's it . . . The result he would write down, sentence by sentence, in longhand. Some sentences, indeed many, he carried around for days, changing them continually. This system of performance-and-repetition had one immense advantage in that psychological discussion was almost entirely avoided. Even the most fundamental gests, such as Galileo's way of observing, or his showmanship, or his craze for pleasure, were established in three dimensions by actual performance. Our first concern throughout was for the smallest fragments, for sentences, even for exclamations – each treated separately, each needing to be given the simplest, freshly fitted form, giving so much away, hiding so much or leaving it more open . . .
>
> The awkward circumstance that one translator knew no German and the other scarcely any English compelled us, as can be seen, from the outset to use acting as our means of translation. We were forced to do what better equipped translators should do too: to translate gests. For language is theatrical in so far as it primarily expresses the mutual attitude of the speakers . . .
>
> Although L.'s theatrical experience had been in a London that had become thoroughly indifferent to the theatre, the old Elizabethan London still lived in him, the London where theatre was such a passion it could swallow immortal works of art greedily and bare-facedly as so many 'texts'.
>
> *(Brecht on Theatre, pp. 165–6)*

Brecht was struck by the realism of Laughton's Galileo, his insistence that the character be rooted in daily life and daily activity.

The first thing L. did when he set to work was to rid the figure of Galileo of the pasty-faced, spiritual, star-gazing aura of the textbooks. Above all, the scholar must be made into a man . . . L. never strayed far from the engineer at the great arsenal in Venice. His eyes were there to see with, not to flash, his hands to work with, not to gesticulate. Everything worth seeing or feeling L. derived from Galileo's profession, his pursuit of physics and his teaching, the teaching, that is, of something very concrete with its concomitant real difficulties. And he portrayed the external side not just for the sake of the inner man – that is to say, research and everything connected with it, not just for the sake of the resulting psychological reactions – these reactions, rather, were never separated from the everyday business and conflicts, they never became 'universally human' even though they never lost their universal appeal.

(GBFA, Vol. 25, pp. 21–2)

Brecht was also struck by Laughton's ability, without theoretical prompting, to defamiliarise, to create *V-effekt*. In the first scene, Galileo gives a lesson in astronomy to the young Andrea:

Washing himself in the background, Galileo observes the boy's interest in the astrolabe as little Andrea circles around the strange instrument. L. emphasised what was novel in G. at that time by letting him look at the world around him as if he were a stranger to it and as if it needed an explanation.

(GBFA, Vol. 25, p. 23)

Laughton also had a great ability to play different aspects of the character simultaneously, to combine the intellectual with the physical:

Some people objected to L.'s delivering his speech about the new astronomy in the first scene with a bare torso, claiming it would confuse the audience if it were to hear such intellectual utterances from a half-naked man. But it was just this mixture of the physical and the intellectual that attracted L. 'Galileo's physical contentment' at having his back rubbed by the boy is transformed into intellectual production. Again, in the ninth scene, L. brought out the fact that Galileo recovers his taste for wine on hearing of the reactionary Pope's expected demise. His sensual walking, the play of his hands in his pockets while he is planning new researches came close to being offensive. Whenever Galileo is creative, L. displayed a mixture of aggressiveness and defenceless softness and vulnerability.

(Materialen zu Brechts 'Leben des Galilei', pp. 72–3)

Laughton also achieved his effects by never merging entirely with the character. In 'A Short Organum' Brecht wrote in section 49:

> This principle – that the actor appears on the stage in a double role, as Laughton and as Galileo; that the showman Laughton does not disappear in the Galileo whom he is showing; from which this way of acting gets its name of 'epic' – comes to mean simply that the tangible, matter-of-fact process is no longer hidden behind a veil; that Laughton is actually there, standing on the stage and showing us what he imagines Galileo to have been. Of course the audience would not forget Laughton if he attempted the full change of personality, in that they would admire him for it; but they would in that case miss his own opinions and sensations, which would have been completely swallowed up by the character.
>
> *(Brecht on Theatre, p. 194)*

Brecht's work with the actor

Angelika Hurwicz

Brecht is a master of method and a great teacher. But it might be useful to set aside his theoretical work, 'A Small Organum', and talk about doing practical work with him. The more so since the present writer six years ago, not a little frightened, went to collaborate with Brecht and his production method. Let it be said at the outset that the first impression Brecht's work gave was that it differed only from the usual production method in that it was more patient. Brecht's originality as a director was to build a large picture bit by bit from small details.

This short article provides an opportunity – and it is the most important thing about it – to discuss the regrettable error of the current opposition between Brecht and Stanislavski. Stanislavski was a great man of the theatre and so is Brecht. Both of them strove for truth on the stage. Instead of creating an artistic contradiction on the basis of both their writings, which needlessly confuses all young people involved in the theatre, we should rather demonstrate the ways in which they agreed. In the final analysis, there can only be one truth. But before beginning an attempt at reconciliation we must point out quite firmly that Stanislavski, who was exclusively a director, was more interested in the use of the smallest details of an actor's performance than Brecht who was above all a writer, and therefore, so to speak, walked with broader strides. It is useful to emphasise that Stanislavski developed his system during the period of naturalism when he was working with Chekhov,* whereas Brecht established his when he recognised that the theatre must show the world as capable of being changed. Once, during a discussion on his productions, Brecht stated that his intention was to show how men behaved in specific circumstances† and he didn't care whether the actor felt involved or not. This means that Brecht was in no way opposed to acting exercises designed to make a performance true to life and warm, but took them for granted. Brecht began simply with what Stanislavski called the actor's supertask.

Stanislavski said somewhere: 'The goal, the purpose of my actions, both as a character in a play, and as an actor in the contemporary theatre, is the foundation of our art. This "why", "for what purpose" is defined by the author's ideas, and the actor's, and in equal measure by the thinking of the age in which they both live.'

And elsewhere: 'But when will you move on from skill and self-confidence to the creative state? – that moment when your human task overrides any of your dramatic tasks, when you share the author's ideas, when you experience them, give them your own warmth and arouse new energy in the audience. This task we shall call the actor's supertask.'

To return to Brecht; everything he said in the 'Small Organum' against the actor's being taken over by his role, and what has caused so much confusion and indignation, is directed against the actor who loses sight of his supertask and only sees his own part, even when the details he brings are interesting and ingenious but work against the content of the play.

The statement that it did not matter whether an actor was involved or not might seem strange and the concept of 'epic theatre' even stranger but they provide the key to understanding the importance Brecht has for a new generation of German actors. His work with young and not so talented actors (the theatre cannot depend on great actors only, all plays contain a greater or lesser number of parts) is of the greatest educational importance.

To act epic theatre means to tell the story. Everything is subordinated to that end. That is why, in the final analysis, it is a matter of indifference to Brecht as a director which particular actor plays a part. Brecht does not cast according to personality. He portrays men as the product of their circumstances and capable of change through their circumstances. For Brecht abstract psychology is unimportant. So, through unusual casting, he expands actors' range and skill.

With actors who cannot manage to find a shade of meaning essential to a reversal in the plot, Brecht tries every possible way to get what he wants. He replaces an emphasis by a gesture, a gesture by a pause, a look by clearing the throat, etc. In this way he trains actors to be exact in their responsibility towards the role and the play as a whole without forcing them.

Equally simple and unusual is Brecht's method of getting actors to abandon the rather bland language of the stage. He encourages the actor to speak in his local

* This is a common misconception. Stanislavsk did not develop the syste until 1906, two years afte Chekhov's death, when he was working on Symbolist plays.
† This was Stanislavski's intention.

dialect. Feelings and thoughts often lose their originality when they have to be expressed in the rather careful language of the stage. He did something similar to good manners that require strong feeling to be expressed with moderation. When speaking in dialect, the actor is freer; unexpected, unusual emphases appear, which must then be carried over, musically, into standard German.

It can be said that in his treatment of stage speech Brecht uses the best naturalistic traditions of the German theatre without allowing 'naturalism'.

It would be a great source of pleasure, if these few, preceding little remarks could make it clear that epic theatre, above all, is the step from naturalism to realism. That is the explanation for its existence and its meaning.

(Errinerungen an Brecht, pp. 172–5)

Brecht in rehearsal: The Life of Galileo

Kaethe Ruelicke

Scene 14

Brecht began by going through the dialogue sentence by sentence, playing special attention to the inflections. He spoke a great deal. The staging was done quickly using the Modelbook from the Californian production.

The scene can be divided into four events each with a different *Gestus*:

- Galileo dictates a letter for the archbishop to Virginia

- Galileo learns that his recantation has worked

- Galileo admits that he has written the 'Discorsi'. Andrea builds a new ethical system

- Galileo analyses his case

Brecht's production notes

Event 1: *Galileo dictates a letter for the archbishop to Virginia*

VIRGINIA: And now let's consider our eyes and leave that ball alone and dictate just a
bit of our weekly letter to the archbishop.

GALILEO: I'm not well enough. Read me some more Horace.

VIRGINIA: Only last week Monsignor Carpula was telling me [. . .] that the archbishop
keeps asking him what you think of those questions and quotations he sends you.
She has sat down to take dictation.

GALILEO: Where had I got to?

VIRGINIA: Section four: with respect to Holy Church's policy concerning the unrest in the Arsenal in Venice I agree with the attitude adopted by Cardinal Spoletti towards the disaffected rope-makers . . .

GALILEO: Yes. *He dictates*: I agree with the attitude adopted by Cardinal Spoletti towards the disaffected rope-makers, namely that it is better to hand out soup to them in the name of Christian brotherly love than to pay them more for their hawsers and bell ropes. Especially, as it seems wiser to encourage their faith rather than their acquisitiveness. The Apostle Paul says 'Charity never faileth'. – How's that?

VIRGINIA: That's wonderful, father.

GALILEO: You don't think a suspicion of irony might be read into it?

VIRGINIA: No, the archbishop will be delighted. He is so practical.

GALILEO: I trust your judgement. What's next?

VIRGINIA: A most beautiful saying: 'When I am weak then I am strong'.

GALILEO: No comment.

VIRGINIA: Why not?

GALILEO: What's next?

VIRGINIA: 'And to know the love of Christ, which passeth knowledge'. Saint Paul's Epistle to the Ephesians, iii, 19.

GALILEO: I am particularly grateful to your Eminence for the splendid quotation from the Epistle to the Ephesians. Stimulated by it I looked in our incomparable *Imitation* and found the following. *He quotes by heart*: 'He to whom speaketh the eternal word is free from much questioning.' May I take this opportunity to refer to my own affairs? I am still blamed for having written an astronomical work in the language of the market-place. It was not my intention thereby to propose or approve the writing of books on infinitely more important matters, such as theology, in the jargon of pasta merchants. The argument for holding services in Latin – that it is a universal language and allows every nationality to hear holy mass in exactly the same way – seems to me a shade unfortunate in that our ever-present cynics might say that this prevents any nationality from understanding the text. That sacred matters should be made cheaply understandable is something I can gladly do without. The church's Latin, which protects its eternal verities from the curiosity of the ignorant, inspires confidence when spoken by the priestly sons of the lower classes in the accents of the appropriate local dialect. – No, strike that out.

VIRGINIA: All of it?

GALILEO: Everything after the pasta merchants.*

* Dialogue trans., John Willett.

First rehearsal, 28 December 1955

Brecht explained Virginia's character, 'For her, basically, everything is hopeless, grey. The basic tone is that the outlook is bleak, he will be attacked by the scientific community, he will be investigated again, will be sent back to prison again. He is an old man, but nasty, he is not easy to deal with.'– 'Understand, Regine [Virginia], that when he won't, he won't. He's a nasty man and that has poisoned the atmosphere for six months.'

When Regine Lutz asked whether she loved her father, 'Yes, but that is something new. He has ruined her life. In Scene 3 she is sent away from court, then he prevents her marriage and so she is now an old maid. After Scene 6, the church has an influence through the father confessor.'

Busch [Galileo] sat leaning back in his chair as he dictated, listening. Regine Lutz was on the bench next to him, eager, but writing mechanically 'this is a business letter'. Brecht was anxious that she should let the audience see – as she did – that Galileo was 'taking the mickey' in the way he phrased the letter to the archbishop.

In general Virginia is seen as having the upper hand. She forces her father to dictate. It emerges that Galileo has underestimated his daughter whom he considers unintelligent. Now she knows her father and can deal with him.

Galileo seems rather childish, old, frail, but with great moments of intellectual insight; Virginia seems elderly and sour.

Rehearsal, 20 January 1956

Brecht rehearsed a completely different reading of the scene. He showed Galileo as a man fully intact intellectually, who gives in to Virgina, in that he dictates a letter but does so with contempt and irony, saying 'I submit to your judgement' with obvious irony.

That makes him negative – he has not only destroyed Virginia, but enjoys himself at her expense. That condemns him.

'Regine, the danger is always that he goes too far, he lays it on with a trowel, he knows no bounds. It's either/or.'

Then Brecht got rid of the hopeless tone established in the first rehearsal. 'Regine, it's as though you had become indifferent to everything. She isn't, she's just gruff, grey and terribly serious.'

But both versions condemned Galileo, instead of showing mercy. In the first version he evoked pity because he was on the defensive with his daughter. In the second his intellectual superiority made his recantation seem courageous. We don't believe he recanted out of fear because even here he 'is paying lip-service'.

Rehearsal, 21 January 1956

Before the rehearsal Brecht had a conversation with Busch in which he explained that the two existing versions

1. Galileo as a childish old man, with huge insights from his former greatness, who is controlled by his daughter whom he underestimates, and
2. Galileo in full possession of his intellectual faculties who maliciously makes fun of his daughter whose life he has ruined

are two sides of the same coin. But Brecht went in another direction: Galileo must be shown as a traitor to society, as a total bastard. His offence is worse because he is in full possession of his intellectual faculties and can analyse clearly. It is no accident that he can analyse himself in a way that he cannot analyse the social aspects of his science. Brecht explained to Regine Kutz how she should read the letter. 'You know, the way many people talk to a dog, quite stupidly.' – 'Not so much voice, it's night, use that . . .'

Lutz: 'I think that when we are sitting with an old man, we are automatically louder. His hearing is bad.' Brecht laughed, 'No, his eyes are bad, he hears perfectly well.' – 'The voice is too bright, you must . . . she is careworn, used up, dried up, deadly serious.'

Lutz: 'You think my posture is too strong?' – 'No, you sit upright but the voice is too bright. Look, she is forty. First you must be a child, then forty, in today's terms sixty. That's not an easy thing to do.'

Lutz: 'Perhaps I could rehearse it sullen?'

'Yes, try it. . . . You know, Regine, you have an awful life – he is a irredeemable glutton. He is overfed and earthly and sinful and fleshy. You must forgive it all, pray, conquer. He is malicious, too, and nobody knows when he is going to explode. Then he is so concerned with Rome and it is always the same thing – comfort.'

Rehearsal, 23 January 1956

Using the analysis of the previous rehearsal, 'a total bastard', Brecht rehearsed the reading.

Note for Regine: 'Regine, he wants to read Horace. It would be a good idea if you were to prepare yourself with great Christian patience. You soon note that the atmosphere is heavy, as always when he speaks about "Christian brotherly love". In his mouth it sounds detestable.' – 'I'll wait for the Horace, look at it for a moment and then speak quietly. So you will only register it a little. Horace is a heathen!' – 'Fight against the outrageous things he says. Does he want poetry? That is pure bodily pleasure!' – 'Now the tone is friendly, now she wants something.' – 'Regine, you are still too good-natured, these religious men are terribly bad-tempered.' –

'You don't even wash any more. Only inwardly you become more beautiful every day. You make sacrifices every day, you sacrifice yourself bit by bit.'

Lutz: 'Isn't that funny?'

'Not at all. She is an instrument, he has ruined her, life is over. You know, there are young women who take every step only for God, otherwise they wouldn't do anything.'

Rehearsal, 20 March 1956

The scene has been basically set.

Virginia starts her line piously and approvingly – the aggression comes from Galileo who is angry and sharp.

About the letter: despite the archbishop's opinion that Galileo has not improved and Galileo's opinion that the archbishop is a fool, and Virginia's doubts about Galileo's repentance, a whole series of positive suggestions concerning the people are made. Admittedly, the people have to pay the cost of the game Galileo, Virginia and the archbishop play, 'soup instead of better pay'. The realisation that in his exile Galileo is amusing himself at the cost of the people helps makes him unsympathetic.

Before she sat, Lutz knocked over Galileo's apparatus so that the globe rolled across the floor. This accident cause a splendid distancing of the object. It acquired another function and lost its own.

Rehearsal, 21 March 1956

Brecht began the rehearsal with a further analysis of Galileo's character. Just as in previous rehearsals he had worked on the 'bastard', now he drew out the positive side. Galileo is shown as a man who has the right to be considered a hero for the next five hundred years during which all opposition is crushed and then falls and becomes a traitor. That is very difficult: to draw the traitor out of the hero. Nevertheless he is a hero and nevertheless he is a traitor. You can't leave that up to the audience. We must make it clear and hope the audience accept it. 'It is not just the man who is guilty, it is society that manufactures traitors. Of course the Inquisition is more guilty than Galileo, he is the victim. But it must be understood that he is a victim because of his change of heart. He is bad-tempered and lazy, will admit nothing, and wants to throw out the pupils who come to see him. He should say something positive but there is nothing. And he is insolent and provocative, 'I'm very healthy, I go towards my spiritual recovery.'

It is noteworthy that in this rehearsal Busch never tried to reproduce feelings, as he might have in some situations, but that by studying the facts and the circumstances he tried to find Galileo's way of thinking and feeling. He never lived through a situation, he thought it through. Throughout the entire rehearsal he spoke of Galileo in the third person, never asked 'What do I do now?' but 'What would Galileo do now?'

ACTION	BRECHT'S PRODUCTION NOTES
VIRGINIA And now let's consider our eyes and leave that ball alone and dictate just a bit of our weekly letter to the archbishop.	*Serious, moderate, pious, resigned.*
GALILEO I'm not well enough. Read me some more Horace.	*He is bored in this villa. The days pass slowly. 'Horace' reproachful.*
VIRGINIA Only last week Monsignor Carpula was telling me [. . .] that the archbishop keeps asking him what you think of those questions and quotations he sends you. *She has sat down to take dictation.*	*Reproachful. He doesn't want to work, or address his conscience. The archbishop knows he is guilty towards you. You should be proud such a great man is interested in you.*
GALILEO Where had I got to?	
VIRGINIA Section four: with respect to Holy Church's policy concerning the unrest in the Arsenal in Venice I agree with the attitude adopted by Cardinal Spoletti towards the disaffected rope-makers . . .	*Virginia reads quickly, writes automatically. It's a business letter Now Galileo is paying for having underestimated her intelligence*
GALILEO Yes. *He dictates*: I agree with the attitude adopted by Cardinal Spoletti towards the disaffected rope-makers, namely that it is better to hand out soup to them in the name of Christian brotherly love than to pay them more for their hawsers and bell ropes. Especially, as it seems wiser to encourage their faith rather than their acquisitiveness. The Apostle Paul says 'Charity never faileth'. – How's that?	*'. . . Christian brotherly love' sounds detestable in his mouth, crude, fast: then comes the sense it would be right and proper.* *Insolent.* *Virginia thinks: he never knows where to stop, but he is helpless. She is lost. 'That should come from the heart.'*
VIRGINIA That's wonderful, father.	*Cautiously: she knows he thinks the archbishop is a fool.*
GALILEO You don't think a suspicion of irony might be read into it?	*Open contempt. The whole thing now becomes a struggle.*

VIRGINIA

No, the archbishop will be delighted. He is so practical.

Mild – it really is wonderful, deadly earnest, then the nonsense appears.

GALILEO

I trust your judgement. What's next?

Virginia knows he is paying lip-service, which is bad, but she has to be content with that.

VIRGINIA

A most beautiful saying: 'When I am weak then I am strong'.

Bad-tempered.

GALILEO

No comment.

For him – he has kicked against the pricks.

VIRGINIA

Why not?

Virginia is cautious. That can't be true from a crook. Galileo buys his comfort with odd jobs. He prostitutes his intellect. Bored, irritated but not without humour.

GALILEO

What's next?

VIRGINIA

'And to know the love of Christ, which passeth knowledge'. Saint Paul's Epistle to the Ephesians, iii, 19.

GALILEO

I am particularly grateful to your Eminence for the splendid quotation from the Epistle to the Ephesians. Stimulated by it I looked in our incomparable *Imitation* and found the following. *He quotes by heart*: 'He to whom speaketh the eternal word is free from much questioning.' May I take this opportunity to refer to my own affairs? I am still blamed for having written an astronomical work in the language of the market-place. It was not my intention thereby to propose or approve the writing of books on infinitely more important matters, such as theology, in the jargon of pasta merchants. The argument for holding services in Latin – that it is a universal language and allows every nationality to hear holy mass in exactly the same way – seems to me a shade unfortunate in that our ever-present cynics might say that this prevents any nationality from understanding the text. That sacred matters should be made cheaply understandable is something I can gladly do without. The church's Latin, which protects its eternal verities from the curiosity of the ignorant, inspires confidence

Look at him. That's not what he means. But you can't understand him. In sentences like these it is not the meaning but the conjunction of theology and selling pasta.

when spoken by the priestly sons of the lower classes
in the accents of the appropriate local dialect. –
No, strike that out.   *Looks at the monk. Spiteful.*
VIRGINIA
All of it?
GALILEO
Everything after the pasta merchants.   *Unwillingly, He has lost the pleasure
                                                        of annoying the church.*

                                                        (*Wer War Brecht*, pp. 191–9)

Brecht in rehearsal: The Caucasian Chalk Circle

Hans Bunge

The scene of buying the milk in the 'Flight into the Northern Mountains'
First rehearsal, November 1953

GRUSHA *to the child*: Noon time, eating time. Now we'll sit here quietly in the grass, while the good Grusha goes and buys a little jug of milk. *She lays the child down and knocks at the cottage door. An old peasant opens it.* Grandpa, could I have a little mug of milk? And perhaps a corn cake?

THE OLD MAN: Milk? We haven't any milk. The soldiers from the city took our goats. If you want milk, go to the soldiers.

GRUSHA: But Grandpa, you surely have a jug of milk for a child?

THE OLD MAN: And for a 'God Bless You', eh?

GRUSHA: Who said anything about a 'God Bless You'? *She pulls out her purse.* We're going to pay like princes. Head in the clouds, bottom in the water! *The peasant goes off grumbling to fetch milk.* And how much is this mug?

THE OLD MAN: Three piastres. Milk has gone up.

GRUSHA: Three piastres for that drop? *Without a word the Old Man slams the door in her face.* Michael, did you hear that? Three piastres! We can't afford that. *She goes back, sits down again and gives the child her breast.* Well, we must try again like this. Suck. Think of the three piastres. There's nothing there, but you think you're drinking and that's something. *Shaking her head, she realises the child has stopped sucking. She gets up, walks back to the door, and knocks again.* Open, Grandpa, we'll pay. *Under her breath*: May God strike you! *When the Old Man appears again*: I thought it would be half a piastre. But the child must have something. What about one piastre?

THE OLD MAN: Two.

GRUSHA: Don't slam the door again. *She rummages a long time in her purse.* Here are two piastres. But this milk will have to last. We still have a long journey ahead of us. These are cut-throat prices. It's a sin.

THE OLD MAN: If you want milk, kill the soldiers.

GRUSHA *letting the child drink*: That's an expensive joke. Drink, Michael. This is half a week's pay. The people here think we've earned our money sitting on our bottom. Michael, Michael, I certainly took on a nice burden with you!*

Content of the scene: during her flight into the mountains Grusha comes across a peasant farmer. She asks for milk. The farmer at first refuses and then asks a horrendous price. Grusha will not pay. But she needs milk for the child and so starts to haggle. Grusha finally gets the milk but it costs her a week's wages.

The action is simple. The characters and staging look simple too. Motherly young Grusha will make any kind of sacrifice for the child. And as to the farmer, he is a man without pity with a bad character who creates undeserved difficulties for her. That is the way the characters would normally be played. And that is how the audience would normally see them: the motherly girl and the wicked farmer.

In fact, that was the first impression given in the early rehearsals of the Berliner Ensemble production. Brecht merely asked the actors to go up on stage and play the scene. And the actors who were used to coping with comments from the director's table and to building their character by trial and error only presented the superficial aspects of the character and their actions. Then came questions like:

'The farmer wants to sell the milk for more than it is worth. Why does he do that? Because he has a bad character? Is the cost of milk determined by a man's character? If someone were to sell a bad man milk at too high a price he would take that badly.'

Brecht warned against seeing actions as the product of individual, inevitable, unalterable traits of character . . .

He then tried to explain the farmer's behaviour in terms of his current situation. 'There's a war on. The soldiers from the city have taken all the goats from the shed. There is now so little milk he scarcely has enough for himself. The price rises because, in these times, goods are scarce.'

The actor then changed his way of speaking. He spoke the lines factually not gruffly as he had before. That sounded, however, as though the price of milk had risen according to some fixed principle and that the farmer had nothing to do with it.

Brecht did not agree. 'There is no doubt that the farmer is very unfriendly towards Grusha. But we don't want to create the idea that he is "rotten to the

logue trans., John
tt.

core". The old farmer is cold and grouchy towards anyone from the city because there are soldiers looting everywhere and those who live through time of war are mistrustful. The fact is that if the farmer had all his milk, he would have too much milk. Can we then question a priori that in this lonely neighbourhood, he might not sell his milk at less than cost, or even give it away? And when in normal times do people come with a child and ask for a glass of milk? Milk is no great riches for a farmer and one litre more or less makes no difference. Can we question either that he can be "generous" simply because he is not being generous right now? Or is the farmer a better character in other circumstances? It is not just the war that is responsible for inflation. The farmer's hut is on the great highway and it would be simple for them to plunder his goods, and they have.'

Then Brecht asked the farmer to do something else, not to come out immediately when he hears the knock but to hesitate a little and then open the door very carefully. He makes sure that Grusha is alone by holding on to the door and looking all around quickly.

That helped even more. Out of a bad character had come a mistrustful one. It would, however, be equally false to assume that this is his 'basic' behaviour, like a deaf man who, being dependent on outward circumstances – puts his hand to his ear when he is spoken to.

Brecht could have then shown how he thought the farmer should enter. But he did not, he wanted the actor to find the *Gestus* himself. He said, 'We need to see that the farmer can be different. If the war has such a decisive influence on his behaviour, how can we play the farmer as he was before the war? Presumably very few people came, and the farmer would be glad to see a stranger rather than suspicious. He probably hopes to get news from other parts, exchange, trade or sell something. If he feels he would like to and the traveller wants to. So he stands happily in front of his door when he sees someone coming across the road.

'We must see how we can show this multilayered attitude. This is now the situation: the farmer has had a bad time. What happened at his hut in the last few days makes him wary. It has cost him dearly and it is only thanks to his cunning that he has managed to hide and save a few goats. The old farmer at the moment doesn't think very much of the townsfolk. They are all traitors as far as he is concerned. Those who ask for milk are the most untrustworthy. That was how it started with the soldiers and then they took the milk and the goats. So how could the farmer think well of Grusha when she is dressed so poorly. People like that have no scruples, the farmer thinks, because they have nothing to lose. And he relies on his "sound understanding of men".'

That was the way the actor played the farmer at the beginning of the scene. To reach a new attitude and show the contradiction in the farmer's behaviour, the actor needed a reaction from his partner that would make a change possible, or cause it. 'Let's see what happens.'

The rehearsal continued and at the end of the scene we concluded: 'The farmer makes a remarkable and unexpected discovery. There is a knock on the door. The farmer thinks it is soldiers but it is only a woman. Just like the soldiers, she asks for milk, but unlike them she really only wants milk. The young girl appears tattered and penniless, yet she has money to pay for the milk. And she does so, although the farmer didn't believe she would. In the last few days everyone has stolen what they wanted but this woman is asking, and asking not for her own sake but for a child. The farmer has one surprise after another and what he took for his "sound understanding of men" is shaken. His attitude changes and he takes Grusha for the most harmless creature in the world.'

The actor suggested that to show this change of attitude he should stand in the doorway after handing the milk over and see how the child was fed. When Grusha continues on her way he watches for a while, shaking his head, he can't sort things out. We suddenly see a warm-hearted man. That didn't match the 'bad character'.

Brecht watched the scene and said: 'It's a good idea for the farmer to watch when the child gets the milk. We discover other things there that are important. The farmer is interested in Grusha but at the same time keeps an eye on the milk jug to make sure it doesn't suddenly disappear.' And: 'The farmer keeps an eye on his milk jug and at the same time shows his interest in Grusha.'

Not all the people watching the scene agreed with Brecht's comments. They had only seen the farmer's generosity and nothing else. 'Why did the farmer simultaneously watch his jug?'

'Because his initial suspiciousness had been overcome but not fully. Attitudes are not always simple, they are made up of contradictory thoughts and feelings.'

'Yes, but that is a question of contradictory facts.'

'Yes, of course, the farmer, whose attitude changes as he watches the child drink, sees the fine clothes it has on. That is the cause of new suspicions because he had not expected it.'

'How is the audience to notice that the farmer had grasped this new fact? Don't they just see how credulous he has become?' . . .

The right action for the actor was found after numerous attempts and was accepted (for this rehearsal).

At first, the farmer stayed by the door and Grusha brought the jug back with the result that no one could see either that the farmer had spied the child's fine clothes or that he was worried about his jug.

Then the farmer came up behind Grusha so that he could see the child close to. Then we were able to believe that the sight of the 'fine child' made him mistrustful again. The picture of Grusha he has just created did not match this somewhat suspicious person. The farmer was mostly worried about his property. So he takes the milk jug from Grusha and puts it quickly back inside the house.

But that was to emphasise the mistrustful attitude too much. There was nothing to stop the farmer from being hostile rather than friendly when he watched Grusha leave from his house. We had to invent something which would retain the warm-hearted element and show in addition his new mistrust. The farmer took the milk jug back but before going back in helped Grusha pick up her bundle . . .

Every action must be shown as a specific action. There are no set conventions, nothing happens 'in general'. We see cause as well as effect. The event of buying the milk can't be allowed to happen any old way or as a polite formality like paying the rent through a standing order at the bank.

Events which are shown on stage must correspond to events as they are played out in life. That's not only true of the milk but must always be so since two things or two actions are never performed in the same way, as the circumstances in which they occur or are observed are slightly different. The theatre must show the audience the conditions in which something happens.

Later discussion between Brecht and Hurwicz

BRECHT (*to Hurwicz*): Think, you are bright and friendly. Now you have decided what to do, you will do it with pleasure (fun). Nothing will hold you back now. You find new pleasure in action because you have a sense of humour. You even understand this dairy farmer. He just wants more money for his milk. That's completely natural.

GRUSHA: Could I have a little mug of milk?

BRECHT: You say that very quietly. It is the most obvious thing in the world. You know, people say things like that in the full expectation of success. For the moment everything is friendly. Relations only get difficult because of the price. As long as friendship costs nothing, it is highly prized.

GRUSHA: How much is this mug?

THE OLD MAN: Three piastres.

BRECHT: There is a *Gestus* from Grusha. A little astonished, as though she hadn't heard properly. People don't really want to understand things like that. You've taken out your purse because you want to pay but the price turns out to be so horrendous that you start to put it away. You will pay because you have to. But you don't want to put money in the old skinflint's fist so simply. [In her own notes, Hurwicz describes how she had one hand on her purse and the other over her ear so as not to hear the price.]

GRUSHA: Three piastres for that drop?

BRECHT: That could almost be a joke. When you were a child were you ever bathed when the water was too hot? You don't have much time, and you want things to go faster because the troops might arrive in the meantime. But now that gives you pleasure. Then you will be able to talk him round.

Without a word the Old Man slams the door in her face.

BRECHT: Stop! See! He has simply shut the door. Look at it; gone. So, it is not the time to joke. The milk has gone. Now it's serious. This oaf is trying to blackmail you!

GRUSHA: Michael did you hear that?

BRECHT: You say that to the child. But in fact you are saying it to yourself. You know, you might have miscalculated. You must find a reason for the pretence. When you speak something like that out loud, it seems more credible. It's right for you to want to pretend to the child quietly. That's your philosophy. How many times have you been hungry and gnawed a single crust of bread as though there were three? You told yourself it really was three and it had to be enough.

GRUSHA: Open, Grandpa.

BRECHT: I think Grusha is now a little faint-hearted. Buying the milk all went wrong and the child was not deceived. It is clear to you that you have landed yourself in it, but now you can't change things.

GRUSHA *under her breath*: May God strike you!

GRUSHA: Don't slam the door again.

BRECHT: Stick your foot in it. It's not a joke any more. You must have milk. You repeated 'one piastre', as much as to say, 'You're a man, so give it here' – but this cut-throat only shook his head and stared straight ahead. And he was still holding the door. The Old Man's strength lies in the fact that he can simply disappear, with you left standing there. And you now know you really need the milk. But he won't give way.

The exchange of money and milk has taken place and as Grusha goes to the child the Old Man follows her, money in hand.

BRECHT: Where are you going to put the money?

THE OLD MAN: Best thing's in my jacket pocket.

BRECHT: And you, a peasant? Aren't you afraid it might drop out? You know only rich men and conmen stick coins in their pockets. You're neither.

THE OLD MAN: Maybe I'm carrying a purse.

BRECHT: In a place where nobody, year in, year out, ever pays with money and it's the first thing the marauding soldiers would take from you?

THE OLD MAN: ?

BRECHT (*after a moment*): First bite it. This piece of riff-raff could be a swindler. It's better for you to keep the money in your hand. It's your Judas money.

The Old Man does so.

BRECHT: Then there's the matter of being warm-hearted. You know, you can be warm-hearted once you have the money. And the woman turned out to be very obliging – finally. Yet the money could be counterfeit. You bite it. But only when Grusha can't see.

(*Wer War Brecht*, pp. 226–40)

13 The 'Ritual' Actor

The 1960s marked a watershed, a major change in the cultural climate. Institutional forms were increasingly mistrusted. They were now seen as ways of masking rather than revealing the truth. It was the age of the drop-out, the commune, the beginning, in terms of New Age philosophy, of the Age of Aquarius, put into general circulation by a highly successful musical, *Hair*.

There was the conviction that the apparent logical flow of life was an illusion, that no real order existed except as a means of oppression, but that there was an essential inner Self which needed to be liberated from the corrupt trappings of society. This was not a new idea. It had already been proclaimed by Jean-Jacques Rousseau and had also been expressed by Wordsworth in his ode, 'Intimations of Immortality', in which the newborn child is seen as 'trailing clouds of glory' but is gradually imprisoned in an ever darkening world.

The youth of the sixties looked to the possibility of expanded consciousness which could be achieved through drugs (LSD), transcendental meditation, yoga, a combination of all three. There was also a conviction that a new human community had to be created, one based on spiritual rather than materialist values. It would not be created by the accepted political process, and that included the communist utopia, which after the 20th Congress of the Communist Party of the USSR and its revelations about Stalin's crimes, and the brutal Soviet interventions in Hungary in 1956 and in Czechoslovakia in 1968, was seen to be a sham.

In art the finished work, the packaged 'product', the emblem of consumerism, was mistrusted. Thus books, plays, paintings had to be referred to as 'research' or 'work in progress'.

Rational, that is consciously organised, discourse was now seen as an instrument of oppression. Rhetoric was a form of lie. The language of persuasion had become the language of advertising. It was the period when the psychoanalyst R. D. Laing was proclaiming the validity of the apparently incoherent statements of a schizophrenic.

Truth was more likely to be revealed through the body, which, unlike the tongue, 'cannot lie'. The way to truth was through developing physical techniques of performance that would in some way release an inner spiritual 'essence'. This led to the development of what often came to be known as 'ritual' or 'total' theatre. This ritual theatre would also create that communion between performer and spectator where they appeared to share a single consciousness, as Nietzsche had envisaged in *The Birth of Tragedy*.

And yet this ideal found its most popular expression not at first in the theatre but at rock festivals, at Woodstock, where tens of thousands of people met, got high, took off their clothes and heard hours of thundering rock music, which was not so much listened to as 'inhabited'.

In the theatre, performance was increasingly conceived as an independent artistic statement, not an 'interpretation' of a text. 'Total theatre' brought together all the expressive means to create an independent theatrical statement. A new awareness of non-European theatre practice seemed to reveal the possibility of a new performance vocabulary.

Just as Formalist theory supplied a theoretical foundation to constructivist theatre, so the newly emerging theory of structuralism provided a more rigorous set of concepts than the undefined and perhaps indefinable Inner Self, and informed new experiments in the theatre. The structuralists saw most human activities in terms of language, systems of signs with a coherent structure. Clothes, table manners, transport systems came to be seen as languages, making specific statements. Theatre itself was interpreted as a coming together of several sign systems – sound, body language, light, etc. – and was subjected to semiological (semiotic) analysis. Structuralism was an extension of formalism and embraced the notion that art was non-imitative, non-mimetic. Works of literature and theatre were seen as self-standing creations depending on the interrelationships among the signs employed, with no external reference except to other writings which were unconsciously quoted or alluded to.

The structural anthropology of Claude Lévi-Strauss became a central discipline. The structure of myth and narrative was examined to find universal elements, and in this sense paid homage to the prevailing notion of the 'other' inner world. Discussing myth, Lévi-Strauss stated: *'Les mythes se pensent à travers nous'* ('Myths think themselves through us').

In these terms, what kind of actor did the theatre require? Who would he be? Performer? Priest? Shaman? How would he prepare himself?

Antonin Artaud seemed to provide the answer. He expressed his ideas in the heady terms the period was looking for. He was a revolutionary, a visionary and poet who found in oriental theatre the beginning of the idea of a universal theatre language.

Part of his appeal, in France at least, was the splendour of his writing, a mixture of metaphysics and metaphor which almost defies translation. Artaud used all the resources of the French language, reforged, reshaped the sense of words, combined them into new meanings.

It was the *idea* of Artaud that inspired and nothing more so than the strange, often wild collection of articles known as *The Theatre and its Double,* first published in 1938. But, above all, in the 1960s, Artaud had the advantage of being considered mad, of having been confined for many years in a mental hospital, which was now seen as a kind of prison in which the creative few were oppressed by the submissive minority. Even the treatments were classified as brutal, which very often they were. He was thus seen as a cultural martyr.

In context, Artaud's work has to be seen as a revolt against the rigidity of French university life and 'official' culture. Official culture remained very strong until the 1960s. The conservatoires of drama and music, the art schools were rigidly academic. There were rules, strict, institutionalised rules. When protest came it had always to be in the form of extreme provocation. Without shock there could be no change. That provocation had come with Alfred Jarry at the turn of the century, Dada in the 1920s and later with the Surrealists. At one Dada exhibition visitors were provided with axes so that they could attack the objects they did not like. On anther occasion, at an evening of readings of Dada poetry and prose, readers and audience pelted each other with chunks of raw meat. When Surrealism came it was perceived as left wing, or communist, certainly anti-establishment. At the same time it attacked the very notion of Cartesian rationality which was at the heart of French culture.

French theatre remained largely a theatre of the spoken word, the text. This remained true even for the great reformers with whom Artaud had worked, notably Copeau and Charles Dullin, a founder member of the Théâtre du Vieux Colombier.

In the background was also the legendary figure of Gordon Craig. Craig had been at the very heart of the English theatrical establishment. The son of Ellen Terry, he worked successfully for ten years with Henry Irving and starred in his own production of *Hamlet*. He suffered increasing dissatisfaction as an artist. He dreamed of an actor liberated from the tyranny of the author, the text and the director, of being an artist in his own right as a creator. His dreams were never fulfilled, which made him all the more romantic as a figure.

Artaud's own efforts as a director were mostly failures, often having not more than one or two performances, but, none the less, he attracted the approval of distinguished devotees, such as Louis Jouvet and André Gide.

Artaud shifted the emphasis radically to the body, to the physical, the explosive, the primally expressive. The emphasis was now on the magical rather than the rational. Many French actors greeted this as a kind of liberation.

Artaud took an essentially Platonic view of the theatre. The theatre we see is only a shadow of the real theatre which exists in another dimension, inside us, and which it is almost impossible to express in physical terms. Yet that is precisely what Artaud attempted to do. The means by which he could achieve this end was the deliberate subversion of theatre language at the very moment it was being uttered, by the use sounds, cries, screams and shouts. There was no room for masterpieces, classic, canonised texts that audiences received in a passive, conventional manner. The theatre must disrupt and re-create.

The theatre
         is the state
       the place
           the point
      at which human anatomy can be grasped
      and through it cure and govern life
         Yes, life with its emotions, its neighings, its gurglings, its empty holes, its itchings, its stoppings of the blood, its sanguinary maelstroms, its fretful showers of blood, its fits of bad humour
             its repetitions
                 its hesitations
                    (*L'Arbalète*, No. 13, p. 7)

As in oriental theatre, it meant creating a fixed theatrical language that would somehow cease to be a language and become a pure act. In this way the mind/body split, which Artaud saw as the central problem for man, would be overcome. It might even be possible, by some mysterious alchemy, to create a new body out of the acting process.

> The theatre has always seemed to me to be the committal of a dangerous and terrible act in which the idea of theatre and performance is wiped out just like that of science, religion and art.
>
> The act of which I speak is intended for the organic, physical transformation of the human body.
>
> Why?
>
> Because the theatre is not that theatrical display in which a myth is virtually and symbolically created
>
> but the crucible of fire and real meat in which anatomically
>
> by trampling down bones, limbs and syllables
>
> bodies are remade
>
> and the mythic act of making a body
>
> occurs physically according to nature.
>
> (*L'Arbalète*, No. 13, p. 15)

Emotion must flow like molten lava erupting from a volcano.

In the 1930s he defined his new theatre as 'the theatre of cruelty'. By cruelty he meant not the cruelty man inflicts on man but absolute, personal emotional honesty on the part of both actor and audience, a ruthless stripping away of lies and evasions, the cruelty of an artist towards himself.

> [W]hen I spoke the word 'cruelty', everybody immediately thought it meant blood. But the *theatre of cruelty* means difficult theatre and cruel first of all towards myself. And, as far as performance is concerned, it is not a matter of the kind of cruelty we can practise on each other by cutting each other to pieces, sawing our personal anatomy or like the Assyrian emperors, sending each other sackfuls of carefully cut-off ears, noses and nostrils through the post, but the much more terrible and necessary cruelty that things can inflict on us. We are not free. And the sky can still fall on our heads. The theatre is made to teach us that.
>
> (*Le Théâtre et son Double*, p.123)

The theatre of cruelty was a purification, a kill-or-cure process from which man emerged nobler and more aware of his true nature.

The theatre like the plague is a crisis which ends in death or a cure. The plague is a better evil because it is a total crisis after which nothing remains but death or an intense purification. The theatre, too, is a crisis because it is an ultimate form of equilibrium which cannot be achieved without destruction. It invites the mind into a state of delirium which simulates its energies; and we can see to finish that from the human point of view, the theatre works like the plague, is beneficial, for by urging men to see themselves as they are, it drops the mask, it reveals the lies, spinelessness, baseness, hypocrisy; it shakes the stifling inertia of matter that reaches deep into the clearest evidence of our senses; and by revealing to groups of men their dark power, their hidden strength, it asks them to adopt an heroic, loftier attitude towards destiny than they could ever have had without it.

(*Le Théâtre et son Double*, p. 46)

In audience terms, the theatre was redefined as a place where the primary connection between actor and spectator, what Artaud called 'the magic chain', could be reforged. As the actor stripped away his lies and evasions, his defences, word by word, movement by movement, gesture by gesture, the audience had to be led through the experience with him. And although Artaud rejected the notion that 'cruelty' was synonymous with 'blood', in his productions he was prepared to use explicit violence and horror to propel the audience into a superior realm. It is no accident that among classical authors his favourite was Seneca.

Artaud defined his new kind of acting in terms of the Kabbalah, ancient Chinese philosophy, the yin and yang and the science of acupuncture: strange and exotic notions for Europeans in the 1930s. He first localised emotions in specific parts of the body. A set of emotional muscles corresponded to physical muscles. The actor required a kind of 'emotional athleticism' that corresponded to the art of the wrestler. The practice of acupuncture proved that such an identification between feeling and the body did actually exist.

The soul thus has a material, physical outlet. The passions cease to be abstract, they become material so that for the audience they are an act, action, rather than an idea.

Central to Artaud's notion of acting was breath, which he derived from the Kabbalah. Breath is at the heart of Creation, it is the breath of life that God infuses into His creatures, into the base material out of which they are formed. Artaud based his own system of breathing on a combination of masculine, feminine and neuter breaths, which depended on the action performed. Outward vigorous actions produce a breath action which is sharp and assertive, while more inward actions result in a breath that is calmer and slower.

Conversely, it was possible that by deliberately controlling the breath, its rhythm and tempo, the soul itself could be influenced.

> I had the idea of using knowledge of the breath not only in the actor's work but training for the actor's profession. For if the knowledge of breath illumines the colour of the soul, it can even more rouse the soul and allow it to blossom.
>
> It is certain that if the breath is an effort the mechanical production of the breath will engender a corresponding quality to the effort in the working organism.
>
> (*Le Théâtre et son Double*, pp. 203–4)

For all his wild poetry, Artaud is restating the age-old notion of the relationship of mind and body and their interaction. Just as inner feelings produce actions so actions produce inner states. The actor can work either way.

Evidence from films and from the radio programmes he made shortly before his death suggest that Artaud was not a good actor. He had put together a kind of personal technique but could not define it. In consequence, he has left us no system of training or rehearsal, or body of exercises that we can use. His ideas, as he himself recognised, were put into practice by others, notably Jean-Louis Barrault who, apart from being a great actor, was also a great mime with total physical control.

In England, his ideas were explored first by Charles Marowitz and then by Peter Brook in preparation for the RSC production of Peter Weiss's *Marat/Sade*. These were, however, local explorations at a particular time for a particular purpose. They have not generally influenced practice, although the name of Artaud is quoted everywhere.

At the same time that Artaud came to prominence outside the narrow circle of a few French intellectuals, Jerzy Grotowski also began to be known, mainly, again, through the work of Peter Brook. His ideas in a way are the natural extension of Artaud's.

Born in 1933, Grotowski was trained, as were all students in the former communist bloc, in a version of the Stanislavski 'system' and the Method of Physical Action. Intellectually, however, he cast his net much wider than communist orthodoxy would allow, to include Meyerhold (unpersoned at the time), Jung, Gurdjieff (both banned), Dalcroze, Decroux, yoga, and t'ai chi. Out of all these sources he forged a new conception of acting and a system of training.

Two key concepts underlay Grotowski's work:

- the notion of an objective art

- the notion of 'sources'

An actor can create a performance out of his own subjectivity, it is personal to him. He can also create out of what he has in common with all other men and artists, a universal aspect to the self. This he can do by taking various traditions and cultural forms of theatre and discovering what is common to them all, a basic core, a universal. Hence his art becomes 'objective'.

Grotowski formulated many of his views before becoming aware of Artaud's writing in the 1960s. He acknowledged his debt in one of the most perceptive and readable articles on his predecessor, 'He Wasn't Quite Himself'. Out of his reading of Artaud he developed his notion of the 'Holy Actor' as opposed to the commercial actor:

> The actor is a man who works in public with his body, offering it publicly. If this body restricts itself to demonstrating what it is – something that any average person can do – then it is not an obedient instrument capable of performing a spiritual act. If it is exploited and to win the favour of the audience, then the art of acting borders on prostitution.
>
> (*Towards a Poor Theatre*, p. 33)

Stanislavski had also castigated actresses who flirted with the audience and actors who were little better than gigolos.

But Grotowski was careful to distance himself from religion.

> Don't get me wrong. I speak about 'holiness' as an unbeliever. I mean 'secular holiness'. If the actor, by setting himself a challenge publicly challenges others, and through excess, profanation and outrageous sacrilege reveals himself by casting off his everyday mask, he makes it possible for the spectator to undertake a similar process of self-penetration. If he does not exhibit his body, but annihilates it, burns it, frees it from every resistance to any psychic impulse, then he does not sell his body but sacrifices it. He repeats the atonement; he is close to holiness. If such acting is not to be something transient and fortuitous, a

phenomenon which cannot be foreseen in time or space: if we want a theatre group whose daily bread is this kind of work – then we must follow a special method of research and training.

(*Towards a Poor Theatre*, p. 34)

The problem that Artaud left unresolved was precisely that of training.

The paradox of Artaud lies in the fact that it is impossible to carry out his proposals. Does this mean that he was wrong? Certainly not. But Artaud left no concrete technique behind him, indicated no method. He left visions and metaphors . . . he probed subtly, in an a-logical, almost invisible, intangible way, Artaud used a language which was almost as intangible and fleeting.

(*Towards a Poor Theatre*, p. 118)

Grotowski also defined acting in structuralist terms. Like Copeau, he placed the actor at the very centre of the theatrical event. In 1964, he was interviewed by Eugenio Barba and expressed views very similar to those noted down in 1940 by Copeau:

Can the theatre exist without costumes and sets? Yes, it can.
Can it exist without music to accompany the plot? Yes.
Can it exist without lighting effects? Of course.
And without a text? Yes: the history of the theatre confirms this. In the evolution of the theatrical art the text was one of the last elements to be added.
But can the theatre exist without actors? I know of no example of this . . .
Can the theatre exist without an audience? At least one spectator is needed to make a performance. We can thus define the theatre as 'what takes place between spectator and actor'.

(*Towards a Poor Theatre*, pp. 32–3)

Grotowski believed the essence of the actor's art was his capacity to give fearlessly and generously. Again like Copeau, he saw that spontaneity was only possible within a rigorous technique, the 'methodical key'.

Creativity, especially where acting is concerned, is boundless sincerity, yet disciplined: i.e. articulated through signs. The creator should not therefore find his material a barrier in this respect. And as the actor's material is his own body, it should be trained to obey, to be pliable, to respond passively to psychic impulses as if it did not exist during the moment of creation – by which we mean it does not offer any resistance. Spontaneity and discipline are the basic aspects of an actor's work and they require a methodical key.

(Towards a Poor Theatre, p. 261)

That key was rigorous training. Grotowski never taught an acting method as such. He did not lay down rules for the creative process. That was the actor's problem. He offered instead a set of principles. These were very similar to Stanislavski's dictum: love the art in yourself, not yourself in art. Much of what he had to say can be found in what has come to be known as Stanislavski's Ethic, of which he would have been made aware as a student.

In an interview with the leading French critric and theatre historian Denis Bablet in 1967, Grotowski declared that his purpose was not to find ready-made, stereotypical answers to routine questions, such as how to show anger, or walk, or play Shakespeare, but to ask the actor what was blocking him and preventing total commitment, physical and mental, to the creative process. The voice and body were trained and developed so that the actor could physically, even facially, transform himself from within, without the artificial aid of elaborate costume and make-up. The actor was never to hide behind the technical trappings of the stage. Using a new system of voice training, by discovering new resonators, Grotowski enabled actors to produce sounds not usually heard in the theatre. He insisted, however, that he only defined the problems, the actors found the answers.

> The physical exercises were largely developed by the actors. I only asked the questions, the actors searched. One question was followed by another. Some of the questions were conditioned by an actress who had great difficulty with them. For that reason I made her an instructor. She was ambitious and now she is a great master of these exercises – but we searched together.
>
> (Towards a Poor Theatre, p. 253)

For all his concentration on the actor's performing skills, Grotowski's theatre remained a director's theatre, in which the actor was one element in an event that Grotowski carefully structured according to his own ideas. Like Stanislavski, Grotowski talked of the 'score', the musical organisation of the performance. This is evident from the account of his treatment of *Akropolis* and Marlowe's *Dr Faustus* in *Towards a Poor Theatre*.

This method of self-revelation and transformation implied a different relationship to the audience. The actor became an object of contemplation, of observation, as he revealed himself from a position of isolation. The normal actor/audience interaction was suspended. What was important was not communication but revelation. Grotowski underlined this new relationship by creating new performance spaces in which the physical relationship was not the normal one of stage/auditorium. Sometimes the audience were separated into groups with the actors among them.

After the closure of the Theatre Laboratory* he abandoned the notion of 'presentation' to explore other aspects of the actor/audience relationship. His work took on a quasi-mystical nature.

Later, in his work in the US, he began to develop Stanislavski's Method of Physical Action, exploring the ways in which inner impulses find physical expression. Grotowski insisted that the coherence of a performance lies within what the actors do. It is not the audience that creates meaning through what it perceives, but the actor who creates the meaning by what he enacts within an organised structure. The actor's internal process thus becomes a matter of prime importance. But it is still not to be explained, or explained away.

Grotowski's influence has been wide but selective, mostly stemming from his work prior to 1969. Directors have taken aspects of his work and used them, but not systematically. His method of training and his exercises produced remarkable results whenever he was in command, but never entered the mainstream of professional practice. One of the reasons is that he never had a general theory of acting, or of the actor's process. Most of the knowledge we have about him comes from accounts by others of his work or interviews. He was frequently enigmatic, gnomic in his language, so much so that even his immediate colleagues at times had difficulty in understanding what he meant. His method could not, therefore, acquire the status of the Stanislavski 'system' or of Michael Chekhov's approach.

The great innovative theatres of the twentieth century – the Moscow Art Theatre, the Vieux Colombier and Brecht's companies – were all initially small and on the margin, but, in time, displaced the establishment to provide the context in which the discussion of the art and craft of acting still takes place. The Theatre Laboratory has never attained the universal status of those theatres, precisely because of the absence of a

* Created in 1965, closed in 1971.

coherent method that can be clearly understood, used and developed by others. Like Artaud, Grotowski is essentially a catalyst but mostly for small theatres out of the mainstream.

The concept of ritual acting has, however, inspired individual directors, and those interested in the theory of dramatic art. It has largely been explored by small companies, usually under an inspirational leader, almost a guru, such as Eugenio Barba, or those like Peter Brook who have become increasingly disillusioned with the industrialised entertainment industry, who see the theatre as some kind of spiritual process in which basic, universal human values are reasserted. This work has been parallelled in university drama faculties where the study of performance merges with that of anthropology and sociology. This is highly specialised.

The general public still finds its rituals of communion at the football match, the rock festival and the rave.

Conclusion

Since Grotowski, no one has worked out a systematic programme of training that is universally recognised. No one has attempted a general theory of the actor's creative process. Perhaps none is necessary. Perhaps the fundamental issues have been fully explored.

It is possible, however, to test out the body of knowledge that has come down to us against the findings of modern science and philosophy, notions of intentionality, the nature of memory and consciousness; but unfortunately, so far, no systematic attempt has been made to apply new research to the study of the actor's process.

But we would need to proceed with caution. When the mechanisms have been defined, acting remains an intense personal activity. We act because we want to, perhaps because we have to, not because someone tells us to. We do not act abstract rules, but the rules may provide means through which we can create more easily. An understanding of the mechanisms of personal and social behaviour could be useful for planning the process of training and rehearsal.

Select Bibliography

The following are the major sources in the original language quoted in the text.

Classical	ARISTOTLE	*Poetics* Edition 'Les Belles Lettres', Paris, 1979 Loeb Classical Library, Harvard, 1999 *The Art of Rhetoric* Loeb Classical Library, Harvard, 2000
	CICERO	*De Oratore* ed. Augustus S. Wilkins, Bristol Classical Texts, 2002 Loeb Classical Library, Harvard, 2001
	LONGINUS	*On the Sublime* Loeb Classical Library, Harvard, 1999
	QUINTILIAN	*Institutio Oratoria* VI–IX Edition 'Les Belles Lettres', Paris, 1977–8 *Institutio Oratoria* XI–XII Loeb Classical Library, Harvard, 2001

Seventeenth Century	BULWER, John	*Chirologia* (1644) *Chironomia*, (1644) Southern Illinois University Press, 1974
	DESCARTES, René	*Traité des Passions*, Editions du Rocher, Paris, 1996

Eighteenth Century	BOSWELL, James	*Remarks on the Profession of a Player* London Magazine, 1770
	DIDEROT, Denis	*Oeuvres* Bouquins, Lafont, Paris, 1994–7

HILL, Aaron	*The Prompter*, 1734–1736
MACKLIN, Charles	*Memoirs of the Life of Charles Macklin Esq.* ed J. T. Kirkman, London, 1799
RICCOBONI, François	*L'Art du Théâtre*, Paris, 1750
RICCOBONI, Louis	*Pensées sur la Déclamation*, Paris, 1738
SAINTE-ALBINE, Rémond de	*Le Comédien*, Paris, 1747

Nineteenth Century

ANTOINE, André	*L'Invention de la Mise en Scène*, Actes sud Papiers, 1999
COQUELIN, Constant	*L'Art et le Comédien*, Paris, 1880 *L'Art du Comédien*, Paris, 1894.
GOGOL, Nikolai	*Izbranie Statii*, Moscow, 1980
SHCHEPKIN, Mikhail	*Zhizn i Tvorchestvo*, 2 vols, Moscow, 1984.
ZOLA, Emile	*Le Naturalisme au Théâtre*, Editions Complexe, 2003

Twentieth Century

ARTAUD, Antonin	*Le théâtre et son double*, Gallimard, 1964 *Aliéner l'Acteur L'Abalète*, No. 13, 1948
BRECHT, Bertolt	*Gesamte Kritische Berliner and Frankfurter Ausgabe*, Vols 21–25, Suhrkamp Verlag *Materialen zu Brecht's 'Leben des Galilei'*, Suhrkamp, 1970 *Wer war Brecht?*, ed. Werner Mittenzwei, Deb., 1977 *Errinerungen an Brecht*, Reclam, 1964.
CHEKHOV, Michael	*Literaturnoe Nasledie*, Vol. 1, Moscow, 1986 *Lessons for the Professional Actor*, Performing Arts Journal Publications, 1985 *On the Technique of Acting*, Harper Perennial, 1991
COPEAU, Jacques	*Registres I*, Gallimard 1974
JOUVET, Louis	*Cours au Conservatoire National d'Art Dramatique*, 1949–1951, Revue d'Histoire du Théâtre, 1987. *Le Comédien Désincarné*, Flammarion, 2002
LEONARD, Charles	*Michael Chekhov's To the Director and Playwright*, Limelight Editions, 1986

MEYERHOLD, Vsevolod — *Stati, Pisma, Rechi, Besedi*, Moscow, 1968

STANISLAVSKI, Konstantin — *Sobranie Sochinenii*, 9 vols, Isskustvo, Moscow, 1989–99

VAKHTANGOV, Evgeni — *Materiali i Stati*, Moscow, 1959

VOLKENSTEIN, V. — *Stanislavskij*, Moscow, 1922

Sources in Translation

WILLETT, John — *Brecht on Theatre*, Methuen, 1964

BRAUN, Edward — *Meyerhold on Theatre*, Methuen, 1969

GROTOWSKI, Jerzy — *Towards a Poor Theatre*, Methuen, 1969

Playtexts

BRECHT — *The Horatians and the Curiatians, Brecht Plays 3*, Methuen, 1997
The Life of Galilei, Methuen, 1980
The Caucasian Chalk Circle, Methuen Student Editions, 1984

Index